Conservation Reconsidered

The Political Economy Forum

Sponsored by the Political Economy Research Center (PERC)
Series Editor: Terry L. Anderson

Conservation Reconsidered

Nature, Virtue, and American Liberal Democracy

Edited by
CHARLES T. RUBIN

ROWMAN & LITTLEFIELD PUBLISHERS, INC.
Lanham • Boulder • New York • Oxford

ROWMAN & LITTLEFIELD PUBLISHERS, INC.

Published in the United States of America
by Rowman & Littlefield Publishers, Inc.
4720 Boston Way, Lanham, Maryland 20706
http://www.rowmanlittlefield.com

12 Hid's Copse Road
Cumnor Hill, Oxford OX2 9JJ, England

British Library Cataloguing in Publication Information Available

Library of Congress Cataloging-in-Publication Data

Rubin, Charles T.
    Conservation reconsidered : nature, virtue, and American liberal democracy /
Charles T. Rubin.
        p. cm. – (The political economy forum)
    Includes bibliographical references and index.
    ISBN 0-8476-9716-9 (cloth : alk. paper) – ISBN 0-8476-9717-7 (pbk. alk. paper)
        1. Nature conservation—United States—History. 2. Nature conservation—United
    States—Philosophy. 3. Conservationists—United States. I. Title. II. Series.
QH76.R83 2000
333.7'2'0973—dc21   99-089576

Printed in the United States of America

⊚™ The paper used in this publication meets the minimum requirements of American
National Standard for Information Sciences—Permanence of Paper for Printed Library
Materials, ANSI/NISO Z39.48–1992.

To my parents

Contents

Preface

Charles T. Rubin

What was conservationism? Perhaps the most influential answer to this question is evident in the very title of Samuel P. Hays's classic 1959 monograph, *Conservation and the Gospel of Efficiency: The Progressive Conservation Movement 1890-1920.* In this work, Hays presented a self-consciously revisionist account of the conservation movement. Previously, he says, conservation had been portrayed as a "noble and stirring enterprise" with "an enviable reputation as a defender of spiritual values and national character." However, this view stands in the way of "careful analysis," which reveals that "the moral language of conservation battles differed markedly from the course of conservation events." A look at those events reveals that conservation "above all, was a scientific movement. . . . Its essence was rational planning to promote efficient development and use of all natural resources."[1] Or again, conservationists "envisaged, even though they did not realize their aims, a political system guided by the ideal of efficiency and dominated by the technicians who could best determine how to achieve it."[2]

From this point of view, the effort of conservationists to gain greater popular support around 1908-09 introduced "a new and somewhat disturbing influence." Those recruited to the cause at this time—the urban middle and upper classes—apparently had bought the "moral language of conservation" enough to see it as a moral rather than an economic imperative, a "religious crusade to save America from its materialistic enemies." Such people actually wanted to "save resources from use rather than to use them wisely."[3] In other words, the moral content of conservationism, which Hays says came to dominate historical interpretation of the movement, was originally a fly in the ointment of rational resource development policy.

ix

This interpretation of events—which the present volume sets out to challenge—has become the basis for the now common reading of conservationism as nothing more than a utilitarian movement in conflict with a moralistic outlook that has come to be called preservationism. This great debate, we are often told, echoes in our own day in the dispute between "reform" or "anthropocentric" environmentalists (heirs to utilitarian conservationism), who seek to save the earth for the sake of the well-being of humanity, and "eco-centric" environmentalists (heirs to preservationism), who seek to save the earth out of an egalitarian concern for the well-being of all ecosystems, their living and nonliving components alike.

The iconic moment for this reading of the conservation movement is the disagreement between Gifford Pinchot, arch-technocrat, and John Muir, prophet of preservationism, over the inundation of the Hetch Hetchy valley for the sake of dam-building. One could hardly ask that two individuals more clearly embody the differing principles for which they have come to stand: Pinchot, the Washington insider born to wealth, with his Ivy League education and special training in the science of forestry, versus Muir, the modestly born man of the mountains, if not precisely an autodidact, then certainly one whose most important education came from experiencing nature first hand.

Like many revisionist accounts of history, Hays's second look at conservationism did the service of filling out a picture that may indeed, as he suggests, have been one-sided. Still, the danger of successful revisionism is the creation of a new one-sided dogma to replace the old, and that seems to have been the fate of conservationism as a "gospel of efficiency." That fate was sealed by Hays's claim to be counterpoising what was merely moral *rhetoric* with the genuine technocratic *action* of conservationists. Yet when he says that conservationists never achieved their technocratic goals, he is admitting that he has highlighted one ideal of conservation over another. As a result, we gain a view of conservationism all but shorn of its moral purposes, aiming at rational efficiency with little sense of political or philosophical nuance. That outlook obscures in particular the movement's complex relationship to contemporary environmentalism, acting in some respects as a precursor and in some as an alternative.

For conservationism was more than a vague prefiguration of contemporary "reform" environmentalism, made for a simpler time and simpler issues. Neither is the only genuinely moral legacy of that period found in preservationism. For as the present volume shows, there are reasons to think that what we have come to call preservationism and conservationism are better understood as two sides of the same coin than as entirely divergent outlooks on nature. And to that extent, the conservation movement understood as an embodiment of *both* outlooks stands as a worthy alternative to much of the more bifurcated thinking about humanity's place in nature that sets the terms of today's debates.

The essays that follow suggest how, as far as the conservationist actors themselves were concerned, there is less than meets the eye to the distinction between preservationists and conservationists. Bruce Pencek and Larry Arnhart remind us that "preservationist" John Muir, and Aldo Leopold, often taken as a key prefigurer of anti-anthropocentrism, both considered themselves conservationists, and were far from advocates of locking away as much wilderness as possible. Teddy Roosevelt, Jeffrey Salmon argues, was no mere rational planner, and was intensely interested in the moral role wilderness could play in a modern democracy. Arch-technocrat Gifford Pinchot, Marlo Lewis suggests, was less a believer in science per se than willing to use science to support a political reform program.

It may be easy to see that the "gospel of efficiency" versus preservationism does not tell the whole story of conservationism. Nevertheless, this volume does not seek to replace one one-sided view with another. Its authors are revisionists, but they come at their subjects from a variety of perspectives. Taken together, they paint a picture of a conservation movement that was hardly monolithic. Still, the possibility that "utilitarian" and "preservationist" tendencies were not regarded as ultimately incompatible emerges subtly from consideration of some themes that recur in these essays. Whatever its strengths and weaknesses, conservationism was rarely intellectually shallow, even though its proponents were not exactly intellectuals in the contemporary sense. Nevertheless, in attempting to define a horizon for political action, conservationism found itself dealing with big questions like that of the proper relationship between the human and natural worlds, and the roles of religion or science in answering such questions. As political actors, the authors considered here had to think about what measures to advocate and about how to popularize them, but also the relationship between their conservation goals and liberal democratic institutions, and the role of conservationism in cultivating a particular kind of citizen or ethical character. An outline of how these various concerns fit together might look like the following.

For conservationism, nature first comes to light as an order beyond human creation, although conservationists may not agree upon the precise character of the natural order. Bruce Pencek argues that Muir sees it as best understood in terms of divine creation, and James Lennox supports this view by showing the anti-Darwinian tendencies in Muir's thinking. Meanwhile,

Larry Arnhart shows how important Darwinian natural science was to Leopold's ideas. Yet despite such differences, the sometimes mystical Muir is enamored of the ability to name creation scientifically, and Leopold the scientist is capable of communion with animals, as in his famous encounter with a wolf in the "Thinking Like a Mountain" chapter of *A Sand County Almanac.* For such authors, the natural order may transcend the normal categories, scientific or religious, we use in attempting to describe it.

Part of the difficulty in understanding nature is highlighted by Theodore Roosevelt's emphatic belief that nature is not one but many, so that there is something misleading about our unreflective use of the term. Jeffrey Salmon shows how for T.R. nature is really the particulars that make it up, and the wide diversity of relationships among those particulars. Such a view makes possible his antireductionism, which wants to see natural particulars as wholes in their own right, neither mere parts of some greater unity nor mere assemblages of uniform parts. It accounts also for Leopold's belief that intimate knowledge of natural surroundings is the proper path to valuing nature rightly. It even fits with Pinchotian managerial aspiration that Marlo Lewis describes, for if nature were not diverse, no expertise would be required to manage it.

The diversity of natural particulars applies as well to human beings, and in a variety of ways. From such a starting point, it is easier to see how human beings could be distinctive *in* nature rather than being distinct *from* it. Whether the things that make us different, primarily our intellectual and moral capacities, distinguish us by degree or by kind from other beings may be something that Roosevelt and Muir could dispute about. But neither ignores the difference. Even as human beings act like others in nature to use their surroundings to their own maximum benefit, our intelligence makes a far wider variety of uses possible. Our moral judgement gives us the capacity to deliberate about such uses, whether that deliberation is premised on Muir's view of our proper place in a divinely created world, Pinchot's effort to maximize the benefit of resource usage, or (as Marc Landy suggests) Frederick Law Olmsted's effort to cultivate nature for the improvement of civic life. Such diversity of outlook, and consequently, of ways of life—which Leopold seems to have been particularly sensitive to—is apparently both in our nature and from nature.

So humanity has the possibility of changing natural particulars beyond what other beings are capable of, even as (like other animals) we use those particulars. That ability opens the door to the improvement of the human condition in material and moral terms, although as Leopold argues there may be diminishing returns. While progress cannot be treated as a given, it is neither the god nor devil of conservationism. Arnhart and Salmon document that Leopold and Roosevelt understood how the diversity of human choices will lead to disagreements about what progress is. T.R., for example, is torn about the disappearance of the vast buffalo herds, a genuine loss, but one necessary to Western expansion. Landy and Lewis show that Olmsted and Pinchot too saw that what we often call progress has both harmful effects on nature's particulars and disadvantages for human affairs more narrowly conceived. For these conservationists, progress is far from a dogma; it requires a nuanced understanding of the good and bad in our capacity to alter the world significantly and repeatedly.

There is thus a limit to what conservationists would expect we can achieve in the progressive improvement of our condition and our relationship with the rest of the natural world, even with the best will in the world. Leopold and Roosevelt acknowledge openly, if regretfully, that there will be tradeoffs between the good of humanity and the good of other beings. They see that this is nothing new within nature, where the benefit of some goes along with harm to others. There is no doubt a great deal at stake, given the distinctive human power to alter and degrade the rest of nature. Keen observers of nature like Leopold, Roosevelt, and Muir were more adept than most of us at noting the vast and subtle impact humans can cause. Stress on the particular makes them cautious of reconciling such tradeoffs in higher syntheses, or in notions of a broad "balance of nature" that somehow makes everything come out all right—or all wrong.

Arnhart shows how Leopold instead took our very regret at the harm we do to suggest our special standing within nature, an opening for a wider sense of responsibility. However, he has no illusion that we can resolve the tension in any once and for all fashion. None of these conservationists is tempted to reify either human progress or nature's well-being, and thereby set the stage for utopian efforts to settle matters once and for all. For all of Pinchot's concern for advancing material prosperity, he knows that it depends on natural fitness. For all of Muir's excoriations of "Lord Man," he wished to deepen civilization, not dismantle it. Conservationists accept the ongoing tension between the good of humanity and the good of the rest of nature as an aspect of human life that is characteristic of the world of nature.

If human life within nature contains irreducible tensions based on natural diversity and human diversity and capacities, then it is only reasonable to expect that the policies and politics of conservationism are going to reflect those tensions. For all our conservationists, the best hope seems to be a properly educated citizenry, but even here problems arise. How is that education to be achieved? We can develop our intellectual capacity through an ever more sophisticated scientific understanding of nature's particulars and their relationships. That knowledge and/or the process of gaining it is not infrequently linked to the education of our moral sense of our place in nature. Yet Pencek suggests that, for Muir, there is something overtly mysterious about how this redemptive process occurs. Is contact with wild nature the best educator, or can wild nature really only be appreciated by one who already has the proper disposition? Is the proper outlook on nature granted to us, or can (even must) we coerce it if necessary? In other thinkers the link between moral education and education about nature may be not much more clear. Can we expect the head to lead the heart, or must the heart lead the head? What role does hunting play in appreciating nature; is it, as Leopold comes to believe, one mode of many to appreciate nature, or is there as T.R. suggests something basic to understanding nature in hunting properly?

Such questions put direct experience of nature first, but almost all our conservationists were inveterate nature writers. Roosevelt, Leopold, and Muir share a writing style that uses their personal experiences to try to convey to the reader as much information as possible about the particulars of nature, in an entertaining and enlightening way. Books are the "hook" to get people to look more seriously at the world around them. That is to say, the best way to popularize conservation was not to write political manifestos, but to educate the eye. Whether it is Lennox speaking of Darwin, or Landy, Pencek, Salmon and Arnhart describing their authors, we come away with a sense that there is a natural delight in knowing about nature, or a pleasure in knowing simply: the open door through which conservation education best passes. Roosevelt and Leopold, to judge by their literary works, seem to have felt that efforts to that end could and should be broad based, democratic in the literal sense. Landy argues that Olmsted shared a like view of the potential impact of his parks. Lewis takes Pinchot—more inclined to the manifesto style—to have also been more inclined to educate the public only to the extent necessary to produce a political consensus for expertise-based governance, legitimized also by popularly shared benefits. To the extent there were different approaches here, they reflect the hoary tension between popular decision making and expertise. But that tension would not be an issue were it not for a shared uncertainty among our conservationist authors about the relationship between scientific knowledge of nature and our diverse moral judgements about how we wish to live in common.

That uncertainty alone would be enough to show the limits of a technocratic interpretation of conservationism. Still, in a variety of other ways, the conservationists keep coming back to character education. Character development is why T.R. defends hunting and other outdoor activities that harden sinews otherwise softened by progress. Roosevelt and Pinchot can seek to nationalize conservation policy because of doubts that the citizenry of the time was prepared to act rightly on their own. Over against this perspective, Leopold can speak up for the efforts of the local landowner, not only because there is a question about where the most useful knowledge of particulars resides, but because a strong sense of "one's own" is part of his "land ethic." Olmsted designed his parks, Landy argued, to build character by enriching and expanding the realm of experience for urban dwellers.

For the thinkers considered here, conservation is thus a kind of cultivation, both of human capacities and of the rest of nature. It is true there is no one view of what that cultivation looks like; it ranges from Muir's cultivation of the soul to Pinchot's cultivation of trees, by way of Leopold's liberally educated game manager, who uses natural means to produce artificial effects. Yet the view could hardly be further from the crude picture sometimes painted of conservationists as dominators of nature. Cultivation requires a cultured cultivator, and it is nature that provides a great measure of that culture. Olmsted's Central Park—a humanly created natural setting—is a better emblem for what they could achieve along these lines than the Hetch Hetchy controversy. Nevertheless, it is still not the whole story.

For conservation had no grand plans for the "pacification of existence," no blueprint for transforming the world into parkland, industrial or otherwise. It is refreshingly bereft of big ideas of this kind. Leopold knows that to an educated eye, a vacant lot teaches much about the wonders of nature. Muir finds the divine hand only most obvious in grand natural settings. Salmon shows how Roosevelt clearly saw the importance of judging and making policies in accord with the full range of particular elements that shape them. That outlook is surely consistent with Leopold's nuanced view of the different kinds of nature recreation, for example, or Olmsted's careful distinctions about what kinds of activities should go on in his parks. The one general rule of conservationism seems to have been to avoid general rules.

Lewis's Pinchot looks more ambitious on behalf of what public policy can achieve than these other figures, with his enthusiastic planning mentality and hopes even for international resource policy. But it is striking that the more comprehensive his vision, the less he could achieve it. Ultimately, Pinchot has his most lasting success in establishing and expanding one relatively small, albeit important, part of the Federal government. If not noted (like Roosevelt or Leopold) for deep insight into natural particulars, he clearly understood human beings and their motives in analogous depth, and could manipulate them accordingly. That is no mean achievement, but it is in strong contrast to the establishment of the ideal of planned, technocratic resource development and exploitation which Hays takes to be his central, and ultimately unrealized, ideal.

Indeed, as Lewis shows, whatever his grand designs Pinchot was master of just the kind of incremental, tightly focused policy development that is most consistent with both the political constraints of American liberal democracy and the necessary tensions that the conservationists saw between human progress and the rest of nature's well-being. Focusing always on the specific merits of particular cases hardly ends conflict, but it is the appropriate arena for conflict that is likely to result in good public policy. It enables both citizens and policy makers to keep in clear view the tradeoffs that will be necessary regardless. And, to return to where this discussion of policy started, citizens liberally educated in the sort of "human ecology" Leopold speaks of will see and understand these tradeoffs, and their necessity, more readily than those without such an education.

The ideas about nature, society, and politics embodied in the conservationist authors discussed so far did not arise overnight, but take their place in a wider discussion of such issues. Landy shows how Olmsted operated within a tradition of Tocquevillian concern about the challenges facing modern democracy. Lennox documents Muir's implicit reaction against the ideas of Charles Darwin. And while scholars widely understand that transcendentalism was another influence on the conservation movement, Charles Rubin and Bob Taylor argue for a serious revision of the terms in which that influence is normally understood.

Rubin suggests how Ralph Waldo Emerson's notion of the unity of nature and culture supplies a basis for understanding the conservationist position that human purposes necessarily mold and are molded by nature. Thus, the opposition between "preservationists" who want to leave nature pristine and "conservationists" who want to use nature for human ends is in Emerson a false dichotomy. There is a complex fit between Emerson's nature and humanity, which not only allows our material needs to be met, but also supplies us with aesthetic, moral, and intellectual educations. Emerson's outlook is thus of a piece with Leopold's human ecology, or T.R.'s picture of nature as a builder of character.

As Taylor sees it, for all of Henry David Thoreau's love and study of nature, he is less interested in nature per se than in the opportunity nature provides to give us perspective on the problems of contemporary democracy, problems stemming from the materialism and conformity of an increasingly commercial society. For Taylor's Thoreau, we can see from the standpoint of nature a life that is egalitarian without sacrificing independent-minded-ness, a theme that resonates in Olmsted's concern for the effects of urban mass society.

Taylor begins his account of Thoreau by documenting the way in which contemporary environmentalist authors have appropriated him, admiring his writings to the extent they can find a confused prefiguration of today's fashionable biocentrism. Taylor's warning against such condescension is a theme of all of the essays, as they attempt to grapple with the complex relationship between conservationism and contemporary environmentalism.[4]

For Lennox and Lewis, Muir and Pinchot mirror important aspects of environmentalism. Lewis sees in Pinchot the forerunner of an environmen-talism that uses crisis mongering and politicized science to centralize power in the national government. In refusing to take the lessons of Darwin seriously, Lennox's Muir develops a static vision of nature, the "delicate balance of nature" vision that environmentalism uses when seeking to accentuate nature's fragility under human assault. From this point of view, conservationism bequeathed to environmentalism some of its most problematic aspects.

Most of the essays in this volume take a different but complementary tack, suggesting as they do that environmentalism differs most from conservation-ism on some of conservationism's strongest points. The contrasts could hardly be more marked. As Salmon shows in his comparison of T.R. and Al Gore, contemporary environmentalism lacks just that emphasis on particulars that tied conservation writing so closely to nature. Conservationism's unwillingness to read humanity out of nature is matched by environmental-ism's fear that it is war to the death between men and nature.[5] Thus, fitting humans back into nature is the grand task that environmentalism is forced to undertake, rather than the more modest effort at cultivation that conserva-tionism essays.[6] Taking its cue from a static picture of nature and humanity, environmentalism must therefore become a comprehensive effort to find the appropriate "niche" for humanity in the global ecosystem. The development of plans for social and economic reform, and the adumbration of large-scale natural processes said to justify them, takes the place of the creation of citizen awareness, and of the cultivation of our appreciation of natural particulars.[7] In short, what is complex and tension-laden in conservationism becomes simple and unitary in environmentalism.[8]

As Taylor and Landy argue, Thoreau and Olmsted were fully aware of, and highly concerned about, the defects of liberal democracy and market economics, and a significant critical distance on the American institutions of their days is evident at one point or another in all of the conservationists examined here. However, unlike too many contemporary environmentalists, their understanding of nature and human beings did not prompt them to seek complete reconstruction of society, economics, and politics.[9] Most seem to have understood that politics has its own ecology, its own delicate balances, that we disturb at our peril.

Rethinking conservationism makes it a test of today's environmentalist ideals—a test that most of the authors presented here suggest they fail. There is no lack of debate within contemporary environmentalism, and between it and its critics, about the key terms on which we are to live in and with nature, but the range of alternatives within that debate is relatively narrow and fast becoming ossified. If this volume widens that horizon, it will have served its purpose.

* * *

The essays in this volume are based on papers presented at a conference at Duquesne University, June 1996. That event and the work necessary to produce this book were generously supported by the Philip N. McKenna Foundation and the Lynde and Harry Bradley Foundation. All conference participants are grateful for their aid. For their extensive efforts in administration of that conference, I would also like to thank Marc Jablonski and Joan Lapyczak. Manuscript preparation was much aided by Leslie Rubin.

Notes

1. Samuel P. Hays, *Conservation and the Gospel of Efficiency: The Progressive Conservation Movement 1890-1920* (Cambridge: Harvard University Press, 1959), 1-2.

2. Hays, *Conservation*, 3.

3. Hays, *Conservation*, 141.

4. To speak broadly of "environmentalism" is to invite criticism on the grounds of generalizing about a movement of great intellectual and political diversity. But that is a charge most frequently leveled against the movement's critics. Those who identify themselves as environmentalists are left free to use the term in a comprehensive manner, to stress the movement's power and intellectual influence.

There is truth on both sides. Serious disagreements separate various wings of environmentalism. But there are shared characteristics as well, some of which are particularly relevant to the themes of this volume. Thinkers like Barry Commoner and Paul Ehrlich, who disagree about a great deal, are equally critical of the politics of liberal democracy and anxious to replace it with more centralized power. From Rachel Carson to E. F. Schumacher, one finds a grave suspicion of free market economics. Deep ecologists and social ecologists agree on little, but join in distrust of the nation-state and private property. Furthermore, in the face of their radical dissatisfactions with the present, the seminal authors of the environmental movement have felt free to imagine wholly new forms of society, politics, and economics—and even wholly new kinds of people to live in them. For a discussion of this utopian strain and the influence it has had on our thinking about nature, see Charles T. Rubin, *The Green Crusade: Rethinking the Roots of Environmentalism* (Lanham, MD: Rowman & Littlefield, 1998).

5. See, for example, Bill McKibben, *The End of Nature* (New York: Doubleday, 1989).

6. See, for example, Bill Devall, *Simple in Means, Rich in Ends: Practicing Deep Ecology* (Salt Lake City: Peregrine Smith Books, 1988).

7. See, for example, Barry Commoner, *Making Peace with the Planet* (New York: The New Press, 1992).

8. The resulting mentality is perfectly captured in best-selling *50 Simple Things You Can Do to Save the Earth* (Berkeley: Earthworks Press, 1989).

9. See, for example, Christopher Manes, *Green Rage: Radical Environmentalism and the Unmaking of Civilization* (Boston: Little, Brown and Co., 1990).

Part One
Conservationists

Saving Wilderness for Sacramental Use: John Muir

Bruce Pencek

> No Sierra landscape that I have ever seen holds anything truly dead or dull, or any trace of what in manufactories is called rubbish or waste; everything is perfectly clean and pure and full of divine lessons. This quick, inevitable interest attaching to everything seems marvelous until the hand of God becomes visible; then it seems reasonable that what interests Him may well interest us. When we try to pick out anything by itself, we find it hitched to everything else in the universe. One fancies a heart like our own must be beating in every crystal and cell, and we feel like stopping to speak to the plants and animals as friendly fellow mountaineers. Nature as a poet, an enthusiastic workingman, becomes more and more visible the farther and higher we go; for the mountains are fountains—beginning places, however related to sources beyond mortal ken.[1]

John Muir would climb trees in howling storms in order to feel more thoroughly the presence of God in nature. He would wander across backwoods America for days and weeks with little more than the clothes on his back and crusts in his pocket. He could navigate unexplored glaciers but professed to get disoriented in hotels. Most people, whether in the second half of the last century, when he flourished, or today, would never think of trying to emulate him. The Muir everyone knows about is a bit too exotic, too wild, for most of us.

The solitary "mountaineer" has become the icon of an urban-based social movement for protection of "the environment." Yet Muir was not simply "John of the Mountains," the anchorite of wilderness. He married into a prosperous family and profitably managed the family ranch, raising hybrid fruit in the upper reaches of San Francisco Bay. He hobnobbed not only with Emerson but also with Republican presidents and a railroad tycoon. With various Bay Area notables he helped found the Sierra Club, presiding over it for twenty-two years until his death. The contrast between the retiring individual and the aggressive social movement he helped spawn are even more striking than his personal paradoxes. This contrast also reveals larger issues within environmental politics that are rooted within the Western intellectual tradition.

John Muir's position is theological and political. In this chapter I argue that we cannot understand his conservation politics without appreciating his strong faith that, on the one hand, nature is part of God's creation, but that, on the other, pride obstructs our ability to apprehend God's order and plan. Culture or civil society is not evil for Muir. It is, however, fallen inasmuch as mundane, social life induces people to think too highly of their wisdom and of their correlative claim to dominion over other creatures. Conversely, society properly constituted in hearts, minds, and culture will teach people to see mankind as a part of nature, not apart from it. We cannot say that Muir had a fully developed political doctrine or prescription, nor can we be sure that he would agree with the political agendas of those who claim to be his ideological descendants. Yet, while Muir's own example suggests that politics must follow, and follow from, a continual quest for fleeting, mystical glimpses into the divine plan, his writings imply principles of this-worldly action, as matters not simply of personal piety but also of enforced public policy.

We must appreciate John Muir's religious thought if we are to understand how he wishes that individuals and public policy should address natural things. In brief, I argue:

1) John Muir's pervasively religious language should be taken seriously on its own terms, not filtered through psychobiographical theory, catch-all characterizations of transcendentalism, nor the environmentalist ideologies of our own time. Muir's publications are unorthodox but nonetheless consistent with the mystical tradition of biblical religion. (They are not consistent, however, with our century's claim that nature—to say nothing of our interpretations of it—is the byproduct of chance interactions.) For Muir, the divine plan of the universe is an evident fact, a given. It can be glimpsed by reading what God has written in natural things. However, the glimpses do not, as in natural science, necessarily cumulate as progress; God's wisdom remains marvelously mysterious, something to be continually sought but never truly comprehended.

2) Muir suggests that nature is a stage in the unfolding of sacred history from Beginning to End, pointing to but not identical with eternal Being, as body points to soul. Human pride obstructs our ability to see the interconnectedness and worthiness of everything in creation. It also obstructs our ability to understand how creation—nature as well as people—is to be revered as God's work and piously protected so that our descendants may read what God has inscribed in it. Nonetheless, the world, as a part of the cosmic plan, is but the penultimate ground for ethics and politics.

3) Experiencing nature does not in itself produce understanding or piety. So far as understanding the divine plan is at all vouchsafed to us, it comes to those who have prepared themselves spiritually and intellectually. People must be taught, as Muir had been taught while still immersed in civil society, to see creation as wonder-full, so that even if they cannot go to the mountain, they can still see around themselves. Like a preacher glossing scripture, Muir writes so that the tourist in Alaska or the teenager in Cleveland may learn to see creation through other eyes than those of proud "Lord Man," who presumes he is the centerpiece of creation.

4) While any part of nature can be a window on the cosmos, wilderness will do it more impressively for more people than, say, a potted plant will. In this sense, wilderness is an instrumental good in Muir's thought. To say that wilderness is an instrumental good, secondary to the creation of the reverent humility that opens us to God, is not to say that it is trivial, any more than one would say that Chartres Cathedral, which has much the same function, is trivial. Piety and politics demand its preservation if humanity is ever to prepare itself for understanding the most fundamental truths. People who, like Muir, already have had a regenerative insight will respect natural things on their own. A question arises, however, in how they are to deal with the people who have not had that revelation or transformation. Muir's thought is insufficiently political to guide policy beyond calling for the protection of edifying natural sites. Trusting to good will and the power of inspiration, it offers little to direct conduct. In this, Muir is more reticent about coercion on behalf of wilderness than some of his followers have been, though his religious rhetoric may inspire zeal that he would regard as excessive.

Muir's Religious Mysticism

Muir emigrated from Scotland with his family as a youth in 1849. He was raised in a sternly evangelical Christian household in the Wisconsin woods before attending the University of Wisconsin. There he had his first quasi-mystical experience, when another student showed him the underlying unity of nature by means of a comparison of pea flowers and locust trees, replete with taxonomy. "Like everybody else I was always fond of flowers, attracted by their external beauty and purity. Now my eyes were opened to their inner beauty, all alike revealing glorious traces of the thoughts of God, and leading on and on into the infinite cosmos."[2] Thus redirected from his interests in engineering and medicine, he never completed his degree.

Muir avoided the 1864 Civil War draft in Canada, where (an incident he published in a newspaper but not in his autobiographical books) he came across a rare flower in the woods, which reinforced his earlier epiphany in Madison.[3] On returning to the United States, Muir was temporarily blinded in a machine-shop accident, another turning point in his practical and spiritual life. Initially trying to emulate the long-admired Alexander von Humboldt by exploring South America, Muir "botanized" his way to Florida on foot in late 1867, where he was nearly killed by fever. After a sojourn in Cuba, he sailed to New York and then west, reaching the Sierra Nevada in California in 1869. The Sierras, especially Yosemite, would be his spiritual home even after he had moved, married, and toured the world. Muir achieved notoriety for articles he published in the popular press that hymned the praises of the California mountains and called for national protection of undeveloped parts of the West. He was a leader in the failed, dozen-year campaign to prevent the damming of the Hetch Hetchy valley, part of Yosemite National Park, for the San Francisco municipal water supply—an event generally held to have catalyzed the distinctively preservationist wing of the conservation movement.[4] John Muir died at age 76 in 1914, the year after Woodrow Wilson approved the Hetch Hetchy dam.

Writers who address Muir's pervasively religious rhetoric customarily begin with the "Calvinist" upbringing his father imposed.[5] One line of analysis, such as Stephen Fox pursues, takes a broadly psychological approach: John Muir rejected his father as well as his father's religion, but either could not entirely free himself of youthful indoctrination or used that language in order not to make enemies in a still well-churched society.[6] The most conventional approach treats him as following a rather undifferentiated transcendentalism.[7] A different line, perhaps trying to appropriate Muir to today's fashions in religiosity, treats him as so pantheistic as to make him a prophet of Gaia and so anti-materialist as to verge on Buddhism.[8] But there have been scholars who, taking his language on its own terms, have seen Muir fitting within Christian traditions. My analysis draws heavily upon them.[9] This approach has the advantage of presupposing the least about the inner workings of Muir's heart and the character and effect of the cultures in which he lived.

It is always hazardous to assert the degree to which upbringing determines an adult's writings. It is reasonable most of the time, nonetheless, to suppose that there is some degree of influence, neither wholesale acceptance nor wholesale rejection. In Muir's case, it is striking how Jesus-free his thought is, whereas his father Daniel's piety made its central tenet the willingness to accept Jesus as Savior. Yet there are striking similarities in the ways John and Daniel Muir expressed their religiosity. "[T]hough [John] Muir's challenge to traditional religion was quite radical, he did not express a completely alien set of ideas," and he rather admired his father's moral fervor.[10]

Most notably, both Muirs became and remained itinerant preachers, moving in and out of their families and mainstream civil society as the spirit moved them. Enthusiasm and a kind of asceticism worked together. "Muir invented a new kind of frontier religion: one based on going to the wilderness to experience the loving presence of God," Charles Worster writes. "Only corrupt, ignorant, arrogant human beings stood outside that divine beauty, spoiling and abusing it. Separating himself from human corruption, Muir found redemption in the wild and he called the rest of the nation to join him. The Sierras became his Cane Ridge revival camp."

Worster calls attention to a long-standing American tradition of "left-wing Protestantism," the characteristics of which apply to Daniel Muir, Campbellite, and John Muir, mountaineer: egalitarian, anti-institutionalist, and anti-creedal, emphatic about the rights of conscience, oriented to hearts more than heads, "unquenched by academic disputations over text or tradition, free from all schism," intensely hopeful that universal brotherhood and virtue will flow once people are shown the Way. "To save humans from their depravity, indifference, and destructiveness became his chief reason for being."[11]

This tradition features a strong sense of the gulf separating humanity from its Creator. Human institutions and laws are then, of course, rendered problematic, even illegitimate, as guides to the most important questions. But so are the things of the visible church. For the Word may be with God, but the words of scripture—to say nothing of the traditions, inferences, commentaries, and disputations that people have made of them—were set down and read by humans. Given these premises, even the noblest of human things are second-rate.

John Muir took some of the precepts of his father's faith and carried them to their logical conclusion. Where the elder Muir called attention to the conscientious, personal study of the Word of God in scripture, unmediated by manmade doctrine and human priests, the younger, recognizing the hand of man in the writing and exposition of scripture, called attention to signs that God wrote in His own hand deeply on the face of the earth. Where Daniel's faith eschewed the dominion of some men over other people, John's rejected the rule of mankind over all the beings he called "people," including plants and beasts.[12] Where the revival tradition continually incited people anxiously to question the validity of presumed signs of grace, the tradition that the younger Muir helped found leads people to question the presumed adequacy of the materialist conquest of nature.

"Muir disavowed Calvinism and retreated to nature, but his relationship with nature is perhaps one that only a Calvinist would truly appreciate. Muir's nature is not earthly or sensuous or material in any significant sense. Rather, what he worships is a purely idealized, spiritual nature," says Taylor, adding that this idealized nature is a reflection of the Calvinist rejection of the sensuous, material world.[13]

Muir writes passionately about nature. Most important, he constantly portrays it as part of the divine order. Conventionally, one reads Muir as if he used God and nature as virtually synonymous, and there is much to be said for doing so. Muir does not say very much about what distinguishes God from Nature; sometimes he conjoins the terms with a hyphen.[14] Yet there are reasons not to accept that equation.

While a transcendentalist might be able to say something about *what* God is—it is implicit in the whole attempt to account for God as a principle of cosmic oneness or the perfection of intelligence—Muir is less confident that he can do more than attest *that* God is, based on the marks He has left on nature. Existence implies a Creator, but getting knowledge of His "methods of creation" is problematic, and communicating it more so. Rather than trust to the man-mediated interpretations put forth by institutional religions, it is better to try to read what God has written in physical nature, at least insofar as we are physical beings.

The transcendentalist rejection of cold rationalism seems one way to do this. Yet, as Max Oelschlaeger notes, the Emersonian notion of universal intelligence looks curiously like a projection onto the cosmos of human ideas of perfection: the conception still bends nature to suit human will. Muir rejects such humanism.

John Muir was raised a Campbellite. He read the transcendentalists as an adult, and they stayed with him always. The question arises: To what degree did his readings in transcendentalism change his understanding of the relation of God to nature? Transcendentalism, according to the mainstream interpretation, folded God into nature, but without the mechanical relation-ship of eighteenth-century deists. Religious language, in this view, is to be read as figurative, as a necessary way of communicating the affective, intuitive understanding of the cosmic order. This is the conventional reading of Muir, typified by Fox and Nash.

The religious interpretation, however, reverses the influence. Transcen-dentalism—working with Muir's unique experiences and thoughts—could allow John to extend the logic of David Muir's principles, so that transcen-dentalism, like institutional religion and scripture itself, appears merely human, though useful as a point of departure. While the New England Mind may have been led historically from Puritanism to Unitarianism to transcen-dentalism, there is no warrant to suppose its social history to have recapitu-lated itself in any one person nor to suppose that the ideas necessarily follow one from the other.[15] Thus the distillation of the conception of God could lead to a sense of His immanence, a sense that every moment and every thing is pregnant with the possibility of God's entry to this world.

This is consistent with a very long, mystical tradition in the biblical religions that treats each moment as uniquely touched, full of the potential revelation of the divine. A new dispensation can come at any time, and it is fitting for people to prepare themselves to receive it. Within American religiosity, this view has come forth among Quakers and Shakers, Millerites and Mormons, Pentecostals and Pat Robertson, Jehovah's Witnesses and John Muir.

Institutional religions constitute themselves upon their answers to the question of which revelation was the last true one; their mystical brethren contend that revelation is an ongoing possibility. Of the latter, Gerschom Scholem notes, "History shows that the great mystics were faithful adherents of the great religions," frequently antinomian but not religious anarchists. Mystics within the biblical religions tell of having "an ecstatic view of the majesty of God and the mysteries of His Realm," and even of gazing upon a mystical Nothing or No-Thing beyond our power to articulate. That is, they continue to understand themselves as created beings, distinct from God rather than merged into Him. This higher cognition causes "an ecstatic experience, the tremendous uprush and soaring of the soul to its highest plane."[16] Words are inadequate to the mystic's task of describing, much less explaining, his new understanding. But they can somewhat prepare their readers to receive their own insights of divine knowledge, God willing.

For John Muir, nature is prophetic, wilderness especially so. Muir says that by standing on a peak in the Sierras—or by studying a flower—anyone

Accounting for This World

Most people read back into nature what is actually the legacy of Lord Man's efforts. They see it as profane, and they profanely deface it for everyone and everything else. The typical person, Muir repeatedly reminds his readers, has been reared to think the rest of creation exists to satisfy his interest and convenience. If one is to approach nature for what it really *is*, a material manifestation of the sacred Mind, Muir suggests, one must appreciate it as part of the larger, interconnected, purposive order. Muir the ecologist teaches us to see the interconnectedness of nature. For Muir the mystic, furthermore, the physical order is interconnected with the metaphysical one, God's plan. The person who has cast off vain presuppositions about where humanity stands in the order of creation can find a new, liberating basis for understanding:

> Our flesh and bone tabernacle seems transparent as glass to the beauty about us, as if truly an inseparable part of it, thrilling with the air and trees, streams and rocks, in the waves of the sun—a part of all nature, neither old nor young, sick nor well, but immortal. Just now I can hardly conceive of any bodily condition dependent on food or breath any more than the ground or the sky. How glorious a conversion, so complete and wholesome it is, scarce memory enough of old bondage days left as a standpoint to view it from! In this newness of life we seem to have been so always.[25]

Despite the newness of this mystical insight, "we" merely *feel* as if the body had disappeared. We still have bodies, and they make their demands upon our attention after the momentary ecstasy has dissolved. Moreover, the mystic must still contend with other people, their bodies, appetites, intellects, and perhaps even their own mystical experiences. That is, one cannot simply reject the material world nor, concomitantly, the social one. The mystical experience gives a longer view that can help one endure life's travails while also undercutting the effectiveness of this-worldly rewards and sanctions.

Muir writes as a precise describer of the natural world. More exactly, he is a precise transcriber of it. Accepting the label of scientist, Muir dwells lovingly on the details of plants and animals and geology, and he goes on and on in giving names—including Latin binomial taxonomy, though few readers would "get it"—because those details and names suggest the comprehensiveness of Creation and the superintendence of God—things humans in their pride forget.[26] For he likens nature to a book, not something to be looked at but studied—read as the more orthodox believers read verses of scripture for what that study offers the soul.

> [The Yosemite Valley revealed itself as] a grand page of mountain manuscript that I would gladly give my life to be able to read. How vast it seems, how short human life when we happen to think of it, and how little we may learn, however hard we try! Yet why bewail our poor inevitable ignorance? Some of the external beauty is always in sight, enough to keep every fibre of us tingling, and this we are able to gloriously enjoy though the methods of its creation may lie beyond our ken.[27]

Translating or transcribing the book of nature, bringing it bit by bit to people who cannot or will not see unvarnished nature on their own, is a form of evangelizing, a way of awakening humanity to the potential of every member to glimpse divine wisdom at work. It is piety for the transcriber; even if the immediate audience reject the message, some reader might be inspired. In brief, reading this "book," even if in imperfect transcript, prepares one to hear the voice of God amid the clamor of life. "Thus," Muir writes of a discussion with a shepherd in the California mountains, "I pressed Yosemite upon him like a missionary offering the gospel, but he would have none of it."[28]

Shepherds, despite experiencing years of life alone in the wild, are in Muir's eye notably degraded people. They have no urge to understand more than they already think they know. There is greater hope for others, who may have had no experience of the wild but who have not had their souls ground down by habitual concern with mere survival's mundane necessities. To these others—these literate others somehow dissatisfied with the American status quo—Muir writes:

> Nowhere will you see the majestic operations of nature more clearly revealed beside the frailest, most gentle and peaceful things. Nearly all [Yosemite] is a profound solitude. Yet it is full of charming company, full of God's thoughts, a place of peace and safety amid the most exalted grandeur and eager enthusiastic action, a new song, a place of beginnings abounding in first lessons on life, mount-building, eternal, invincible, unbreakable order; with sermons in stones, storms, trees, flowers, and animals brimful of humanity. During the last glacial period, just past, the former features of the range were rubbed off as a chalk sketch

from a blackboard, and a new beginning was made. Hence the wonderful clearness and freshness of the rocky pages.

But to get all this into words is a hopeless task. The leanest sketch of each feature would need a whole chapter. Nor would any amount of space, however industriously scribbled, be of much avail. To defrauded town toilers, parks in magazine articles are like pictures of bread to the hungry. I can write only hints to incite good wanderers to come to the feast.[29]

While John Muir can say for himself, "Going to the woods is going home"—that is, a way of recovering for oneself mankind's lost cognition of God's thoughts—he writes of, and perhaps for, many people who plainly do not feel as he does.[30] He can only hint about what others may discover when they set out to understand nature. He can, however, say what has been vouchsafed to him during his immersions in nature, pointing the way for others, as a Moses or John the Baptist.[31]

How consuming strong the invitation [the Sierras] extend! Shall I be allowed to go to them? Night and day I'll pray that I may, but it seems too good to be true. Someone worthy will go, able for the Godful work, yet as far as I can I must drift about these lovemonument [sic] mountains, glad to be a servant of servants in so holy a wilderness.[32]

The experience of understanding nature is a window on new beginnings, which point our minds beyond nature.

Surely a better time must be drawing nigh when godlike human beings will become truly humane, and learn to put their animal fellow mortals in their hearts instead of on their backs or in their dinners. In the meantime we may just as well not learn to live clean, innocent lives instead of slimy, bloody ones. All hale, red-blooded boys are savage, the best and boldest the savagest, fond of hunting and fishing. But when thoughtless childhood is past, the best rise the highest above all this bloody flesh and sport business, the wild foundational animal dying out day by day, as divine, uplifting, transfiguring charity grows in. [Emphasis added.][33]

The wild and animal in our nature yield to divine charity among the best, not necessarily among the rest. In context, "childhood" would be read literally. Yet the view toward a future time for human beings in general, combined with the resignation to Providence implied by saying "we may just as well not learn to live clean, innocent lives" suggests that the "transfiguration" of the species is out of our hands. This passage would suit the transcendentalist interpretation of Muir but for that curious *not learn.*

Our best people and our best behavior are simulacra, foreshadowings of true good to be realized later. Meanwhile, the bulk of humanity remains estranged from the order and harmony glimpsed in God's work. Indeed, this world is more harmonious in concept than it is as we and our fellow creatures experience it. Consider:

> I can't understand the need of their ferocious courage; there seems to be no common sense in it. Sometimes, no doubt, they fight in defense of their homes but they fight anywhere and always wherever they can find anything to bite. . . . When I contemplate this fierce creature so widely distributed and strongly intrenched [*sic*], I see that *much remains to be done ere the world is brought under the rule of universal peace and love.* [Emphasis added.][34]

There is nothing overtly metaphorical about this passage. Muir is discussing the virtual "master existence of this vast mountain world": ants. It seems unlikely that they will read Emerson nor receive God's word nor benefit from human moral progress. We can discern that they have their function in the divine plan, of course. They are food for bears and "Digger Indians." As such, they remind us that the harmony of the world is a great cycle of creatures coming into being and passing away: "Thus are the poor biters bitten, like every other biter, big or little, in the world's great family."[35] Peace, love, and Being are out of this world; within created nature there is a place for ways of life that are, if not solitary, at least nasty, brutish, and short.

Human pride is the great impediment to reconciliation with God and with the rest of the cosmos. Pride manifests itself in all parts of human life, but especially in our various ways systematically of accounting for life. It is pride to suppose that people are more important than ants. It is also pride to suppose that human industry or ingenuity can stop the world's biting, attractive though that goal may be. Sentimental environmentalists might be distressed by Muir's recognition that the natural world is an arena of slaughter. In most instances, geological and biological death and life are part of one great cycle. Man in his pride puts himself out of that loop. As a natural being, he is in it, but as a moral and intellectual being, he does not know nor understand it very well. Thus he sometimes kills gratuitously, sometimes innocently, sometimes purposively. But it remains part of his lot to be a destroyer; the trick is to destroy in accordance with the divine plan rather than as merely human notions suggest.

Muir's longest continuous exposition of the contrast between human presumption and pious humility makes up the last pages of the sixth chapter of *A Thousand-Mile Walk to the Gulf,* the posthumously published journal of his first great trek. Notably, it is here Muir says Lord Man least deserves, of all creatures, to survive; "more than aught else, mankind requires burning, as being in great part wicked, and if that transmundane furnace can be so applied and regulated as to smelt and purify us into conformity with the rest of terrestrial creation, then the tophetisation of the genus Homo were a consummation devoutly to be prayed for."[36] The discussion has two major parts, a brief summary of smug, bourgeois doctrines about God and a longer discussion of smug, bourgeois suppositions that the world and everything in it were created for the sake of mankind as it currently understands itself.

Muir is more ironic and more critical here than usual. Clearly an attack on the hypocrisy of at least a certain type of public Christian, the passage has been read as the consummation of Muir's rejection of Christian orthodoxy.[37] Yes and no. Non-believers can easily attack vainglorious clergy, false prophets, and congregants of little faith and fewer good works, but so can convinced reformers—Jeremiah trumping Voltaire. Attacking self-serving teleologies is not the same thing as denying the possibility of *telos.* Muir's Jesus-less God and his discounting of received scripture certainly place him outside the Christian mainstream. While he often speaks rather confidently of the eternal (i.e., uncreated) universe of which mankind is a small part, he is not so confident as to say that any human should strike the match for "the tophetisation of the species Homo." Rather, in closing the discussion he says he is "glad to leave these ecclesiastical fires and blunders." The Gospel principles of humility and love are fundamental to his critique of the ways of Lord Man, so it may be that he is glad to leave the discussion open lest he commit the equal and opposite vice, common to ecclesiastics, businessmen, and some scientists, of projecting his vision on the universe, when human knowledge simply will not extend so far.

God is real to John Muir. But what is He, really, beyond a negation of the bourgeois idol? Muir speaks too often of divine agency and plan for us to think that Muir's God is an organic answer to the deists' universal clock maker or a Gaia prototype. To paraphrase Hobbes, on first inspection, it is difficult for the reader to know whether Muir talked to God in a dream or he dreamt he talked to God. If Muir's God is more than a transcendentalist's metaphor for perfected intelligence or a cosmic prime mover, how could he—or we—tell? That is, how can one distinguish between the transcendentalist "religious" experience, a psychological transformation, from an authentically religious experience, a metaphysical one? No wonder institutional religions have become established. "[T]he hills and groves were God's first temples, and the more they are cut down and hewn into cathedral and churches, the farther off and dimmer seems the Lord himself."[38]

Muir is not explicit about the resolution of such uncertainties. Insofar as he is a mystic, or at least insofar as he tries to avoid pretending he knows more than he can, he could not be expected to be explicit. Perhaps he does not have to be. John Muir cannot be a proxy for someone else's mystical experience. Religious sentiments aside, observation and experience of how settled opinions have become unsettled by new evidence and insight counsels that we not reject possibilities simply because they do not fit our convenience, vanity, or systems.

Cultivating Souls and Civil Society

Throughout his writings, Muir especially criticizes city-dwellers for boorishness and world-weariness. Moreover, they provide the market for industrial destroyers of nature. Yet it would be a mistake to say that it is city life that debases them. Urban life exacerbates a prior malady: the brute fact that people are social animals who inadequately reflect on their place in the world they willy-nilly transform through their practices and theories. Social life writes large the moral and intellectual vice of pride, whether it takes the form of optimism about human mastery and progress or the opposite form, cynicism. Such certitude obstructs individuals' glimpsing the divine mind.

Aside from a passing discussion of ants, already mentioned, two species of social animals have a thematic presence in Muir's writing: people and sheep. All three are destroyers, though the ones who seem the most willfully destructive, ants and people, seem to be so naturally, as if it were as necessary as their interdependence to complement their social natures.

The sheep cannot be blamed for what human craft has bred into them; modern sheep are the decayed remnant of "wild wool." It is not their fault that they are "horned locusts" eating all plant life in their path. Driven to be destroyers of nature's bountifulness, desecrators of the wilderness temple, and utterly stupid, domesticated sheep are a scourge or plague that Muir can use to chastise human pride, greed, and shortsightedness.

Muir addresses a common distinction between the goodness of wild and of the cultivated in "Wild Wool" (1875), an article sometimes cited to support a claim that Muir thought natural things simply superior to manmade ones. It is more accurate to say that Muir thought that natural things have their place, manmade things have their place, and that neither can be ranked intrinsically superior within the divine plan.

Throughout the essay, Muir contrasts the fitness of natural creatures in their own appointed niches with the chance effects that characterize human cultures' attempts to improve nature. Implicitly acknowledging that it is part of human nature to transform physical nature and to wonder about the rightness of doing so, Muir says that terms like "wild" and "tame" "are not properly comparable, nor are they in any correct sense to be considered as bearing any antagonism toward each other; they are different things, planned and accomplished for wholly different purposes."[39]

Muir initially uses the language of the marketplace in discussing wool, and by extension the rest of nature, before he introduces the idea of divine order and harmony. Wild wool, he says, is "finer," though nevertheless a "manufacture."[40] That is, after using a utilitarian argument to unsettle the utilitarian assumptions of Lord Man, Muir contends that use cannot be separated from the question of intrinsic qualities of the object and the user. He ends the essay with a call "for someone to go back as far as possible and take a fresh start" in raising wool.[41] This is a call for the continued *use* of sheep, specifically wild ones, because they will better serve human ends—fulfilling our nature as the hawk fulfills its in eating a songbird.

Both John Muir's contemporaries, who thought that the untamed was inferior, and our own, who think the un-wild corrupt, presume to know too much about how God chooses to go about "the attainment of [His] definite ends."[42]

> We are governed more than we know, and most when we are wildest. Plants, animals, and stars are all kept in place, bridled along their appointed ways *with* one another, and *through the midst* of one another—killing and being killed, eating and being eaten, in harmonious proportions and quantities. And it is right that we should thus reciprocally make use of one another, rob, cook, and consume, to the utmost of our **healthy** abilities and desires. . . . Wild lambs eat as many wild flowers as they can find or desire, and men and wolves eat the lambs to just the same extent. The consumption of one another in its various modifications is a kind of culture varying with the degree of directness with which it is carried out, but we should be careful not to ascribe to such culture any improving qualities upon those on whom it is brought to bear. [Italics original, boldface added.][43]

It is not one's environment (much less "the environment") that makes a person good or base but rather something else, a quality of soul that one brings into one's situations. Muir, recall, entered the wilderness already prepared. He had learned from his father the scriptural lesson that God's hand was at work in nature; it was only later that he learned at the university a natural theology with a similar purport. That is, Muir manifestly carried a slice of culture and learning with him, so that the heightened experience of wilderness could complete his transfiguration. Other white people, notably shepherds and derelict Forty-Niners, had lived longer than he in the same mountains, but they remained boors the whole time, as unaffected by the mountain cathedral as by Emerson or Humboldt. American aborigines lived in the wild, but they had become so effectively degraded that it is not clear they could have had the religious insights Muir seeks, nor that they ever could. Conversely, the elderly Emerson came to visit and seemed inclined to camp out, but he succumbed to the pleas of companions solicitous of his health: manners prevailed over the champion of (abstract) Nature.

Not only is society necessary to our species' physical survival, but its concomitant acculturation (or at any rate a certain kind of culture: literate, scientifically informed, familiar with the biblical revelatory tradition) seems to be necessary to prepare people for the experience or event that will, however briefly, abolish their estrangements. Certainly it was so in Muir's own case, and it seems likely, given the style and audience of his public writings and the nature of his associates in conservation, that he thought some sort of culture would make it possible for others. Society, full of evils and hope, is at once our fated state and a phase.

Nature serves to elevate society, working both on individuals through opening them to regenerative experiences, and more generally as an idea of fitness, that is, of fitting-ness, each creature existing its own way without presuming to be wise about what is best for others.

> To the sane and free it will hardly seem necessary to cross the continent in search of wild beauty, however easy the way. Like Thoreau they see forests in orchards and patches of huckleberry brush, and oceans in ponds and drops of dew. Few in these hot, dim, strenuous times are quite sane or free; choked with care like so many clocks full of dust, laboriously doing so much good and making so much money—or so little—they are no longer good for themselves.[44]

Wilderness is that part of nature that will impress itself most on the greatest number of people who have not sought out the natural wonders in their own back yard or, finally, in themselves. Even in the most majestic wilderness, many people must be shown—educated—what to see and how to interpret it.[45] The essential nature of nature is less important as an educator or shaper of souls than a fit *concept* of nature is.

> We saw another party of Yosemite tourists today. Somehow most of these travelers seem to care but little for the glorious objects about them, though enough to spend time and money and endure long rides to see the famous valley. And when they are fairly within the mighty walls of the temple and hear the psalms of the falls, they will forget themselves and become devout. Blessed indeed, should be every pilgrim in these holy mountains![46]

No mere human can fully communicate his glimpse of the thoughts of God, much less lead another to a full understanding of the divine mind. The experience is deeply personal, perhaps privileged. Nor does one necessarily receive that experience spontaneously. One must struggle to come to the mountain with the right frame of mind and heart. One should not go seeking some undifferentiated "experience," no matter how breathtaking. Rather, one goes open to know, to replace intellectual prejudices with new insights. Otherwise, the would-be salvation seeker is merely a tourist, someone who would go to a cathedral simply to admire the craftsmanship of the windows and whine about the air conditioning. As Muir had been prepared by the teachings of his father, of natural scientists, and of transcendentalists, though accepting none wholly, so his mission as author and activist is to inform the larger society.

Preservation, Use, and Politics

It is human nature as well as part of divine command that humans use nature, that they transform it by their efforts. What matters to Muir is how they use it: for what ends, with what frame of mind and heart. That is, people need to appreciate, by experience of nature, how creation is not merely an array of objects of utility but rather something as uplifting and meaningful as a temple or illuminated manuscript. This lesson in turn transforms their appreciation of human things as part of the whole. The experiences themselves may be small, but even a footprint on the trail makes an imprint that would not otherwise be there.

For Muir, the use of nature can be reverent or blasphemous. Muir's own example certainly seems to offer advice about how to do the right thing to our fellow humans, to other living creatures, and toward inanimate nature, yet living in imitation of Muir has never been an option for most people. The predisposition to use nature piously, it appears, comes from outside nature—from intellectual or affective preparation, as by reading Muir, or from accidental sources in culture and personal experience. Muir's life alternated between solitary immersion in the least developed parts of the country and participation in civil society. While Muir's character in some sense made it possible, or even demanded it, he also had opportunities—as the right man in the right places at the right times—that most people could not enjoy, save vicariously as readers. What gives the moral compass to people who share neither his internal moral guidance and cognitive framework, nor his peculiar formative experiences? This is the question underlying his conservation politics.

Muir was not an antinomian nor a Luddite. He did not discard his clothes nor his manners—nor his scientific frame of mind and tools—to live a quasi-Rousseauan fantasy. Muir praises great, roaring campfires in the forests, gardens and groves in the fruited plain, and even the incidental (providential) benefits of timber-harvesting and exotic trout in alpine lakes. He even praises roads and railroads that make the wilder parts of the country more convenient to city people.[47] Moreover, the woods and rocks of the Sierras that he so loved were not virginal when he arrived; they had been combed by miners and shepherds, lumbermen and trappers, and by the Indians before them. They had become even more administered and tamed by the time he wrote his guidebooks and led the Sierra Club.

Wilderness already had one meaning—resource—which conservationism sought to change. Fortuitous conversions are unlikely to break society's collective pride. Preparation requires not only preachments like Muir's that direct people to see nature differently but also a kind of structuring of people's experiences: setting aside particular sites that will have the most impressive effects. "[C]hoked in the sediments of society, so tired of the world, [in wilderness] will your hard doubts disappear, your carnal incrustations [sic] melt off, and your soul breathe deep and free in God's shoreless atmosphere of beauty and love."[48] Hence, the goal of wilderness preservation policy is not hermetic quarantine of "the environment" but rather the preservation of awe, not non-use of natural resources but rather sacramental use of didactically significant places.

There is a tension in Muir's writings between his loving meditations on plants, animals, and natural phenomena, in which people appear at best intruders and often desecrators, and his celebration of national parks and forest reserves as tourist destinations. As anyone knows who has been caught in a traffic jam at the Grand Canyon, this is a real tension. Yet even in traffic, seeing the Grand Canyon can inspire jaded urbanites, who may take a little of that inspiration with them to their own back gardens.

To realize the goal of preservation, Muir seems to place his greatest hope in the cultivation of a public mind that is receptive to the divine, hence protective of the mountain temples. For John Muir himself, a retreat from society and, especially, from mundane political compromise and coercion, may be warranted. His experience and character allow him to live decently in both realms. But what of others? Some will be elevated by the experience of God's landscape. Others, who have not been prepared to encounter nature with reverent humility, may bring their proud, exploitative ways with them to the wilderness.

Some sort of human management of nature, in the name of access to revelation, seems to be a necessary evil that Muir would accept, for he says that even a garden or a weed can point one upward if one looks at it with the right heart.[49] But hoping that moral sensitivity will prevail over exploitation and greed is admittedly a pretty slim hope.

Muir's discussion of the need for enforcement of nature policy is indirect. It is most evident in his praise of the Army's protection and administration of the national parks, yet it is not clear whether he praised it so much because the protectors were an army as because they were *there*.[50] It would be no surprise if Muir were simply ambivalent, caught between his belief that the national government is least likely to be corrupted, on the one hand, and a sense that it would be impious presumption to impose his will upon the rest of the country, particularly through the notably prideful hierarchy of the military.

Centralized power, we see, is a problematic option, inconsistent with the evangelical atmosphere of his upbringing and the mysticism of his writings. It cannot be humble, nor it is likely to be bound together by love. Congregational forms, and their political complement, voluntary association, are much more compatible. Private action to preserve natural sites for public inspiration and enlightenment is especially compatible with the mystic's sense that the regenerative experience comes to people as individuals who must continually explore it.

The idea of a private obligation to preserve nature has various problems. Legitimacy of private actions, especially when they conflict with others' rights and the law, is an obvious one. Consistency and effectiveness are others. Muir had his own mystical experiences. He stayed within the laws, which is consistent with the religious injunctions to be humble and to love one's neighbor. On the other hand, supposing that God exists and works as

Muir indicates, there is the possibility that others might interpret their similar experiences differently, and still others might have different experiences with different lessons. And many will not have any revelations at all and, albeit in error, disdain religious and aesthetic arguments for nature. Muir's mystical premises could lead to conclusions more akin to an environmentalist Savonarola's than to Muir's own. If his premises are fundamentally wrong but still believed, there remain the problems of the deluded enthusiast and of the false prophet manipulating believers to his own, wicked ends. Muir's writings offer little to inspire moderation, humility, and charity among the secularists, unregenerate, and differently regenerate who would follow him.

Indeed, an undertone in Muir's biblical rhetoric suggests grim retribution if people do not mend their materialism. Will tophetisation be directly from the hand of God? The result of natural, wolf-eat-lamb processes? The result of humans acting (or believing they act) on God's or nature's behalf? In all these possibilities, there is the political and moral question of how people will be led to mend their ways, a transformation that might, regrettably, require coercion. In the first two possibilities, the retribution is not within the power of people to carry out; we may assume that Muir himself would eschew such human agency as another presumption of Lord Man. The third retributive possibility, however, invites zealots to say, "vengeance is mine."

Consider a passage that seems very like many others in transcendental fervor:

> A thousand Yellowstone wonders are calling, "Look up and down and round you!" And a multitude of still, small voices may be heard directing you to look through all this transient, shifting show of things called "substantial" into the truly substantial spiritual world whose forms flesh and wood, rock and water, air and sunshine, only veil and conceal, and to learn that here is heaven and the dwelling-place of the angels.[51]

The "still, small voices" are a biblical allusion, referring to an encounter in the wilderness between the prophet Elijah and God. According to I *Kings* 19, as the Kingdom of Israel passed through the final stages of corruption (specifically the worship of the nature-god, Baal), Elijah fled Israelite persecution and encountered God in the wild at Mt. Horeb. God sent storm, earthquake, and fire to announce Himself, awe-fully, to Elijah, though His actual communication comes in a "still, small voice." In his encounter, Elijah notes that he is the last zealot for God, the rest of Israel having forsaken their covenant, whereupon God sends him forth to anoint kings and another prophet, Elisha, to kill all the idolaters. Later, after Israel is destroyed, Elijah makes his spectacular ascent to heaven.

Muir, it appears, describes his Yellowstone communion in order to educate the suitable souls among potential wilderness visitors. The "thousand Yellowstone wonders" are, of course, natural phenomena. So are the natural disasters of the biblical passage.[52] The Bible to which Muir alludes pointedly tells us that "the Lord was not in" any of them. Nature is not God, and it is idolatrous to act as if it were. The phenomena are separate from the message, the Word. They are attention-getters, awakening the spectators so that the subtle and splendid will be all the more impressive once the clamor has stopped.[53] Muir's reference to Elijah here stands as a reproach, not only of capitalist exploiters but also (before the event) of environmental enthusiasts who would treat the earth as itself sacred.

Muir also invokes Elijah and the still, small voice in "Summer Days on Mount Shasta"[54] to a similar end but from the opposite direction, contrasting them with the wonders of modern engineering: the voices will be lost in the din of steam locomotives taking tourists up Mt. Shasta as if "in a chariot of fire or a whirlwind." It is not surprising that Muir would note instances of human technology obstructing a revelation that requires relatively great human effort to perceive and interpret correctly. God is not in the steam engine any more than He is in the mountain. On the other hand, He may not be there any less. In likening the railroad to the vehicle of Elijah's ascent to heaven, Muir implies that human ingenuity, appropriately used, gives ordinary people a direct route to the divine mind such as formerly had been granted to a great prophet.

But we cannot all be Elijah, even if we go to Yellowstone or Shasta, and there is more to the Elijah story than the still, small voice. The story reminds us that the saving remnant of the faithful, who piously obey the revealed Law and glorify the True God, is small, and that the number of prophets who can hear the still, small voice themselves is smaller still. Elijah did not make himself a prophet, and he was already one before the voice came to him. For the rest of us Muir seems to present a painful alternative, not necessarily a choice: regenerate yourself (though this might put you in the thrall of false prophets and doctrinaire zealots) or face the fate of the Kingdom of Israel, destruction.

The contrast is striking between Muir's allusions to Moses, Elijah, and John the Baptist, on the one hand, and his portrait of natural harmony and a God of Gospel love. These prophets were sent by God to impose, or reinstall, order and fidelity among inharmonious people, and they were not genteel about it. They were stern and austere voices in the wilderness. (Note that Elijah heard these voices at the same place as Moses had delivered the Law and that the Gospels treat John the Baptist as Elijah reincarnate.) Moses and Elijah were agents of the divine retributive slaughter of idolaters and covenant-breakers; John urged repentance before an even greater One would do it again on a grander, final scale.

Is the still, small voice calling the regenerate to arms? Probably not. But the proud who think themselves prophets may suppose they hear themselves called. Moreover, among those who take mystical understanding seriously, there remains the possibility of successor prophets and new revelations less pacific than Muir's.

Of course, one can read John Muir's biblical allusions simply as metaphors, figurative rhetoric chosen to persuade a biblically literate public. The message would be something like this: it is bad to abuse nature; consequently something bad (such as a wholly natural catastrophe) will happen if you do not change your ways. It would be bad business to risk the consequences of staying that course.

However, it is not clear how mere repentance would bring in the reign of love and harmony, unless we are to suppose that it too is all figurative speech. For once lordly men see the references as simply figurative, once they understand that warnings about what must come are merely statements of remote probabilities in the natural world, they need simply recalculate their situations. Repentance, humility, and the opening of one's soul to the transformative experience lose their potency in the face of utilitarian forecasts of more concrete costs and benefits.

So there remains the need for a credible enforcer beyond calculated self-interest, to persuade the recalcitrant, but also for a creditable one, who will not misbehave. Muir's advocacy of a national parks policy is a compromise that it does not solve the problem, familiar in crowded parks today, that parks and natural areas have become so popular that visits reproduce the lessons and habits of civil society. In order to preserve edifying sites for visitors who are prepared to glimpse God in nature, park rangers carry firearms and lay down the law for tourists. Policy having succumbed to the ways of society, we are led back to Muir's concern for cultivating souls.

Mere Nature

John Muir sought the conservation of wilderness because wilderness promoted immediate human contact with the divine mind, an experience that is as close as mortals can bring themselves to redemption. Appropriately, the methods he sought to assure conservation try to win over the heart to the general principle. Utilitarian concerns about what to preserve, how, and to what degree, along with the problem of coercion, enter at the far end of conservation policy, enforcement. In part, of course, we can suppose that this relegation of practical politics is prudential, inasmuch as relative utilities and political players vary from case to case. There is a deeper reason as well, rooted in John Muir's theology.

The mystical insight into the divine order calls into question the necessity and rightness of all human things, from physical structures to social institutions to intellectual systems. Perhaps, too, it calls into question the precept that wilderness preservation is an eternal human obligation. If the temporal world is part of the larger sequence from the Beginning to the End then it is inappropriate to suppose an unchanging case for preserving all things that exist in history. If so, then it is easier to reconcile Muir's advocacy of wilderness with his own activities as sawyer and rancher and his promotion not only of tourism but of some of the extractive uses Pinchot advocated. This case is rather different from the claim, popular among today's environmentalists, that this or that tree, grove, or forest deserves to remain unaffected by human activity simply because it is "natural."

We can appreciate Muir's analogy of wilderness to temple better if we consider a very old, familiar critique of external piety before returning to Muir's theological-political conservationism. Religious buildings and ritual are this-worldly pointers toward understanding and unity with God. People who follow these pointers can, if appropriately inspired, eventually appreciate that the pointers are merely pointers, instruments whereby the unregenerate can be made to look toward God, rather than ends in themselves. Piety does not require the church building nor even the visible social institutions called churches and denominations. Most people, however, suffer from pride and spiritual sloth. They are practically indifferent to essential piety, merely going through the motions. Rather than surrender themselves to God, they make piety satisfy their prejudices and interests. This can range from a sincere but largely legalistic piety (as, notably, in the case of Muir's father) to raw hypocrisy. But at least these consumers of religiosity come through the church door, where the right sort of exhortation may lead them to open their hearts. The people who never enter are a larger problem, for their own ultimate good as well as for their ability to persecute and destroy. And even the regenerate need ongoing participation to avoid backsliding and prepare for further insights.

For John Muir wilderness is like a church building; experiencing wilderness is like participating in the church service. Neither location nor activity is God. Neither makes one righteous, absent a suitable inward inclination to open oneself to things above those of this world. Wilderness is the most accessible path for most people's redemption. Love of wilderness—but also love of nature in even the commonest forms—is an outward manifestation of an inward potentiality. For most people would not, owing to the degrading effects of culture, or could not, owing to brute necessity, see the reflection of God in all the parts of creation. They must be led and shown. Once shown, however, they see that wilderness is not so much for their sake as for future generations and for God. Just as one can prepare to hear the still, small voice of God by piously reading the books of prophets, perhaps mediated by a preacher or teacher, one can appreciate the cosmos by reverently studying a potted plant, perhaps mediated by Muir's wilderness transcriptions. For those who are already inclined it is the thought that counts. For the others, there are threats in this world and the next.

If unadulterated wilderness is essential to redemption, then compromise with despoilers is unacceptable. If, however, it is instrumental or, more to the point, if we cannot know that its virginity is the essential requirement, then there may be room for negotiation and the exploration of alternative paths to the insights that wilderness brings.

Muir's conservationism, his political thought both theoretical and practical, turns on our inability to measure up to our presumptions. Muir's awareness of our essential ignorance of the being of God suggests an awareness that we cannot feel certain whether nature is on the one hand eternal, hence the proper basis of our moral judgments and laws, or on the other hand created, in which instance it is of limited authority, a special case derived from the higher authority of the Creator. That, in brief, is the theological-political question. The possibility that it cannot be conclusively answered by us means, among other things, that wilderness may not be the absolute good that Muir's ideological heirs assert but rather an instrumental one, a good that may indeed be subject to political deliberation and even to some sort of utilitarian calculus, provided it be piously informed. As important as protecting wilderness is, it is only *next* to godliness.

Notes

1. Reprinted in *John Muir: The Eight Wilderness-Discovery Books* (London: Diadem, and Seattle: Mountaineers, 1993), 248. Unless otherwise noted, all references to Muir's publications will be to this anthology. The Sierra Club has made most of Muir's books available on the World Wide Web at www.sierraclub.org/john_muir_exhibit/writings/.

2. *The Story of My Boyhood and Youth*, in *Eight Wilderness-Discovery Books*, 110. The story of this experience is the last anecdote in the book, nearly the last page of it. Muir's autobiographical books, *My Boyhood and Youth* (published only in 1913), *A Thousand-Mile Walk to the Gulf* (1916), and *My First Summer in the Sierra* (1911), are significant inasmuch as his accounts of humans in them provide the setting for geological and biological discussions rather than being nearly incidental to them; the *Thousand-Mile Walk* is his lengthiest commentary on—and in many respects harshest indictment of—civil society. The autobiographies are mature reflections; though based on journals and recollections from his early years, these works were prepared for publication late in his life, after he had already become something of a public figure as popularizer of, and fighter for, Yosemite and other national parks.

3. Stephen Fox discounts the mystical elements of the Madison experience, treating it as simply Muir's discovery of botany. He represents Muir's rustic encounter with *Calypso borealis* as the primary revelatory experience. (Stephen Fox, *John Muir and His Legacy: The American Conservation Movement* [Boston: Little, Brown, 1981], 40, 43-45, 51.) Note that placing the first revelation in the woods makes it appear that it was precipitated by Muir's rejection of civil society, whereas a revelation at the state university suggests that the flight from society may have been the effect of the revelation—whose receipt and interpretation may have been made possible by civil society.

4. While some elements of Muir's thought are consistent with Progressivism (notably the national outlook, suspicion of laissez-faire capitalism, and a kind of missionary impulse whereby the educated WASPs save the world for—and from—less gifted stock), I will not press the affinities here. Moreover, as Bob Pepperman Taylor notes, Muir's "lifelong project is to give an account of his rejection of the democratic and utilitarian tenets of progressive conservation" (Bob Pepperman Taylor, *Our Limits Transgressed* [Lawrence: University Press of Kansas, 1992], 85.) On the Progressive elements of the Sierra Club during the two decades of Muir's association with it, see Michael P. Cohen, *The History of the Sierra Club: 1892-1970* (San Francisco: Sierra Club Books, 1988), esp. 8-22.

5. Daniel Muir was a Campbellite. This sect, which became the Disciples of Christ, diverged significantly from Calvin in its rejection of the doctrine of predestination and the permanence of original sin, and it rejected the institutionalism and hierarchy of its ancestral Scottish Presbyterianism in the name of the greater unity of Christians. Louis and Bess White Cochran summarize the Campbellites' fundamentals, Thomas Campbell's "Declara-

tion and Address," in *Captives of the Word* (Garden City, NY: Doubleday, 1969), 6-7, 23. See also Donald Worster, *The Wealth of Nature: Environmental History and the Ecological Imagination* (New York: Oxford University Press, 1993), 191; Daniel G. Payne, *Voices in the Wilderness: American Nature Writing and Environmental Politics* (Hanover, NH: University Press of New England, 1996), ch. 5; and Mark Stoll, "God and John Muir: A Psychological Interpretation of John Muir's Journey from the Campbellites to the 'Range of Light,'" in Sally Miller, ed., *John Muir: Life and Work* (Albuquerque: University of New Mexico Press, 1982).

6. Fox (ch. 2, throughout) succumbs to this temptation, especially in his tendentious discussion of Muir and Christianity. Muir's generally unflattering portrayal of his father in *My Boyhood and Youth* certainly makes him a tempting target for psychologizing, though doing so trivializes his ideas. For correctives, see the chapters on Muir in Taylor and especially Worster. In not taking seriously the history of American religiosity, Fox moreover misreads both Muir's distinction between "the facts" and common interpretation of the nature of God, and the anti-institutional tradition in Christianity. Compare Fox, *John Muir*, 51-52, with the portion (ch. 6, 160-61) of the *Thousand-Mile Walk* on which he hangs his claim that Muir rejected religion. See also Dennis Williams, "John Muir's Christian Mysticism and the Spiritual Value of Nature," in Miller, *Muir: Life and Work*, 86-88.

7. In addition to Fox, see Roderick Nash, *Wilderness and the American Mind*, 3d ed. (New Haven: Yale University Press, 1982), 123-28, and Richard F. Fleck, "John Muir's Transcendental Imagery," in Miller, *Muir: Life and Work*, esp. 139, 149, and citations.

8. See Max Oelschlaeger, *The Idea of Wilderness: From Prehistory to the Age of Ecology* (New Haven: Yale University Press, 1991), 184-95; see also 172-80, 203. Oelschlaeger takes pains to distinguish Muir from categorization as a "lesser Transcendentalist"—i.e., an anthropocentrist *malgré lui*—portraying him rather as a proto-postmodern pantheist.

9. In addition to Worster and Taylor, already cited, see Stoll, "God and Muir," and Williams, "John Muir's Christian Mysticism" both in Miller, *Muir: Life and Work*.

10. Worster, *Wealth of Nature*, 194.

11. Worster, *Wealth of Nature*, 194, 195.

12. This anthropomorphism pervades Muir's writing. See, e.g., *My Boyhood and Youth*, 53-54 (oxen), 59 (a horse), 63 (various meadow flowers).

13. Taylor, *Limits Transgressed*, 89. As should become clearer below, Professor Taylor and I disagree about the degree of the rejection, though not about the implications of solipsistic environmentalism.

14. See, e.g., Taylor, *Limits Transgressed*, 87.

15. Worster, *Wealth of Nature*, 189, 196, 199, develops the cultural implications of the Reformed tradition on American conservationism even after the theological stream had turned elsewhere.

16. Gershom Scholem, *Major Trends in Jewish Mysticism* (New York: Schocken, 1961), 5-6.

17. Muir, *Our National Parks*, 496.

18. Muir, *First Summer*, 238.

19. Scholem, *Major Trends*, 10-11.

20. Muir, *Thousand-Mile Walk*, 168.

21. Scholem, *Major Trends*, 18.

22. Muir, *First Summer*, 256. The account of the incident occupies the bulk of ch. 7, "A Strange Experience."

23. Muir, *First Summer*, 260.

24. Arguably, the return to civil society is also an occasion for Muir to learn from *that* part of creation. Simon Schama contends that the longstanding arguments between wild and idyllic conceptions of the unbuilt landscape, such as the contest between preservationism and conservationism, are "mutually sustaining," noting that it was Thoreau who was "quite right to insist" that salvation lay in wilderness—and also quite right to speak his passion to intellectuals in "picket-fence New England." Simon Schama, *Landscape and Memory* (New York: Knopf, 1995), 525.

25. Muir, *First Summer*, 196. See also the epiphanies he describes in *Boyhood and Youth*, 109-11, and *Thousand-Mile Walk*, 182-85 (which he likens to his "resurrection day").

26. Bryon G. Norton locates Muir within a tradition of amateur scientist-naturalists, whose science was holistic and aesthetic rather than analytic, instrumentalist, and professionalized. Bryon G. Norton, *Toward Unity Among Environmentalists* (New York: Oxford University Press, 1991), 31-35. See also Stoll, 74.

27. Muir, *First Summer*, 227.

28. Muir, *First Summer*, 244.

29. Muir, *Our National Parks*, 490.

30. Muir, *Our National Parks*, 498. Muir reuses favorite phrases: "The mountains are fountains, not only of rivers and fertile soil, but of men. Therefore we are all, in some sense, mountaineers, and going to the mountains is going home." "Summer Days at Mount Shasta," (1874-88) in

the 1918 posthumous compilation, *Steep Trails,* in *Eight Wilderness-Discovery Books*, 887-88.

31. Worster, *Wealth of Nature*, 195, quotes from one of Muir's journals: "John the Baptist was not more eager to get all his fellow sinners into the Jordan than I to baptize all of mine in the beauty of God's mountains." For further discussion of the Christian analogy, see also Stoll, "God and Muir," 74, and Nash, *Wilderness,* 129. For a possibly Mosaic analogy, consider the quotation following this note.

32. Muir, *First Summer*, 196.

33. Muir, *My Boyhood and Youth*, 80.

34. Muir, *First Summer*, 206.

35. Muir, *First Summer*, 207.

36. Muir, *Thousand-Mile Walk*, 161.

37. Fox, *John Muir*, 52-53.

38. Muir, *First Summer*, 243-44. Throughout *Landscape and Memory*, Schama (esp. chs. 4 [trees] and 8 [mountains]) notes that using figurative speech identifying trees or other natural features with sacred buildings and artifacts is very old. Even at the time of Muir's settlement in California, the "cathedral grove" of big trees was already becoming a "pious cliché" (197).

39. Muir, "Wild Wool," *Steep Trails*, 875.

40. Muir, "Wild Wool," 871.

41. Muir, "Wild Wool," 876.

42. Muir, "Wild Wool," 873.

43. Muir, "Wild Wool," 874-75.

44. Muir, *Our National Parks,* 459. Examples are most abundant in this guidebook to the national parks, where he consistently juxtaposes the advantages roads and the like will bring to wildness-lovers against the destruction they work. See, e.g., *Our National Parks,* 463, 465, 472, 479-80. Note too the trip itineraries he suggests in *The Yosemite*, ch.12, throughout. Railroads were, of course, also politically useful: the Southern Pacific virtually ran California politics, and its aid, bolstered by a personal friendship between Muir and E. H. Harriman (who ran the Southern Pacific), was instrumental is securing Yosemite as a park.

45. Fox, *John Muir*, 120, notes that Muir was frustrated by the insensitivity to nature of even Sierra Club members on hiking trips he led for them.

46. Muir, *First Summer*, 228.

47. See, e.g., Muir, *Our National Parks*, 460, 472. Muir does not break ranks with scientific forestry in his call for less-wasteful forest management in the closing chapter (10) of that work, which is perhaps his longest

discussion devoted to public policy. On Muir's initial acceptance of, and break with, the "wise use" of forests for yield, so long as their esthetic, spiritual qualities are not impaired, see Norton, 31-38, Taylor, *Limits Transgressed*, 91, and Nash, *Wilderness,* 134-35, 137-38.

48. Muir, *Thousand-Mile Walk*, 183.

49. The arrow may even point from nature to artifice while still pointing upward. In *The Mountains of California* (296), Muir says, "the park valleys of the Yosemite" are "diversified like artificial landscape-gardens." Recall Muir's repeated temple-and cathedral-imagery for the same region. Schama repeatedly calls attention to how much the tradition of "natural" writing is couched in terms of human creations.

50. See the discussion of military enforcement in Fox, *John Muir*, 112-13.

51. Muir, *Our National Parks*, 488. For gently correcting the more flagrant errors in my exegesis of this allusion, and for clarifying certain points in Reformed and evangelical doctrine and usage, I thank the Revs. Gilmore Ott and John Jaeger.

52. Cf. Taylor, *Limits Transgressed*, 89: "Storms actually serve, for Muir, as the best metaphors of his experience of God's love in the wilderness. We know that we are becoming more like the wild things—for which God cares completely—when we can 'lean fully and trustingly on Nature' not only for the 'infinite tenderness,' but also for the equally infinite 'power of her love.'"

53. For those too desensitized by mundane interests, Muir has a different prophetic image: the scenery in Yellowstone is "wild enough to awaken the dead." *Our National Parks*, 475. Muir again contrasts the still, small voices with storms in "A Great Storm in Utah" (1877), *Steep Trails*, 913. Note that recent radical environmentalists, often using Muir's birthday as an occasion, have resorted to direct action and stunts to provoke attention, evidently because God was not effective enough at it when left to His own devices.

54. Muir, *Steep Trails*, 887.

2

"With Utter Disregard of Pain and Woe": Theodore Roosevelt on Conservation and Nature

Jeffrey Salmon

> There are four categories of outdoors men: deer hunters, duck hunters, bird hunters and non-hunters. . . . The deer hunter habitually watches the next bend; the duck hunter watches the skyline; the bird hunter watches the dog; the non-hunter does not watch. [1]

The roots of Theodore Roosevelt's political thought on conservation are readily available in his writings and are inseparable from his character. Seldom have thought, action, and personality been so closely tied. It is hard to think about Roosevelt and ignore his hunting, his curiosity about wildlife, or his impact on the national effort to conserve and protect natural resources. "By interest, training and knowledge," one author argues, "Theodore Roosevelt was a conservationist. No one before or since was so well prepared to lead a national conservationist movement."[2] But there is a deeper connection between his character and his concern for nature. Roosevelt was a vigorous explorer and adventurer, a man driven by his willful personality and his passion for taking on the elements.

If one had to use a single word to describe Roosevelt, it might well be "will," the root of the word "wilderness," uncontrolled nature. [3] A sickly child, Roosevelt seemingly willed himself to robust health through physical exertion. When he was twenty-six his mother and his wife, Alice Lee, whom he worshipped, died on the same day in the Roosevelt family home in New York City. In deep despair, Roosevelt fell into "a state of cataleptic concentration" on the work of overcoming the grief, according to Roosevelt biographer William Morris. "Like a lion obsessively trying to drag a spear from its flank, Roosevelt set out dislodging Alice Lee from his soul," writes

Morris.[4] On some level, at least, he was successful. Roosevelt never even mentioned her in his autobiography. Again, nearly thirty years later, as a half-blind and portly former president, Roosevelt set out on an unimaginably arduous journey on a previously uncharted tributary of the Amazon for the purpose of discovery and scientific research. The trip very nearly killed him. Roosevelt called all this the "strenuous life." It was certainly a life dedicated to overcoming, conquest, and testing.

It is doubtful that even the rough and tumble of American politics would have been strenuous enough for T.R. Roosevelt needed the challenge and unpredictability of the outdoors—of nature and wilderness—to be complete. He regarded those challenges as necessary not just for himself, but for building and maintaining a democratic character in the American people. To lose wild nature was to lose the opportunity for creating the independent spirit and toughness he thought were needed in a free people.

Roosevelt was drawn to the outdoors as a place to test himself and, at least in his youth, to help restore his health through physical exertion. But his attraction to the outdoors quickly became more serious. Early on he began to collect specimens and to study wildlife in the manner of a naturalist. To collect specimens meant hunting, a sport his father introduced him to, and the two activities—serious scientific field study and hunting—became a significant part of his life. They were in fact the explicit source of his intense interest in, and his influence on, the American conservation movement.

Roosevelt's progressivism has been noted by Samuel P. Hays and others as the source of his conservationism.[5] Roosevelt's place in the conservation movement, however, is somewhat ambiguous for Hays, at least as compared to the role played by Gifford Pinchot. He clearly identifies T.R. as one of the "apostles of the gospel of efficiency [who] subordinated the aesthetic to the utilitarian."[6] Starting from his famed 1908 speech to the Conference of Governors, in which the president argued "that the conservation of natural resources . . . is yet but part of another and greater problem . . . the problem of national efficiency,"[7] Hays has strong justification for placing Roosevelt in the conservationist camp, which believed that "preservation of natural scenery and historic sites . . . remained subordinate to increasing industrial productivity."[8]

Later, however, in describing the battles between conservationists and preservationists, Hays finds T.R. in the latter's camp. The preservationists, he notes, included such groups as the Boone and Crockett Club, an organization founded by Theodore Roosevelt.[9] Hays credits the president, "himself a natural historian of no mean ability" with aiding John Muir and other preservationists by helping them accomplish "much during the early years of the century," and refers to his efforts to put federal wildlife research on a "firm basis" by enhancing the bureaucratic clout of the Biological Survey and to his establishment of "a host of bird sanctuaries."[10]

Seen in light of his outdoor writings, Roosevelt's faith in the gospel of efficiency appears even less solid than Hays suggests, and the sources of his dedication to natural resource conservation more complex than a simple adherence to the progressive movement. Including his wildlife, ranching, and hunting stories in a study of T.R.'s political thought makes it more difficult to conclude that he "subordinated the aesthetic to the utilitarian" since these writings often elevate the former over the latter. A full picture of T.R.'s thinking, then, should include both his progressive politics and his books about the western wilderness.

He was a prolific author. His writings on the outdoors, hunting, the American West, and field studies of wildlife occupy seven volumes in the twenty-volume National Edition of his published works, in addition to essays, correspondence, and speeches on these topics scattered throughout the rest of this collection. And this does not even include his vast correspondence, much of which concerns his outdoor life. *Hunting Trips of a Ranchman, Ranch Life and the Hunting Trail,* and *The Wilderness Hunter* were published between 1885 and 1893 and primarily concern his life as ranch owner and western game hunter. During the same period—between 1889 and 1896—Roosevelt wrote *The Winning of the West,* a massive history of America's western expansion, a work he believed to have been his best. *Outdoor Pastimes of an American Hunter* was published while he was president, with *African Game Trails, Through the Brazilian Wilderness,* and *A Book-Lover's Holiday in the Open* appearing between 1910 and 1916. Before he died in 1919 he compiled a body of writings that offers not only a considerable amount of science, history, and adventure, but also provides a window though which we can see the origins and evolution of his thinking about conservation of natural resources.

Roosevelt embodied on many levels the tension many have pointed to in the conservation movement between the romantic views of the pre-servationist school and the rational enlightenment roots of the resource management school. While the essays in this volume suggest that conservationism cannot be reduced to this simple conflict, it does seem clear that these inclinations frequently define the basic alternatives, not least of all in today's environmental debate. Roosevelt did not provide a simple guide for how one should reconcile the clash between a dedication to human progress and a desire to preserve wild nature as a source of strength and wisdom in the human character. He did, however, live this tension, giving each element its due in his writing and in his politics. In so doing, Roosevelt undermines the view that these two perspectives are incapable of reconciliation. He represents, as a result, a deeply interesting, practical, and thoughtful source of thinking about our relationship to nature.

A present-day challenge to Roosevelt's conservationism comes from Albert Gore. An examination of Gore's thought helps us understand more fully both the conservation movement of Roosevelt's time and modern environmentalism. Here we have two public men with self-professed concerns about nature engaged in serious writing that is intended to shape public attitudes toward the environment. Both write with an eye toward long-term opinion and prejudices, and each develops a characteristic literary style to lay out his political intentions.

Moreover, it is clear that Roosevelt and Gore consider the environment a proper arena for presidential leadership. To varying degrees, both emphasize the requirement for a level of national and international leadership on environmental questions that only the president can supply. Both raise serious questions about the extent of federal authority that should be brought to bear on this issue.

Roosevelt stood, as Gore now stands, at the end of one century looking to mold the next. This chapter examines the ideas the former employed to help create the American conservation movement and those the latter is asking us to adopt in hopes of creating a new global environmental ethic.

Roosevelt as Naturalist

Roosevelt's curiosity about wildlife and natural history showed itself at an early age and never left him. "I remember distinctly the first day that I started on my career as a zoologist," he wrote in his autobiography. When still a young boy he encountered a dead seal laid out in front of a store in his New York City neighborhood. "That seal filled me with every possible feeling of romance and adventure," he recalled. He set about recording "utterly useless measurements," of the seal and he developed "vague" hopes of "owning and preserving" the animal.[11] He eventually even acquired the seal's head and began the "Roosevelt Museum of Natural History" in his room. Subsequently, Roosevelt was drawn to natural history books and he learned taxidermy at age thirteen.

T.R.'s autobiography explicitly connects these recollections with receiving his first rifle. His initial attempts at hunting revealed that his companions often saw things to shoot at that he could not, and he soon learned his eyesight was poor. "I had no idea how beautiful the world was until I got those spectacles," he writes after his father had given him a pair of glasses (20:17).[12] From the beginning, then, Roosevelt's passion for hunting was closely tied to his desire to collect and to understand—to hear, see, and smell—the things he hunted. Hunting was his most immediate access to nature. At the age of fourteen, Roosevelt was taken on an extended trip to the Middle East, which included a trip down the Nile. The Nile trip gave him the chance to become an expert on the birds of the region and to exercise his interest in taxidermy. "Bird collecting gave what was really the chief zest to my Nile journey," Roosevelt noted, estimating that he killed between one and two hundred birds during the journey. [13]

Roosevelt's interest in collection and taxidermy pointed beyond a mere hobby, suggesting a desire to see things remain whole, even after death, so that an animal's physical shape and color could be thoroughly studied. Autopsy did not engage his mind; rather, he wanted to collect and display the creature whole. Indeed, the practice of taxidermy at a young age foreshadowed a major turn in Roosevelt's life away from a career in science as it was practiced in the laboratory.

When he entered Harvard, Roosevelt's ambition was to become a "scientific man of the Audubon . . . type—a man like Hart Merriman . . . today." He did not do so because science as taught at Harvard was entirely reductionist. He observed that scientists had made a "fetish" out of the microscopic study of "minutiae." "They treated biology," he notes, "as purely a science of the laboratory and the microscope." There was a "tendency . . . to treat as not serious, as unscientific, any kind of work that was not carried on with laborious minuteness in the laboratory." "My taste was specialized in a totally different direction," T.R. wrote. He completely "abandoned all thought of becoming a scientist" (20:27).

Breaking things down to their constituent parts, useful perhaps for certain aspects of scientific exploration, nevertheless obscured the reality of the living creature for Roosevelt. It was not only that his restless temperament did not suit him for the laboratory; more importantly, he believed that microscopic study missed a large part of the truth and was "a very small part of the biological field" (5:389). C. Hart Merriman, founder of the United States Biological Survey, observed that science in Roosevelt's time "seemed to overlook the fact that the instrument is not the only road to knowledge—forgetting that it takes no account of the higher forms of life and fails utterly to explain the interrelations of life and the environment." [14]

Roosevelt's view that the whole could not be explained by its parts, or that the whole was at least more interesting than its parts, was a theme he returned to often during his life. In a review essay entitled "The Origins and

Evolution of Life" published a year before his death, Roosevelt argued that
the origins of life as understood by biology do not explain the consequences
or the end result of the evolutionary process. There are, he said, "plenty of
phenomena unquestionably proceeding from natural law which nevertheless
have in them an element totally incomprehensible" to us. Evolution appeared
to be such a phenomenon for Roosevelt. He noted that "a line of
uninterrupted and gradual causative changes may result at the end in
something of which there was no vestige at the beginning" (12:157-58).
Roosevelt provided an example: "The tracing of an unbroken line of descent
from the protozoan to Plato does not in any way really explain Plato's
consciousness, of which there is not a vestige in the protozoan. There has
been a non-measurable quantity of actual creation. There is something new
which did not exist in the protozoan. It has been produced in the course of
evolution" (12:157-58). Roosevelt concluded that there were things in nature
that we might not be able to understand through quantification.

This situation did not trouble him. He was aware of the discoveries being
made in biology, but those findings never captured the truth for him because
microscopic investigation could not explain the whole of which the cells
were a part. So far as Roosevelt was concerned, the whole was made up of,
but not explained by, its parts. Nature interested him only so far as it
presented itself to humans as fully formed, heterogeneous objects.[15]

Roosevelt pursued those fully formed objects with a vengeance.
Merriman, himself one of the leading scientists in the field of mammalogy,
called Roosevelt "the world's authority on the big game mammals of North
America."[16] Roosevelt's knowledge of bird songs was considered authorita-
tive, as were his writings on deer.[17] Merriman recalls that "one evening at my
house (where I then had in the neighborhood of five thousand skulls of
Northern American mammals) [Roosevelt] astonished everyone—including
several eminent naturalists—by picking up skull after skull and mentioning
the scientific name of the genus to which each belonged."[18]

Roosevelt's reputation was built on the solid ground of years of experience in the outdoors. Virtually every trip was recorded in detail and later
published, as any good scientist would seek to do with research. If anything,
his interest in science increased as he got older, to which the character of his
two greatest outdoor writings, *African Game Trails* and *Through the
Brazilian Wilderness*, attested.

African Game Trails is an account of a nearly year-long expedition T.R.
led to East Africa on behalf of a number of major museums in the United
States. The adventure took place in 1910 just after Roosevelt left the White
House. Beginning in Mombasa, his safari moved northeast to Lake Victoria

and then north to Sudan and up the White Nile. At the time, the various species of mammals, reptiles, birds, and plants of Africa were poorly understood in America, a deficiency that was largely corrected by Roosevelt's energetic safari. He described the expedition as a "trip through the Pleistocene," so varied were the wildlife. His narrative, like many of his other outdoor adventures, weaves dramatic hunting tales with detailed descriptions of flora and fauna. As one reviewer noted of *African Game Trails*, "the essence of Roosevelt's book is an overwhelming account of the natural history of Africa not easily available in one volume; but he also moves on to ethnology, lessons in game protection, and an astute record of the beginnings of European civilization in Eastern and Central Africa." [19] Mixed with history, ethnology, and gripping narratives of lion hunts in which several of the hunters are mauled, Roosevelt's story also offers the naturalist's view of a less exciting kind: "There were eland on the high downs not far from Meru, apparently as much at home in the wet, cold climate as on the hot plains. Their favorite gait is the trot . . . when alarmed [they] bound with astonishing agility for such large beasts—a trait not shown by other large antelope, like oryx" (4:243).

Natural history is woven seamlessly into discussions of hunting techniques, native culture, or the proper extent and means of wildlife preservation. Indeed, preservation is a recurrent if muted theme, one Roosevelt discusses here, as elsewhere in his outdoor writings, with a combination of scientific detachment and a passion for action. His discussion of the African elephant was typical. T.R. notes how the ivory-hunters and traders have "penetrated Africa to the haunts of the elephant since centuries before our era," leading "well-nigh to bring about the mighty beast's utter extermination" (4:203). "Fortunately, the civilized powers which now divide dominion over Africa have waked up" and established "large reserves . . . on which various herds of elephants now live what is, at least for the time being, an entirely safe life." He continues by describing regulations in the game preserves, noting that "it would be a veritable and most tragic calamity if the lordly elephant, the giant among existing four-footed creatures, should be permitted to vanish from the face of the earth" (4:204). Still, he argues, "it would be not merely silly, but worse than silly, to try to stop all killing of elephant," since "the unchecked increase of any big and formidable wild beast, even though not a flesh-eater, is incompatible with the existence of man when he has emerged from the state of lowest savagery" (4:204).[20] Roosevelt gives a detailed account of how and under what circumstances elephants can become a danger to man. He also notes the difficulty presented in preserving rhinoceros and hippopotamus (due to its destruction of crops) when they live in such close quarters to humans (4:204-5). These discussions are significant because they hint at how Roosevelt might connect the world of field study with the world of politics. Since the character of wildlife differs, so too must the policies designed to protect them. Underlying distinct approaches, however, is an underlying principle: Government power should be used to protect wildlife.

Roosevelt's knowledge of nature, gained as it was from the ground up, gives him an appreciation of wildlife that goes beyond its usefulness as mere sport. When speaking of the value of the elephant, Roosevelt explicitly separates its value as a "trophy" from its value "as such":

> [T]he elephant has always profoundly impressed the imagination of mankind. It is, not only to hunters, but to naturalists, and to all people who possess any curiosity about wild creatures and the wild life of nature, the most interesting of all animals. Its huge bulk, its singular form, the value of its ivory, its great intelligence—in which it is only matched, if at all, by the highest apes, and possibly by one or two of the highest carnivore—and its varied habits, all combine to give it an interest such as attaches to no other living creature below the rank of man. (4:199)

The elements of awe and cool necessity are combined in Roosevelt's writing to the extent that they come to form a single view. *Through the Brazilian Wilderness* is an excellent example of T.R. attempting to hold these two views of nature together. It is a study of nature in all its fearsome indifference and its beauty.

In 1914, at the age of fifty-five, overweight and blind in one eye, the former president undertook the exploration of an uncharted tributary of the Amazon known at the time as the River of Doubt. Roosevelt and his companions set out into jungles that few humans had ever even seen. The difficulties and dangers of this adventure are hard to imagine. It took his party sixty-seven days just to reach the starting point of the river trip and then an additional ten weeks to reach the Amazon. The team nearly starved; all were brought down at one time or another with some sort of hideous jungle disease; a native guide was murdered by a fellow guide; and one of the group was drowned. Roosevelt never mentioned in his own accounts of this adventure that at one point the injuries and diseases he suffered during the trip made it impossible for him to travel under his own power and that he insisted the party leave him behind to die. [21]

Through the Brazilian Wilderness shows Roosevelt at the height of his art as a nature writer. "No other book ever written," a commentator remarked, "conveys with more exactitude the fascinating horror of the South American jungle."[22] The tale itself is enough to dissuade readers from a romantic embrace of nature, though Roosevelt generally allows them to draw their own conclusions from the straightforward narrative. After describing the "sinister and evil in the dark stillness" of a grove of palms strangled by the predatory vines of the fig tree, an attack of maribundi wasps, and the effects of the "loathsome berni flies" on man and animal, T.R. concludes that

> In these forests the multitude of insects that bite, sting, devour, and prey upon other creatures, often with accompaniments of atrocious suffering, passes belief. The very pathetic myth of 'beneficent nature' could not deceive even the least wise being if he once saw for himself the iron cruelty of life in the tropics. Of course 'nature'—in common parlance a wholly inaccurate term, by the way, especially when used as if to express a single entity—is entirely ruthless, no less so as regards types than as regards individuals, and entirely indifferent to good and evil, and works out her ends or no ends with utter disregard of pain and woe. [23] (5:120-21)

Interestingly, Roosevelt's comments about "nature's indifference" are directed primarily at how that indifference affects "other creatures" not mankind. Mankind is a part of nature, threatened as are others by jungle forces. But mankind, although at danger in the jungle, can also recognize its beauty:

> We passed through wonderfully beautiful woods of tall palms, the onaouaca palm—wawasa palm, as it should be spelled in English. The trunks rose tall and strong and slender, and the fronds were branches of twenty or thirty feet long, with the many long, narrow green blades starting from the midrib at right angles in pairs. Round the ponds stood stately burity palms, rising like huge columns, with great branches that looked like fans, as the long, stiff blades radiated from the end of the midrib. One tree was gorgeous with the brilliant hues of a flock of parti-colored macaws. Green parrots flew shrieking overhead. (5:120)

This description, which appears just three paragraphs before the "iron cruelty" passage, would almost make one want to join Roosevelt on the journey if one did not happen to know what was coming a few paragraphs later. He is both drawn to and repelled by what the parts of nature have to offer. Indeed, because he sees nature as a collection of distinct entities each with peculiar characteristics and each needing to be given its due, rather than as a single entity, Roosevelt can embrace a view of nature that recognizes its beauty as well as its horror. If there are seeming contradictions in his thought and action with respect to conservationism, those contradictions can probably be understood as growing out of this view of nature.

But Roosevelt's understanding of nature derived from the serious field studies of a naturalist was not the only influence on his conservationism. Roosevelt's access to nature, the road he traveled to come to see nature as heterogeneous instead of homogeneous, was through the violence of hunting. To understand Roosevelt's conception of nature and his views of conservationism, we must also understand his hunting.

Roosevelt as Hunter

Roosevelt's hunting is a "knotty problem for the modern reader."[24] Morris reports that in a six-week hunting trip after graduation from Harvard the young Roosevelt shot some 200 animals,[25] which works out to about five a day if he hunted every day. Morris wonders if Roosevelt's hunting in his youth might not properly be termed "carnage," given the list of kills.[26] "How such a lover of animals could kill so many of them . . . is a perhaps unanswerable question," Morris suggests.[27] This is a particularly vexing issue, given Roosevelt's preoccupation with the proper limits of hunting and his frequent condemnation of "game butchers." What explains this tension?

Hunting was a common and uncontroversial sport for men of Roosevelt's time and class and the number of kills he recorded when he was young would probably not have been regarded as excessive by his contemporaries.[28] Moreover, what measure of criticism Roosevelt might have met with could be offset with reference to the character of young men. What separated Roosevelt from his contemporaries, however, was that excess in the blood sport did not survive his youth. Indeed , the awareness that his own actions were at the least self-defeating and perhaps even immoral seemed to have come to him by the time he had completed *Hunting Trips of a Ranchman*, his first outdoor book.

In *Hunting Trips* (published in 1885 when he was just twenty-seven, about the same time he was recording the large bags questioned by Morris) Roosevelt calls man "the destroyer" of the elk, an animal he believes may well be on its way to extermination at the hands of the hunter. While Roosevelt the hunter is racking up large bags, Roosevelt the naturalist is recording the overhunting of certain species and the changing western landscape. It was not too long before the scientist's insights tamed the youthful hunter.

The book itself is distinguished from other hunting stories of this era for its deep, textured look at the changing West and for avoiding a "mere recitation of kills."[29] Roosevelt, in fact, was one of the first to recognize and to report on the threat to western wildlife from unrestrained hunters and fur traders, especially buffalo hunters, whom he regarded as one of the lowest forms of life. "Finding and killing game is but a part of the whole," he wrote in his preface to *The Wilderness Hunter*. The "free, self-reliant adventurous life, wild surrounding, beauty of the scenery, the chance to study the ways and habits of the woodland creatures" are all part of the reason for hunting. What is more, hunting "cultivates vigorous manliness for the lack of which in a nation, as in an individual, the possession of no other quality can possibly atone" (2:6).

Hunting, for Roosevelt, points beyond itself to science, education, and character building. These themes recur in Roosevelt's writing, building from his earliest reflections in *Hunting Trips of a Ranchman* to their most thorough coverage in *Outdoor Pastimes of an American Hunter*. The very title of the book—emphasizing hunting as a "pastime" not a way of life—suggests the theme of limits. The hunter, he argues, must be a sportsman, not a "game hog" and must be humane (e.g., 12:428). "The big game hunter should be a field naturalist," Roosevelt explains, "carefully studying and recounting the habits of the wild creatures, especially when in some remote regions to which trained scientific observers but rarely have access." He is contemptuous of hunters who make no field notes, but simply record their kills. "Hunting should go hand in hand with the love of natural history, as well as descriptive and narrative power," Roosevelt argues (3:117).

Hunting is also an important avenue for toughening character. "No nation facing the unhealthy softening and relaxing of fiber," which is a tendency in civilized counties, he writes, "can afford to neglect anything that will develop hardihood, resolution and the scorn of discomfort and danger. But if sport is to be made an end instead of a means, it is better to avoid it altogether" (3:22). Indeed, the manner in which one hunts is equally a reflection on a person's character. In a stinging rebuke to an acquaintance who had taken up bear and mountain-sheep killing as a business written two years before publication of *Pastimes*, Roosevelt scolds, "You are a Christian at heart; why don't you become a Christian in your ways, instead of a ruthless butcher of defenseless animals. . . . Killing game the way you are doing it is not just wrong; it is cowardly and contemptible and wicked. It ought to be a criminal act, besides, and it will be when the people wake up to the facts."[30]

Hunting was not a sport Roosevelt took lightly. He took it seriously enough to preach its limits and to explain the consequences of exceeding those limits. The game butcher and those whose hunting was lazy degraded themselves. Proper hunting was a nearly comprehensive activity for Roosevelt. It challenged the intellect to study and understand nature, tested the body against the harshness of terrain and weather, and built character through the manner of one's hunting. In Roosevelt's time, hunting also gave him an exceptionally clear glimpse into the western landscape. This was essentially the theme of his early outdoor books and articles. Hunting, and to a certain extent ranching, brought him face-to-face with the devastation being wrought by civilization on large game and on the wilderness itself.

"For we ourselves and the life that we lead," Roosevelt writes in *Hunting Trips*, "will shortly pass away from the plains as completely as the red and white hunters who have vanished from before our herds. . . . It is scarcely a figure of speech to say that the tide of white settlement during the last few years has risen over the West like a flood; and the cattlemen are but the spray from the crest of the wave, thrown far in advance, but soon to be overtaken" (1:21).

The change is irreversible, Roosevelt believes. While he regrets the passing of the old, he regards this change with some ambivalence. His discussion of the extinction of the large buffalo herds in *Hunting Trips* is especially poignant in this regard. Roosevelt recounts the natural history of the buffalo in North America in considerable detail, noting that "the rapid and complete extermination of the buffalo offers an excellent instance of how a race that has thrived and multiplied for ages under conditions of life to which it has slowly filled itself by a process of natural selection continued for countless generations, may succumb at once when these surrounding conditions are varied by the introduction of one or more new elements" (1:188). He suggests that the mountain buffalo is "better fitted to 'harmonize with the environment' to use the scientific cant of the day" even though this species, too, is destined to die away "unless very stringent laws are made for its protection." Here is one of the few suggestions found in *Hunting Trips* that positive measures might be taken to save an endangered species. The tension between his desire to keep the wilderness wild and his realization that to a large extent that desire is unrealistic is played out throughout this book and in his other outdoor literary efforts.

In *The Wilderness Hunter,* Roosevelt notes that the extension of the railroad to the American West resulted in "such a slaughter of big game as the world has never before seen" (2:182). In *Hunting Trips* he writes that "the extermination of the buffalo has been a veritable tragedy of the animal world" (2:186). But he also notes that:

> While the slaughter of the buffalo has been in places needless and brutal, and while it is greatly to be regretted that the species is likely to become extinct, and while, moreover, from a purely selfish standpoint, many, including myself, would rather see it continue to exist as the chief feature in the unchanged life of the Western wilderness; yet, on the other hand, it must be remembered that its continued existence in any numbers was absolutely incompatible with anything but a very sparse settlement of the country; and that its destruction was the condition precedent upon the advance of white civilization in the West. . . . From the standpoint of humanity at large, the extermination of the buffalo has been a blessing. The many have been benefited by it and I suppose the comparatively few of us who would have preferred the continuance of the old order of things, merely for the sake of our own selfish enjoyment, have no right to complain. (2:191)

Roosevelt never changed his mind about the buffalo. Not long after writing these words he did, however, begin to place greater emphasis on ideas that were only germs here. For example, he started to assert the need for positive steps by government to protect the wilderness and the species it supported. Morris argues that at the time of *Hunting Trips*, in 1885, Roosevelt "took the conventional attitude that some dislocation of the environment must occur when civilization enters a wilderness."[31] But that attitude did not last long. By 1887, Roosevelt had undergone a significant shift in his thinking about the fate of the wilderness West.

Building a Conservation Constituency

When he returned to the East in 1887 after another extended trip to the Dakotas, Roosevelt invited a dozen influential animal lovers to dinner and persuaded them to form the Boone and Crockett Club, an organization dedicated to greater understanding of the American wilderness and to preserving its resources. In typical Roosevelt fashion, Boone and Crockett was conceived to do more than simply raise the general awareness of poor natural resource practices and of the plight of endangered wildlife. He formed the group to galvanize influential quarters to push for legislative change. This was Roosevelt's first important political move toward conservation and it had considerable consequences.

The club became an effective lobbying organization for the new conservation movement. Among its many accomplishments, it pushed for and succeeded in extending protection of Yellowstone in the Lacey Act and most importantly was instrumental in the passage of the bill granting wide authority to the president to establish federal lands for protection. The importance of the following section of that bill can not be overstated. "The President of the United States may, from time to time, set apart and reserve in any States or Territory having public lands bearing forests, any part of the public lands, wholly or in part covered with timber or undergrowth, whether of commercial value or not, as public reservations, and the President shall, by public proclamation, declare the establishment of such reservations and the limits thereof." A decade later, President Roosevelt used that power to great effect.

One might have expected, given his newfound political activism, that Roosevelt's outdoor writings would begin to reflect more sharply his involvement in the conservation movement. By the time Boone and Crockett had been founded, he had already become a well-known chronicler of western life and landscape. What better vehicle could there be for arguing the need for policy change and for pro-conservationist polemics?

Curiously, the character of his outdoor writings changed very little after the formation of the influential Boone and Crockett Club. While hardly devoid of politically charged rhetoric, his hunting and outdoor adventure stories must have had a broader education purpose than just attempting to persuade readers that certain legislative actions were required to preserve western wildlife. Otherwise the post-Boone and Crockett writings would surely have taken on a more argumentative tone or would have come to fit more closely with his political writings and speeches. That they did not, or that Roosevelt did not reshape his nature writing, is further indication of how seriously he took his responsibilities as recorder of nature.

These works remained largely a vehicle to describe in detail the beauty, diversity, and wonders of the American West and only occasionally did he use these writings to urge readers of the need for conservation. His literary intentions remained set even as his political intentions changed, because he saw his outdoor writings as fulfilling a necessary part of his overall political goal of changing the way people regarded nature. By describing in compelling prose precisely what nature offered in the West and therefore what was to be lost, Roosevelt built a case for conservation and preservation.

"It is an affectation of the man who is praising outdoors," Roosevelt writes in his autobiography, "to sneer at books." But, he notes, "usually the keenest appreciation of what is seen in nature is to be found in those who have also profited by the hoarded and recorded wisdom of their fellow men" (20:308). Indeed, "hunting should go hand in hand with the love of natural history, as well as with descriptive and narrative power" (3:117). "A really first-class hunting book," Roosevelt notes, "ought to be written by a man of prowess and adventure, who is a fair out-of-doors naturalist; who loves nature, who loves books, and who possesses the gift of seeing what is worth seeing and of portraying it with vivid force and yet with refinement" (12:410).[32] Hunting stories lacking this quality disgusted him. "I doubt if there is a less attractive type of literary output," Roosevelt writes in his essay "A Hunter-Naturalist," "than an annotated game-bag, or record of slaughter, from which we are able to gather nothing of value as to the lives of the animals themselves" (12:370).

The very compounding of details about the West found in his hunting stories allow Roosevelt to present "with refinement" a picture of what might be sacrificed to unchecked expansion. Taking the seven books generally regarded as his major outdoor corpus, one could hardly extract a thin chapter dedicated to the requirements for conservation measures. But the overall impact of the books is to inspire a reverence for the land by providing the reader with a deep understanding of the wilderness features that have already been lost and of those that yet remain unspoiled.

A good example of his descriptive powers can be found in *Outdoor Pastimes of an American Hunter*, a book he wrote while he was president. Among many other things, Roosevelt provides an in-depth survey of Yellowstone Park. As in his work of this kind, he spends relatively little time in direct commentary on conservationism. When he does address the issue directly, he does so with considerable power. "The most striking and melancholy feature in connection with American big game is the rapidity with which it has vanished," he writes in *Outdoor Pastimes*. "At the present moment," he continues, "the great herds of caribou are being butchered, as in the past the great herds of bison and wapiti have been butchered." Roosevelt concludes that "every lover of nature, every man who appreciates the majesty and beauty of the wilderness and of wildlife, should strike hands with the far-sighted men who wish to preserve our natural resources, in the effort to keep our forests and our game beasts, game-birds, and game fish—indeed all the creatures of prairie and woodland and seashore—from wanton destruction" (3:85-86).

But passages such as this are rare in his outdoor writing, the main purpose of which appear to be to teach a hunting ethic and to explain to the politically influential East what was being lost in the wilderness West. He viewed this changing western landscape with the detachment of a naturalist combined with the passion of the hunter. This combination could never translate into a simple posture toward conservation because both science and hunting convinced him to reject the idea of nature as an abstract principle and to adopt a view that regarded nature as heterogeneous. Circumstances, as much as abstract principles, guided his conservationist thinking. The central role played by the distinction between parts and wholes in Roosevelt's thought becomes clearer with an investigation of his conservationism.

Roosevelt as Conservationist

Roosevelt listed conservation as one of the four primary accomplishments of his presidency along with the expansion of American naval power, building the Panama Canal, and terminating the Russo-Japanese War.[33] Under Roosevelt, government land reserves were increased from 45 million acres in 1901 to 195 million acres in 1909. He signed the first appropriation for the preservation of the buffalo and established in Yosemite the first herd of buffalo owned by the government. He created the first national game reserve, established fifty-one national bird reservations, pushed through the National Monuments Act of 1908 that preserved areas of scientific interest including Muir Woods, and added 150 million acres of timberland to reserves.[34] Equally important, Roosevelt raised conservation to the level of a presidential, and therefore national, concern. Roosevelt has had more influence on public attitudes toward the land and nature than any other president in American history.

As president, Roosevelt employed a different set of rationales for conservation than he did in his outdoor writing. Taken together they present his comprehensive argument for natural resource conservation.

Roosevelt's political rhetoric stressed the material benefits that would be lost to America if it wasted its natural resources, while in his outdoor writing he was concerned with the erosion of character that will take place if democratic citizens no longer have access to the testing and harsh qualities of wild nature. His political arguments face people with the practical economic consequences of a failure to embrace conservationism. His writings about nature face people with the moral and ethical dimensions of putting excessive demands on nature. Even his speeches, however, and even in those that were influenced or drafted by Gifford Pinchot, the moral dimension is not entirely ignored.

In perhaps his most important conservation speech as president, "Natural Resources—Their Wise Use or Their Waste," which he gave in 1908 at the opening of the Pinchot-organized and -controlled Governor's Conference on the Conservation of Natural Resources, Roosevelt stresses how the advance of civilization increases societies' dependence on nature. "With the rise of peoples from savagery to civilization," the president noted, "and with the consequent growth in the extent and variety of the needs of the average man, there comes a steady increasing growth of the amount demanded by the average man from the actual resources of the country. Yet, rather curiously, at the same time the average man is apt to lose his realization of this dependence upon nature" (16:120). While "very primitive peoples" can subsist on nature's bounty using its surface resources, it is only more advanced cultures, according to T.R., that need to slash the ground, thus making use of and threatening all that nature has stored. Indeed America's "position in the world has been attained by the extent and thoroughness of the control we have achieved over nature." However, that growth has been built on the "rapid destruction of our natural resources," a destruction that Roosevelt argues must cease if the prosperity of the U.S. is to be sustained.

Although clearly structured to fit the conference goals as conceived by Pinchot, Roosevelt's remarks at least suggest that conservationism may have a purpose beyond providing a sustainable economic base. He pointed, if only briefly, to the broader implications of resource destruction that were more fully examined in his outdoor writings when he noted that "So great and rapid has been our material growth that there has been a tendency to lag behind in spiritual and moral growth: but that is not the subject upon which I speak to you today" (16:123).

Returning quickly to the political task at hand, Roosevelt continued with a vivid description of the waste and destruction of natural resources that had taken place since the founding of the nation. After recounting the devastation of the land, forests, coal-fields, iron reserves, and natural waterways, he concluded that "we have thoughtlessly, and to a large degree unnecessarily, diminished the resources upon which not only our prosperity but the prosperity of our children must always depend" (16:124). Here again, Roosevelt tried to convince his audience that its own self-interest was intimately connected to the success of conservation efforts. Not only your prosperity, but your children's and children's children's prosperity rests on how we treat nature today, Roosevelt argued.

He ended this address, which had been largely given over to a dark view of the future of America's natural resources, on an optimistic note—that is, man can in fact improve on nature by "compelling the resources to renew and even reconstruct themselves in such manner as to serve increasingly beneficial uses" (16:125).

What is clear from Roosevelt's speech is that, as president, he selected a different set of arguments for conservationism than were developed through his experience as scientist/naturalist and hunter. As president, Roosevelt tended to stress self-interest over moral requirements. As field naturalist, hunter, and author he incorporated both self-interest and ethics into a single view of nature and man's relationship to nature.

His outdoor writings reveal conservation as a reflection of a nation's and a people's maturity. As hunting reflected on the morality of the hunter, so conservation reflected on the character of a nation. "Above all, we should realize," he wrote in *Outdoor Pastimes*, "that the effort toward [preserving wildlife] is essentially a democratic movement" since wild creatures should be enjoyed by everyone "whether he is or is not a man of means" (3:87). Accordingly, "if unchecked popular rule means unlimited waste and destruction of natural resources—soil, fertility, water-power, forests, game, wild life generally . . . then it is sure proof that the present generation is not yet really fit for self-control." Roosevelt notes that "'for the people' must always include the people unborn . . . or the democratic ideal is not realized."

The contrast here between "a democratic movement" and "unchecked popular rule" is worth noting. The democratic inclinations or ends of conservationism can be undermined, Roosevelt notes, by popular excess. The check, it seems from the example of Roosevelt himself, is executive power. As will be discussed below, Albert Gore presents an alternative solution to the zeal of a nation to soil its own nest.

Later in *Outdoor Pastimes*, Roosevelt connects the goal of a politically feasible democratic conservationism with the character building of hunting:

> The only way to secure the chance for hunting, for the enjoyment of vigorous field-sports, to the average man of small means, is to secure such enforced game-laws as will prevent anybody and everybody from killing game to a point which means its diminution and therefore ultimate extinction. Only in this way will the average man be able to secure for himself and his children the opportunity of occasionally spending his yearly holiday in that school of hardihood and self-reliance—the chase. (3:379)

Character, moral conduct, and democratic leadership are necessary if the conservationist movement is to succeed. Conservation not only signals the maturity to look beyond one's immediate self-interest; it reflects on the degree to which a nation as a whole is capable of self-government. "Foresight," Roosevelt argued, "should be one of the chief marks of any people calling itself civilized." [35] Clearly, however, nations do not preserve everything. Some things are saved, others are not. Is it just a matter of expediency to decide what part of nature will be ravaged by civilization?

At the Grand Canyon in 1903, Roosevelt told his audience to "keep this great wonder of nature as it now is. . . . You cannot improve on it; not one bit. . . . What you can do is keep it for your children, your children's children and for all who come after you." [36] Yet, Roosevelt was a major force in western land reclamation and sided against John Muir in the famous Hetch Hetchy dam controversy.[37] He favored conservation though scientific management of forests because trees are renewable resources and because their control was necessary for agriculture. At the same time, he favored preservation of parts of nature that could not be renewed if lost. Roosevelt's principle of action seems to have been determined by his understanding of particulars, certainly by the politics, but clearly not by an abstract commitment to either resource exploitation or preservation.

In *The Wilderness Hunter*, for example, Roosevelt discusses in great detail the rate of extinction of various species, focusing on the special, individual circumstances that influence the survival of particular animals. While he is concerned by extinction and the threat of extinction, he appears most interested in explaining the multiple levels of particularity that must be considered before one can understand fully the reasons why a particular species dies out.

Why Roosevelt worked to save one species (or one wilderness area) and not another is a question of particulars and political judgment, with what is best for humans weighting the balance. But the value of a particular has to be measured in both material and nonmaterial terms. Roosevelt regarded certain parts of nature as "art" in much the same way as did Aldo Leopold. Leopold argued that if we can "live without goose music, we may as well do away with stars or sunsets or Iliads. But the point is that we would be fools to do away with any of them." [38] Roosevelt also pointed to art to explain the value of nature to man:

> Birds should be saved because of utilitarian reason; and, more-
> over, they should be saved because of reasons unconnected with
> any return in dollars and cents. A grove of giant redwoods or

sequoias should be kept just as we keep a great and beautiful cathedral. The extermination of the passenger-pigeon meant that mankind was just so much poorer; exactly as in the case of the destruction of the cathedral of Rheims. And to lose the chance to see frigate-birds soaring in circles above the storm, or a file of pelicans winging their way homeward across the crimson afterglow of the sunset, or myriad terns flashing in the bright light of midday as they hover in a shifting maze above the beach—why, the loss is like the loss of a gallery of the master-pieces of the artists of old time. (3:377)

Far from holding to a simple materialist view of nature—a view that might well have come to him through science and hunting—Roosevelt saw nature's benefits to man as going beyond the utilitarian. Such an understand-ing, as with that developed in Leopold's writing, transcends the distinction between preservationism and conservationism because it is neither abstract moralism nor abstract exploitationism, although it strives toward morality and wise use. The view attempts to include the insights of both while avoiding their natural extremes. What is more, as was clear from his discussion in *Through the Brazilian Wilderness*, Roosevelt scorned the notion of nature as a "single entity." He loved nature in its particularity and it was in its particularity that he judged its value. An abstract value judgment on nature was close to meaningless for T.R., since he knew of nature only as it presented itself in peculiar circumstance. His politics, therefore, demanded to the extent feasible case-by-case judgments and decisions flowed with the benefit of a single abstract principle.

Systematic field studies gave Roosevelt the tools he needed to understand the great diversity of wildlife and wilderness in the American West. Hunting gave him immediate access to nature and taught him to respect its parts for their individuality. Both convinced him that nature was heterogeneous and unequal, and that conservationism had to take into account both commercial and aesthetic values.

As will become clear from a comparison of Roosevelt with Albert Gore, an alternative approach to understanding nature, one that does consider it as a "single entity," results in different political thought and action.

The Environmental Thought of Albert Gore

No other contemporary politician can claim the mantle of "defender of the environment" with as much confidence as Albert Gore. His Senate career was marked by leadership in bringing the issues of global warming and ozone depletion to national prominence. As vice president, Gore is generally recognized as the environmental conscience of the Clinton Administration in which he directs a variety of environmental initiatives for the White House, including international negotiations on the full range of global ecological questions. It is his writing, however, and especially his best-selling book, *Earth in the Balance: Ecology and the Human Spirit* (1992), that established Gore in the public mind as a leading, articulate, and persuasive environmentalist. Given the book's scope (Gore covers the history of science, philosophy, and religion), Gore clearly intends to build an intellectual framework for environmentalism in the twenty-first century.

A century earlier, Theodore Roosevelt was helping to do the same for the conservation movement. Gore's book, however, presents a fundamentally different view of nature than the one held by Roosevelt, and Gore explicitly means to supplant the earlier view with his own concept of nature. These varied understandings of nature have a significant impact on how we view our responsibility to the environment and therefore how we structure policy on the use of natural resources.

Despite their many important differences, T.R. and Gore share important common ground. Both, for example, argue that the destruction of natural resources undermines human character. As we have seen, Roosevelt believed the end of the wilderness, or at least wild settings, would deny American citizens an arena for self-testing and toughening of character. Technological progress, he argued, while to be encouraged, also carried with it an almost inevitable weakening and slackening of soul that could be counterbalanced only by meeting nature head-on, or by war. Roosevelt believed experiencing nature was necessary for building democratic citizen who were not only willing, but also capable, of making personal sacrifices.

Gore too is concerned with how society's callous attitude toward nature has undermined individual character. "The froth and frenzy of industrial civilization," he writes, "masks our deep loneliness for that communion with the world that can lift our spirits." [39] Our large commercial civilization, according to Gore, has separated us from nature and caused a deep spiritual crisis and void that erodes society. "The accumulation of material good," he argues, "is at an all-time high, but so is the number of people who feel an emptiness in their lives." [40] For Gore, the solution to this "inner crisis" seems to lie with each individual. Each of us, he believes, must restore a balance within ourselves between who we are as humans living in the world and who we are as a part of nature. Once this balance is restored within the self, we can begin to take steps to restore the balance in nature itself.

But Gore does not spend a great deal of time in this book developing a therapy for individual self-healing. He appears to be primarily concerned with the "dysfunctional civilization" in which we live and the global manifestation of the individual's spiritual degradation. He compares our dysfunctional global society to the national pathologies that have seized peoples in the past and led to brutal totalitarian rule. Just as these totalitarian regimes posed a threat to world peace, our technologically driven and materialistic civilization poses a threat to the earth itself. "The real solution will be found," Gore contends, "in reinventing and finally healing the relationship between civilization and the earth."[41]

On the issue of individual corruption by materialism, Roosevelt might not strongly disagree with Gore's analysis. But *Earth in the Balance* is interested in the corruption of the individual by technology primarily for how that distortion of the human soul has caused pathological behavior profoundly to degrade the global environment. Roosevelt is concerned with the connection between nature and a democratic character. He urged the nation to ensure that it would always have an avenue for testing because he was interested in maintain strong democratic citizens. Gore's perspective is global and looks beyond the individual to the good of human society as a whole.

This difference in perspective is worth noting because it is part of a large disagreement over nature itself. This becomes clearer when looking at another area in which Roosevelt and Gore begin with a shared concern—the defects of modern science.

In the 1880s, Roosevelt turned away from "establishment" science—especially biology—because it was rooted in microscopic study of cells and ignored what the cells create when they formed a whole. Gore finds the same problem with science in the 1990s. "We organize our knowledge of the natural world," he writes on the first page of *Earth in the Balance*, "into smaller and smaller segments and assume that the connections between these separate compartments aren't really important. In our fascination with the parts of nature, we forget to see the whole."[42] One of the primary reasons, according to Gore, for this failure to see the whole is the dominance of reductionism aided by the scientific method. While the "scientific method gave us a powerful . . . way to investigate natural phenomena and reduce them to a collection of smaller bits of information, each one susceptible to explanation, repetition—and manipulation,"[43] it has the destructive effect of separating the "observer" from the "observed," leading to an amoral detachment.

> The very act of intellectually separating oneself from the world in order to observe it changes the world that is being observed—simply because it is no longer connected to the observer in the same way. This is not a mere word game; the consequences are all too real. The detached observer feels free to engage in a range of experiments and manipulations that might never spring to mind except for the intellectual separation. In the final analysis, all discussions of morality and ethics in science are practically pointless as long as the world of the intellect is assumed to be separated from the physical world. That forced separation leads inevitably to the separation of mind and body, thinking and feeling, power and wisdom; as a consequence, the scientific method changed our relationship to nature and is now, perhaps irrevocably, changing nature itself. [44]

Reductionism, argues the vice president, has caused us to embrace a distinction between facts and values, between what science lets us see and the ethics of how we should treat what we see. Gore argues that by breaking nature down into its parts we lose respect for, and attenuate our moral obligations toward, the whole. Scientists must be more than observers; for Gore, they must have a commitment to the whole. [45]

The interplay between Roosevelt and Gore on the limits of modern science is revealing. As with Gore, T.R. thought nature was more than matter in motion. Both argue that the observer needs to understand that what he observes demands respect and some kind of moral obligation. But Gore asks us to address that respect and moral obligation to an abstraction—nature—while Roosevelt is committed to the hard things in nature, or to the parts of nature which taken together form the whole. When T.R. rejected a career in science he did so because it told him nothing of interest about birds, rocks, trees, streams, big game, sunshine, or rain. When he rejected the idea of nature as homogeneous, he did so because the idea itself was an abstraction. Roosevelt's commitment to the environment grew from his interest in the parts of the environment. He experienced awe and reverence during his time outdoors, but it was awe and reverence born of a respect for the distinctiveness that he encountered rather than a reverence for a whole that transcended the parts. In *Hunting Trips of a Ranchman* he writes:

> Each animal that I saw had its own individuality. Aside from the thrill and tingle that a hunter experiences at the sight of his game, I by degree grew to feel as if I had a personal interest in the

> different traits and habits of the wild creatures. The characters of
> the animals differed widely, and the differences were typified by
> their actions; and it was pleasant to watch them in their own
> homes, myself unseen, when, after stealthy, silent progress
> through the somber and soundless depths of the woods, I came
> upon them going about their ordinary business. (1:223)

Here Roosevelt moves from a knowledge of the individuality of wildlife, to a "personal interest" in their individuality, to a pleasure in observation of individuals. For T.R., diversity was the attraction, and it imparted both respect and concern.

Gore, however, objects to modern science because it fails to understand, or engender an obligation toward, a threatened earth—itself an abstraction. He argues that it is precisely the T.R.-like focus on particulars that has caused civilization to push the environment to the brink by blinding us to a larger crisis. Gore explains that it is important to look "beyond simple questions about what we are doing to the various parts of the environment," to "consider the complex nature of our interaction with the whole environment."[46]

He uses the example of a computer-generated mosaic of Abraham Lincoln, which is recognizable only at a distance, to suggest that looking at only parts obscures the whole. "In order to recognize the pattern of [ecological] destruction," he contends, "we have to see it from a distance, both in time and space. Since the pattern is truly global, we have to see the entire world in our mind's eye."[47] And "much of our success in rescuing the global ecological system will depend upon whether we can find a new reverence for the environment as a whole—not just its parts."[48]

The Politics of Environmental Reform

A reverence for the whole is necessary for Gore because it is the whole of nature that is threatened. Accordingly, "the entire relationship between humankind and earth has been transformed because our civilization is suddenly capable of affecting the entire global environment, not just a particular area."[49] What he calls "strategic threats" to the environment (e.g., chlorine disruptions of the atmosphere, global warming) encompass nothing less that the "bulldozing of the Garden of Eden" or the transformation of the entire Earth into an unlivable and barren wasteland.

Environmental regeneration requires that we aspire to a "comprehensive command of the way in which the environment functions."[50] This amounts to a kind of universal human knowledge of nature, a comprehension of the whole. From that knowledge we can begin to restore the health in our own souls and the earth we inhabit.

The consequences for politics of Gore's view of nature and of the threat humankind now poses to nature are worth discussing. Gore calls for a fundamental reshaping of human civilization. Technology, he argues, has made mankind a "coarchitect of nature." It can certainly help us turn the tide back. But technology alone cannot solve the problem of environmental degradation, because the destruction of the earth is at root a consequence of our collective unhealthy relationship to nature. Therefore, while technology can help, it is only a tool used in a larger project—the transformation of civilization and each individual's posture toward nature.[51] Failure to recognize the scope of the impending global disaster will itself generate crisis. "We now face the prospects," Gore writes, "of a kind of global civil war between those who refuse to consider the consequences of civilization's relentless advance and those who refuse to be silent partners in the destruction."[52] To avoid this catastrophe Gore contends that "we must take bold and unequivocal action: we must make the rescue of the environment the central organizing principle of civilization."[53]

In policy terms for Gore:

> Adopting a central organizing principle—one agreed to voluntarily—means embarking on an all-out effort to use *every* policy and program, every law and institution, every treaty and alliance, every tactic and strategy, *every* plan and course of action—to use, in short, *every* means to halt the destruction of the environment and to preserve and nurture our ecological system.[54]

This is strong medicine. Now, Gore's insistence that a new organizing principle be adopted "voluntarily" is in apparent tension with the manner in which he tends to characterize those who have yet to see the global crisis. In addition to claiming that the recalcitrant could cause global civil war, on at least three occasions in *Earth in the Balance* Gore compares those who have yet to awake to environmental crisis, or actively work against his solutions, to those who turned their backs on Nazi aggression and the Holocaust.[55] If this is truly the case, what would be the justification for waiting, and perhaps waiting too long, for a voluntary consensus on action to be brought to bear on the ecological crisis? This passion inclines the reader to question whether Gore sees a place in the political community for compromise with those who are, in effect, responsible for a global crisis. Given Gore's conclusion, that we face an unprecedented global tragedy unless we make saving the environment the controlling principle of government, it is difficult to see how his political objectives could be achieved short of a basic change in the democratic process. This would entail the nation voluntarily agreeing to shift the focus of government from its primary function, to secure rights, to a new locus of concern, rescuing the environment. Individual rights including property rights would then be secondary to the rights of nature, and the actions of government would be directed first toward protecting the environment and then toward protecting human rights. In principle, at least, there is nothing necessarily undemocratic in this proposal, though it must be noted it is not liberal democracy as understood by the Framers of the Constitution.

A comparison to T.R. on this point is again revealing. Roosevelt contends that conservationism is precisely a sign that a society is *ready* for democracy. If society demonstrates, however, that self-governance and restraint with respect to its natural resources is beyond it, Roosevelt might be inclined to answer with strong presidential leadership, rather than a rethinking of the constitutional order. Gore certainly believes that the chief executive must lead society—and indeed perhaps the global community—to a recognition of the ecological crisis. He seems to imply the need to go beyond the constitutionally restrained executive power, however, when he demands a fundamental change in the goals of democracy. He stands alongside T.R. in demanding self-rule, restraint, and moderation with respect to human desires. But he departs from Roosevelt when he argues that solving the problem of environmental degradation may demand a turn away from individual rights as the end of government and leaves himself open to the charge that his "voluntary" agreement (a plebiscite?) on a new central organizing principle for society could lead us away from limited government. Especially in his political rhetoric, Roosevelt was not beyond speaking of a grave environmental crisis, but he does not take the next step, as does Gore, to say that the nature of the political community is incapable of facing this crisis and must be changed, perhaps because Roosevelt was satisfied that executive leadership (and its bully pulpit) was sufficient. As president, Roosevelt used the bully pulpit to exhort the nation to take better care of its natural resources, interpreted presidential power broadly, and exercised that power vigorously. Gore speaks little about the powers of the president, although he speaks at length about programs (e.g., a "global Marshall Plan") that government can undertake. But his zeal leaves one wondering if he would be willing to entertain a change in the nature of democratic rule in order to avoid what he believes to be an impending environmental nightmare.

Gore has come to these conclusions and has begged these questions as a direct result of his abstract view of nature and his depreciation of the heterogeneity of nature. When nature is separated from the things that humans can experience, it becomes an idealized object of almost religious proportions. When that object is threatened to the degree Gore believes, taking "every means to halt the destruction" without much concern for how those means might affect the discrete segments of nature—the phenomena actually observed by humans—appears to be an appropriate response. This approach necessarily devalues the needs, excellences, virtues, vices, and requirements for those parts of nature that mankind confronts each day. What is more, Gore's single-minded preoccupation with taking action to solve the ecological crisis must certainly fly in the face of his own experience as a legislator. Has Gore forgotten the law of unintended consequences?

Finally, Gore's book begs another question: what are the consequences for human beings, let alone fish, deer, and mountain streams, for reinventing civilization and aiming all powers of the state (even if agreed to by a majority) as well as all our individual energies toward saving the abstraction called the "environment"? Can we all now agree as to what is an environmental problem?

Take the example of climate change. Gore considers global warming a "powerful symbol of the larger environmental problem." But viewing this problem solely from the global perspective obscures the fact that, even if the most dire predictions came to pass, some regions and some species would probably benefit, some might not be affected at all, and some might suffer considerable harm. This in turn raises simple questions policymakers face everyday—is the race worth the candle? Does the good to be had from attempts to prevent climate change outweigh the possible consequences? None of these questions is given an adequate answer in *Earth in the Balance*. There is something apolitical about Gore's abstract approach. Gore stresses that ecology is complex, yet abandons complexity when it comes to environmental impacts on particular parts of nature because he has paid too little attention to the particulars themselves.

Abandoning the local aspects of nature in favor of a concern for a comprehensive environmental understanding leads Gore to an additional problem. It is possible to love or hate an abstract entity with great passion, but it is more difficult to hold extreme attitudes when presented with the segments that make up that entity. Roosevelt could see the necessity, the bleakness, the ugliness, and the beauty in nature, but did not give these things moral content. They simply "were." Gore's view of nature, however, leads him to an undifferentiated embrace of the environment with less thought to the amoral functionings of nature itself.

How, then, will Gore be able to make distinctions—a necessary requirement for politics—between the actual things in nature? For example, should we (even if we knew how to do so) save every endangered species, and at what cost? Because his standard for making political judgments is an abstraction, Gore's answer to basic questions such as these has the tendency to to run to extremes.

T.R.'s view regarded some parts of nature as more important than others, with man, not earth, in the balance. This approach is not without its problems: why save the Grand Canyon and not Hetch Hetchy? In other words, what is Roosevelt's principled ground for deciding in favor of one and letting the other be dammed, so to speak? Principle may be so closely tied to prudence on these kinds of questions that they are difficult to separate. However, it seems clear that Roosevelt believed economic prosperity was not the only or most important value, that material human progress could rightfully be sacrificed to the non-material and unmeasurable value of preserved wild nature. This is not the kind of clear-cut principled argument found in Gore. Roosevelt's prudential approach is by definition subject to significant tempering by the pulling and hauling of politics. And certainly injustice can and often does result from such pulling and hauling. But the dangers inherent in Roosevelt's mixture of prudence and principle are less to be feared than those attached to Gore's embrace of principle at the expense of prudence. Gore points, for example, to overpopulation as a major global environmental concern and lays down rather conventional approaches to handle the problem.[56] But in the background of all his benign proposals stands his more basic and ultimately ruling position, that *any* means can be used to solve global distress if agreed to "voluntarily."

Conservationism and Environmentalism

The objection can be raised fairly that Roosevelt faced dramatically different circumstances with respect to threats to the environment than we do today and that therefore, while Gore's view of nature may have defects, his policies may well be an imperative. Moreover, it could be argued, we simply know more about ecology today than in Roosevelt's time, knowledge that clearly points to comprehensive global trouble for nature: All "distinctions" fade in the face of impending ecological calamity.

There are several possible ways to think about these important objections. First, Gore's openness to alterations in the liberal democratic process and his seeming resistance to compromise are troubling. The consequences for human beings as well as for our environment of a shift away from a government based on individual rights must be taken seriously and must indeed be the primary question addressed to Gore. One need not be a partisan of America's large commercial republic to at least acknowledge the advances in environmental clean-up it has made relative to other regimes. This progress certainly places an obligation on Gore's part to explain in detail how a turn away from limited government will in fact help the environment. Reinventing civilization is a utopian scheme, the end result of which is not at all clear.

Second, there is simply enough doubt about Gore's primary contention—that the earth is near ecological collapse—to wonder whether radical political change is required. For virtually every environmental disaster he discusses, from ozone depletion to species extinction, there is a host of professionals who believe the threat is either nonexistent or can be managed with policies pointed directly at the specific environmental problem and that are far less radical than those Gore believes are required.

Third, the possibility of global environmental disaster was not in fact unknown to Roosevelt's generation. "It is evident," Roosevelt wrote, "that natural resources are not limited by the boundary-lines which separate nations, and that the need for conserving them upon this continent is as wide as the area upon which they exist." Roosevelt also discusses the need to hold an international conference "for an inventory of the natural resources of the world and to [devise] a uniform scheme for the expression of the results of such inventory, to the end that there may be a general understanding and appreciation of the world's supply of the material elements which underlie the development of civilization and the welfare of the peoples of the earth." Roosevelt noted that the "project lapsed" after he left the White House (20:401-2). Still, despite his interest in the international aspects of resource management, he cautioned his fellow conservationists not to exaggerate threats. "Sometimes . . . " he argued, "in endeavoring to impress upon a not easily aroused public the need for action, [conservationists] in their zeal overstate the need. This is a very venial error compared to the good they have done; but in the interests of scientific accuracy it is to be desired that their cause should not be buttressed in such manner" (3:125).

Utopianism and exaggeration of threats to move policy in a special direction may be checked by Roosevelt's view of nature, which begins with particulars, makes distinctions between the requirements of different parts of nature, and is prepared to differentiate the parts of nature in terms of their value to human beings, since it is precisely concerned with constructing specific policies to fit peculiar circumstances. Roosevelt's conservation policies, while sweeping in several respects, were always tied to the requirements of a specific part of nature. Roosevelt could talk about the importance of wilderness and the need to preserve it. But to do so in the policy context for T.R. meant knowing whether the aim was protecting the Grand Canyon or Hetch Hetchy Valley. The decisions in this regard were highly political, of course. Roosevelt laid down no unyielding principle that can guide us in making these kinds of decisions today. But by beginning with the local situation of the environment and asking questions about how different outcomes would affect humans both materially and spiritually, Roosevelt turns our attention away from abstractions and toward the particular. He provides less an all encompassing blueprint than a way of thinking.

Roosevelt respected nature because he saw it for all its harshness and beauty. He witnessed its changes and flux first-hand, as few have done. He recognized, with Gore, the awesome impact of civilization on nature, but he also realized that man was not the only, or always the most powerful, force that changed the environment. In fact, change and uncertainty were some of the things that most attracted Roosevelt to the outdoors. If we know anything about Roosevelt, it is that—with all his capacity for reflection—he was a man of action, of doing, of motion. An unchanging nature would not have interested him.

But this is precisely what Gore appears to desire—nature at rest. His idealized view of nature leads him to see it as an entity that could be perfect if humans could only understand it better and let it find balance. When he sees an environmental threat, therefore, he tends to see it not as isolated challenges to a locality, but as a threat to the whole, since local problems are only proxies of a more fundamental menace, the individual's diseased relationship to nature. Yet, he fails to offer the reader eager to know about or get closer to nature much more than an abstraction. For all their violence and bloodshed, Roosevelt's hunting tales leave the reader with a greater respect for and interest in nature than Gore's moving call for regeneration and renewal.

Notes

1. Aldo Leopold, *A Sand County Almanac* (New York: Ballantine Books, 1966), 223-24.

2. Paul Russell Cathright, *Theodore Roosevelt, the Making of a Conservationist* (Urbana: University of Illinois Press, 1985), 211.

3. See, for example, Roderick Nash, *Wilderness and the American Mind* (New Haven, CT: Yale University Press, 1982), 1.

4. Edmund Morris, *The Rise of Theodore Roosevelt* (New York: Ballantine Books, 1979), 243.

5. Samuel P. Hays, *Conservation and the Gospel of Efficiency: The Progressive Conservation Movement, 1890-1920* (Cambridge: Harvard University Press, 1959).

6. Hays, *Gospel*, 127.

7. Hays, *Gospel*, 125.

8. Hays, *Gospel*, 127.

9. Hays, *Gospel*, 189.

10. Hays, *Gospel*, 189.

11. *The Works of Theodore Roosevelt*, National Edition, 20 Volumes (New York: Charles Scribner's Sons, 1926), 20:16. All citations in the text are to this collection, referenced by volume and page number.

12. It is certainly possible that one of the reasons Roosevelt became such an expert on bird songs is that he could not see well enough to easily identify species by sight alone.

13. Morris, *Rise of T.R.*, 66.

14. C. Hart Merriam, "Roosevelt the Naturalist," *Science* Vol. 75, No. 1937 (February 12, 1932): 183.

15. His major interest was in life forms rather than geology or forestry.

16. Edward Wagenknecht, *The Seven Worlds of Theodore* Roosevelt (New York: Longmans, Green & Co., 1958), p. 42.

17. Cathright, *Making of a Conservationist,* 252-57.

18. Merriman, "T.R. the Naturalist," 183.

19. Aloysius A. Norton, *Theodore Roosevelt* (Boston: Twayne Publishers, 1980), 109.

20. Roosevelt often employed this argument for hunting.

21. This information only came to light in accounts of the trip from the other naturalists traveling with Roosevelt. Norton, *Theodore Roosevelt,* 113.

22. Norton, *Theodore Roosevelt*, 116.

23. See also, *Nat. Ed.,* 4:169-70 where Roosevelt notes, "Death by violence, death by cold, death by starvation—these are the normal endings of the stately and beautiful creatures of the wilderness. The sentimentalists who prattle about the peaceful life of nature do not realize its utter mercilessness; although all they would have to do would be to look at the birds in the winter woods, or even at the insects on a cold morning or cold

evening. Life is hard and cruel for all the lower creatures, and for man also in what the sentimentalists call a 'state of nature.'"

24. Paul Schullery, ed., *Theodore Roosevelt: Wilderness Writings* (Salt Lake City: Gibbs M. Smith, 1986), 19.

25. Morris, *Rise of T.R.,* 132.

26. Morris, *Rise of T.R.*, 285-86.

27. Morris, *Rise of T.R.*, 299.

28. Morris, *Rise of T.R.*, 299.

29. Norton, *Theodore Roosevelt*, 91.

30. Quoted in Wagenknecht, *Seven Worlds of T.R.*, 18.

31. Morris, *Rise of T.R.*, 382.

32. This is a fair description of Roosevelt himself.

33. Cathright, *Making of a Conservationist*, 232.

34. Cathright, *Making of a Conservationist*, 222.

35. Quoted in Cathright, *Making of a Conservationist*, 218.

36. Schullery, *T.R.: Wilderness Writings*, 217.

37. Hays argues that the president was "torn between the two uses" [i.e., water for San Francisco and preservation of the valley] and "supported Pinchot only with indecision." (Hays, *Gospel*, 193.)

38. Leopold, *Sand County Almanac*, 230.

39. Albert Gore, *Earth in the Balance: Ecology and the Human Spirit* (Boston: Houghton Mifflin Co., 1992) 220-21.

40. Gore, *Earth in Balance*, 221-22.

41. Gore, *Earth in Balance*, 35.

42. Gore, *Earth in Balance*, 1-2.

43. Gore, *Earth in Balance*, 199.

44. Gore, *Earth in Balance*, 253.

45. Gore, *Earth in Balance*, 254-59.

46. Gore, *Earth in Balance*, 8.

47. Gore, *Earth in Balance*, 45-46.

48. Gore, *Earth in Balance*, 204.

49. Gore, *Earth in Balance*, 30.

50. Gore, *Earth in Balance*, 204.

51. Gore, *Earth in Balance*, 35.

52. Gore, *Earth in Balance*, 269.

53. Gore, *Earth in Balance*, 273.

54. Gore, *Earth in Balance*, 274. Emphasis added

55. Gore, *Earth in Balance*, 177: "Once again, [as in the 1930s] world leaders waffle, hoping the danger will dissipate. Yet today the evidence of an ecological *Kristallnacht* is as clear as the sound of glass shattering in

Berlin." On page 196, Gore plays Winston Churchill warning Britain to prepare for war with Nazi Germany to George Bush's Neville Chamberlain. On page 274, Gore writes, "Minor shifts in policy, marginal adjustments in ongoing programs, moderate improvements in laws and regulations, rhetoric offered in lieu of genuine change—these are all forms of appeasement, designed to satisfy the public's desire to believe that sacrifice, struggle, and a wrenching transformation of society will not be necessary. The Chamberlains of this crisis carry not umbrellas but 'floppy hats and sunglasses'—the palliative allegedly suggested by a former secretary of the interior as an appropriate response to the increased ultraviolet radiation caused by the thinning of the ozone layer."

56. Gore, *Earth in Balance*, 309.

3

Gifford Pinchot, Founder:
A New Look at *Breaking New Ground*

Marlo Lewis Jr.

"Sustainable development" has become the unifying theme of the modern environmental movement.[1] The overarching rationale for everything from the United Nations Framework Convention on Climate Change to Federal habitat conservation plans to local zoning ordinances and recycling mandates, sustainable development is one of those gauzy phrases to which even the most hard-boiled businessman may feel obliged to pay lip service, if not homage. Yet the phrase implies a radical critique of the market economy, and betokens a radical program of "reform."

According to sustainable development advocates, population growth and consumerism are placing unnatural burdens on the earth's "carrying capacity" and life-support systems. To meet the growing demands of an increasingly global economy, modern industry and agriculture are depleting the world's non-renewable resources, denuding its forests, and obliterating wildlife habitat. At the same time, the byproducts of industrial civilization are contaminating the air, poisoning the water, and dangerously altering the climate.[2]

It is not too late to "save the planet," sustainable development advocates contend, but only if the world's governments cooperate to establish new controls on population growth, consumption, technology development, and trade. Thus, implementing a sustainable development regime would require massively expanding the powers of government and creating new institutions of "global governance." Far from being a moderate alternative to "command and control" regulation, sustainable development is natural resource planning, family planning, and industrial policy all rolled into one. What sustainable development advocates seek is centralized ecological planning, on a global scale.

By all accounts the conservation movement was as concerned with the threat of resource depletion as today's advocates. Did it pursue a more sensible approach to stewardship questions than the present sustainable development agenda, with its totalitarian implications? Could a thoughtful encounter with the founders of the conservation movement suggest new directions for environmental policy today?

This chapter will examine the early career of the man who was at the center of founding conservation as a national policy and as a political movement. By attempting to understand Gifford Pinchot (1865-1946) as he understood himself, we may gain a deeper insight into the alternatives available to policy makers in our time.

Founding Ambitions

In an oft-quoted passage of his autobiography, *Breaking New Ground*, Gifford Pinchot explains his delight in gaining the title "Forester" instead of "Chief of the Forestry Division." In Washington, chiefs of division were a commonplace; foresters were not. Besides, says Pinchot, "I was a forester in fact before that happy day. I have since been a Governor, every now and then, but I am a forester all the time—have been, and shall be, all my working life."[3] But Pinchot was no ordinary forester. He founded American forestry, both as private practice and as public policy. And founding is a political act.

To found means to introduce "new modes and orders."[4] The founder shapes the moral and political horizon within which later generations think and act. To overcome the partisans of the old order, the founder may lay claim to special knowledge, authority, or integrity transcending the venality and partisanship of politics. But founding is politics at its most intense and the founder is the most political of men. Gifford Pinchot was a governor—as well as a senatorial candidate and a presidential hopeful[5]—"every now and then," not because he was a forester, but because he was a politician. Pinchot's ambition was a princely ambition. His genius lay not in the realm of theory but in that of action. He helped launch the conservation movement not by developing a doctrine a là Marx or Freud but by building coalitions, creating institutions, implementing strategies, and stage-managing events. Pinchot's autobiography is his "personal story of how Forestry and Conservation came to America" (xv). More than anything else, it is the story of a remarkable political career.

Pinchot's book is political in more than one sense. There is in it almost nothing about Pinchot's private life. In 510 pages, Pinchot never mentions the names of his parents (James and Mary). He does not tell us that he was the eldest of four children, one of whom died of scarlet fever at the age of two. Nor does Pinchot reveal whether he ever fell in love, married, or had children of his own.[6] *Breaking New Ground* is the public record of a public man. Political events and actions form the core of the book; all else is background or context. The book has a political intention: to renew public support for the Forest Service and the conservation movement. Finally, it is written in a politic manner. Things are not always spelled out.

Consider, for example, Pinchot's discussion of his reading habits:

> So far as my bad eyes would permit, reading has always been to me an enormous relaxation and relief. But I have read for escape more than for information and improvement, and have wasted time beyond counting. I have spent much time with books, but I have never gained in knowledge anything approaching what the time expended might easily have yielded. I am not, I am sorry to admit, what is called a well-read man. (229)

At one level, this is a confession of ignorance. At the same time, it implies that Pinchot knows whereof he speaks, that his insights are not borrowed from other sources but grounded in experience. He makes this explicit in the final chapter: "What I have learned in more than half a century of active life, whatever else it may be, is not mere book theory. The conclusions I have reached are based on what I have lived, and seen, and known, and had to fight" (504). Pinchot's autobiography never lets us forget that conservation was a political project—the brainchild, program, and legacy not of armchair theorists but of men in the arena.

Pinchot was of course not born a politician but he was born into a prominent family whose connections and wealth he used unapologetically to get ahead in the world and make his mark upon it.[7] The seeds of Pinchot's ambition were planted early by his father. "'How would you like to be a forester?' asked my foresighted Father one fortunate morning in the summer of 1885, just before I went to college." This was an "amazing question" for that day and generation. At the time, not a single American had made Forestry a profession. Not one acre of timberland was being managed under the principles of Forestry anywhere in America (1). There was no market, no public demand, for the services of foresters.

Pinchot explains the situation as follows. "Forestry is Tree Farming. Forestry is handling trees so that one crop follows another. To grow trees as a crop is Forestry" (31). Most Americans, if they thought about forest perpetuation at all, considered it unnecessary and "even ridiculous." Public opinion held forests to be "inexhaustible and in the way" (1). Lumbermen in particular "regarded forest devastation as normal and second growth as a delusion of fools." The idea of "sustained yield" had never "entered their heads" (27).

Accordingly, there were no schools of Forestry in the United States, nor any courses in forest management in any American universities. During the winter of his senior year at Yale, Pinchot conferred with some of the leading academic and government experts—Dr. George Loring, former secretary of agriculture; Dr. Bernard Fernow, chief of the government's Forestry Division; Professor Charles Sargent, editor of *Garden and Forest* and the foremost advocate of forest preservation. These men saw no future for a forester in America and advised Pinchot to pursue another profession. "Nevertheless and notwithstanding," says Pinchot, "my Father strongly advised me to stick to my guns. With his support I did stick to them" (5). Pinchot offers no explanation, but apparently the difficulty and originality of the path he had chosen—plus the prospect of leading a profession by pioneering it—made him all the more determined to stay with it. After learning from his professors that no science of forestry existed in the United States, Pinchot wrote to his mother: "[I]t seems to me that I shall have not only no competitors, but even a science to found. . . . This is certainly as good an opening as a man could have."[8] There is honor and distinction in doing what is hard and different—in breaking new ground.

Pinchot conceived this ambition without having any clear idea what Forestry was. Forestry was "new and strange and promised action," and that was enough (5). Although knowing little about Forestry, he was eager to profess his faith in it. His first opportunity came at commencement. Pinchot had carefully prepared a speech on another subject. "But on the spur of the moment I dropped it, my future profession welled up inside me and took its place, and I made to the exalted graduates of Yale (in June of 1889) my first public statement on the importance of Forestry to the United States" (6). If a politician is someone who can speak well about a subject without knowing what he is talking about, Pinchot already had the gift.

Pinchot's father believed Forestry could have a bright future in America because he had seen it flourish in France and other European countries. After graduation, Gifford went to Europe to learn Forestry. Although family and Yale connections undoubtedly helped, young Pinchot showed a talent for what is today called "networking." Arriving in London, Pinchot met W.N. Sturt, a high official of the Indian Civil Administration, who took an interest in him. Sturt got his chief, Sir Charles Bernard, to write letters of introduction for Pinchot to Sir Dietrich Brandis, founder of Forestry in British India, and Sir William Schlich, head of the British Indian Forest Service School. Although Pinchot enrolled in the French Forest School in Nancy, he became a protégé of Dr. Brandis, who lived in Bonn. Brandis arranged for Pinchot to spend a month with Forsmeister Meister, a Swiss forester in charge of the city forest of Zurich (6-15).

Pinchot acknowledges only two formative influences in his life—his father, whose "tenacity and foresight" in guiding and encouraging Gifford "were responsible, in the last analysis, for bringing Forestry to this continent" (2), and Dr. Brandis, to whom "I owe more than I can ever tell." Of Brandis, Pinchot wrote: "I doubt whether any other man in Europe could have been as wise a guide. Moreover, he could scarcely have taken more trouble with me than if I had been his own son" (17). But of even greater importance, Brandis was the "founder" of Forestry in British India: "[H]e had done great work as a forest pioneer, had made Forestry to be where there was none before. In a word, he had accomplished on the other side of the world what I might hope to have a hand in doing in America" (9). Did Brandis nurture this ambition in his protégé? Pinchot suggests as much: "As I look back, I think he saw in this long-legged youngster a possible instrument for bringing Forestry to a new continent" (17).

A successful politician must be a quick study, and after spending a year at the French School Pinchot decided he had learned enough. Brandis and other European foresters urged Pinchot to stay on for two more years to complete the full course of instruction. In Pinchot's view, his teachers did not understand how different political and economic conditions were in the United States. There was no Forestry in America. Introducing the rudiments would be challenge and achievement enough. It was time to get started.

Private Demonstration Projects

When Pinchot returned from Europe in 1890, he found "the most rapid and extensive forest destruction ever known . . . in full swing." America was "obsessed . . . by a fury of development. The American Colossus was fiercely intent on appropriating and exploiting the riches of the richest of all continents—grasping with both hands, reaping where he had not sown, wasting what he thought would last forever" (23). Pinchot was appalled at the devastation of America's forests. Forests that could have been managed to produce a steady harvest were simply destroyed, either to supply wood for homes, fuel, and railroad ties, or simply to clear space for development. The woodman's "reckless ax" had despoiled millions of acres of productive forestland. Forest fires, allowed to rage unchecked, had ruined millions more.

What accounted for the stark difference between European and American practices? Why was there no American Forestry? According to Pinchot, the vastness of our continent had spawned the myth that America's forests were "inexhaustible." If there would always be plenty of timber, then there was no reason to regulate cutting or manage the forests to assure future productivity. The inexhaustibility myth excused and encouraged waste on a gigantic scale. America was killing its own future and robbing posterity, and nobody seemed to care (27-28).

There is, however, an alternative explanation that Pinchot never considered. Pinchot prided himself on adapting European Forestry to American conditions. In France he visited a forest "where peasants carried away every scrap of dead wood, and where branches down to the size of a pencil could be made into fagots and actually sold." Pinchot chides those who sought to replicate such practices in America's forests, "where settlers were still rolling logs into piles and burning them to get them out of the way" (14). But a case can be made that Forestry *as such* was largely inappropriate to American conditions in the nineteenth century. Europe practiced Forestry because it had to—nearly all the old growth forests had been cut down centuries ago. The only way to supply timber was to grow trees as a crop. In America, there were still hundreds of millions of acres of virgin forest. Cutting without replanting would have been wasteful in Europe but might make perfect economic sense in America for long stretches of time. Where timber is plentiful and labor scarce, labor expended on forest management might represent a net waste of resources.

As Robert Nelson points out, Pinchot made no attempt to adapt the concept of sustained yield to American conditions. To Pinchot and other European-trained foresters, sustained yield meant steady or increasing production from the same tract, year after year. But where forests are vast, clear-cutting of even large tracts may not destroy the forests' capacity to regenerate. Furthermore, it is arbitrary to assume that timber stocks should always remain constant or increase over time. In a society of industrious pioneers, it may be perfectly rational to draw down timber stocks for decades or even generations before taking steps to conserve and replenish them. As long as the market eventually provides for the renewal of timber resources, sustained yield harvesting is achieved.[9]

Pinchot, however, had little faith in the self-correcting powers of the marketplace. He feared that declining timber stocks would make homes more expensive, so he was not unaware of the relationship between price and supply. Yet he apparently had no inkling that rising prices could induce people to economize on the use of wood, develop substitutes for wood products, or even, for purely commercial reasons, begin growing trees as a crop. Nor did he imagine that market-driven technological progress might come to the rescue of the forests, which is in fact what happened. Technology dramatically increased the productivity of U.S. agriculture. American farmers met the nutritional needs of a growing population and produced enormous quantities for export without expanding the total amount of cropland. In fact, since 1950, total farmland has declined by almost 200 million acres, allowing wild and forested areas to return on much of this land. Indur Goklany and Merritt Sprague estimate that if farmers today were still using the technology of Pinchot's era, they would have to plow an additional 925 million acres to match current output. In other words, an additional area four times larger than the entire national Forest System (including the State of Alaska) would have to be put under the plow.[10]

It was as a student at the French Forest School that Pinchot became "convinced of the imperative need of Government control" of timber cutting in America—a conviction, he says, "which has grown steady with the years and has never been as strong as now" (14).[11] Brandis persuaded him that Americans would never see the light "until some State or large individual owner makes the experiment and proves for America what is so well established in Europe, that forest management will pay." This opinion, says Pinchot, was his "lodestar" for years (15).

To change public sentiment, deeds count more than words. Initially, Pinchot chose action over exhortation. Following Brandis' advice, he proposed and ran what today might be called "pilot" or "demonstration" projects. The idea was to "put Forestry into actual practice in the woods, prove that it could be done by doing it, prove that it was practicable by making it work" (30). Once again, his family connections and talent for befriending important people served Pinchot well. In 1891, he held "several conferences" with George W. Vanderbilt, one of America's wealthiest men, and Frederick Law Olmsted, the "first and greatest of America's landscape architects" (about whom more is said in chapter 8). Vanderbilt had hired Olmsted and Richard Hunt, the "foremost" American architect of the time, to create for him, near Asheville, North Carolina, the "most beautiful and elaborate country estate in America" (47). Known as Biltmore, the estate had a small farm, an arboretum, and a 6,000-acre forest. Pinchot proposed to manage the forest for sustained yield. Vanderbilt agreed.

Biltmore House was a magnificent chateau of Indiana limestone; with terrace and stables, it measured a thousand feet in length. "Its setting was superb, the view from it breathtaking, and as a feudal castle it would have been beyond criticism, and perhaps beyond praise." "But," says Pinchot,

> in the United States of the nineteenth century and among the one-room cabins of the Appalachian mountaineers, it did not belong. The contrast was a devastating commentary on the injustice of concentrated wealth. Even in the early nineties I had sense enough to see that. (48)

Whether he also saw that "concentrated wealth" was what made it feasible for Vanderbilt to take a risk on an unproven youngster with unconventional ideas is not evident from the text.

Biltmore became "the beginning of practical Forestry in America" (50). It was the first tract of woodland in the United States managed in such a way as to generate revenue while improving the forest. For example, instead of clearing out the young growth to make logging cheap and easy, green trees were left standing to perpetuate the forest. Large trees were spared at regular intervals to produce seeds for future crops. The first year's work showed a positive balance of $1,220.56. "To that extent we made it [Forestry] pay" (54).[12] But did it pay as much as the usual cutting methods? Was this really a relevant test? Wasn't it Vanderbilt's "concentrated wealth" that made Pinchot's experiment "practical"? Vanderbilt wasn't in the timber business. Most of the wood produced in Biltmore forest was for use on the estate rather than for sale in the marketplace (66). Vanderbilt was an art lover, and Biltmore was his "heart's delight" (48). He wanted Biltmore and its forest to remain lovely for generations to come. Vanderbilt had aesthetic reasons for experimenting with Forestry—motives a timber company would not have. The long view comes easily to men of dynastic wealth.

Be that as it may, Pinchot, at the 1893 Chicago World's Fair, presented a photography exhibit on Biltmore Forest, "the first exhibit of practical Forestry ever made in the United States" (57). Soon afterwards he persuaded Vanderbilt to buy 80,000 acres of an adjacent forest called Big Creek. Unlike Biltmore Forest, which supplied wood for the estate, Big Creek's product was sold on the open market. "The first year showed a profit. Unfortunately," concedes Pinchot, "later years did not. Whether the fact that

I had turned to other works had anything to do with it, I cannot say" (68-69).[13]

The truth is, it didn't matter. His arrangement with Vanderbilt left him "free to take on additional work." Pinchot set up office in New York City and put "Consulting Forester" on his door (69). The Vanderbilt credential attracted business. In fact, Pinchot's second client was Vanderbilt's brother-in-law, Dr. W. Seward Webb. Webb owned a "superb tract of 40,000 acres" in the Adirondacks in New York, which he named Ne Sa Ha Ne Park, and hired Pinchot to manage it. Webb's objective was to produce a "fair" rate of return while increasing the value of the land (74-75). Pinchot succeeded, but this was still baby steps and a long way from settling the issue. What makes financial sense to a man of independent means may not be practical for a lumber company with competitors and a payroll to meet.

Public Forestry Activist

For Pinchot, however, the real point of building a resume and a clientele was to gain the credibility required to shape public policy.

> By far the larger question in those days, and the chance for swifter progress, had to do with the public lands of the United States, whose forested portions covered areas to be measured not in thousands but in millions of acres. These public forests held this enormous attraction for a forester—they were under one and only one ownership and control. In contrast with the slow process of inching along from private owner to private owner, which I knew so well, Congress by a single act could open the way for the practice of Forestry upon these enormous stretches of public lands. No wonder they caught and held my keen interest and attention. (79)

The U.S. government owned nearly two billion acres—"a domain richer in soil, water, forage, timber, and minerals than any other similar area on earth" (79). The Federal Estate dwarfed Biltmore or any other private holding. He who defines and enforces the rules of this realm presides over a mighty empire indeed! We may suppose that this, too, was part of the attraction. Here was a domain worthy of a man of princely ambition.

Pinchot and other members of the small but growing band of forest reformers had one thing going for them—fraud and theft were rampant on the public lands, and it was only a matter of time before brazen illegality and scandal aroused public indignation and sparked demands for legislative remedies. Needless to say, Pinchot and his allies publicized the abuses and led the charge for reform.

The general theme they pushed was that "the vast common heritage of land fit for and intended for American homes was falling, in huge quantities, into the crooked, mercenary, and speculative hands of companies, corporations, and monopolies" (82). Monopolists, greedy speculators, and outright crooks were cheating and robbing the honest citizen of his birthright. This theme was a moral claim, not a technical assessment by scientific foresters. It was an emotionally charged framing of a controversial issue—exactly what it takes to launch a political crusade in a country with a strong egalitarian ethos.

Pinchot recounts several examples of outrageous fraud that must have jarred public opinion at the time. Under the Homestead Act of 1862, any citizen could acquire 160 acres of public domain by living on it five years and making certain improvements. At a minimum, the homesteader had to build a dwelling on the land. To evade this requirement, many a claimant would build a toy house, swear to the existence of a dwelling "14 by 16 in size," but omit to say that the dimensions were in inches rather than feet (81). Under the Timber and Stone Act of 1878, an individual could purchase up to 160 acres of timberland at $2.50 per acre if he swore in writing that he had not entered into any agreement to transfer title to another party. The intent was to disperse ownership among a large number of independent loggers. To get around the act, big lumber companies took "trainloads" of tourists from distant states on free trips to the Redwood forests. Each visitor swore he wanted to buy a tract for his own use—and then immediately signed a paper transferring title to a lumber company. The company then completed the transaction by paying $2.50 per acre to the local Land Office, which did nothing to stop the fraud (82).

To Pinchot, the main problem with the Homestead Act, the Timber and Stone Act, and other federal land laws was that they were "badly and, more often than not, corruptly administered" (79). He elaborates:

> [T]he General Land Office in Washington, under the Department of Interior, and the local Land Offices under it were dripping with politics. They early adopted the general idea that their business was not to safeguard the Public Domain, but to pass Government lands into private hands as fast as possible, without regard to actual compliance with the law, as long as the papers were in order. Congress, moreover, under political pressure from the land fraud profiteers, declined to appropriate money enough for special agents to go-look-see whether the law had actually

been complied with on the ground as well as on paper. Stealing
public lands became a regular business. (80)

A few years later, Pinchot, trumpeting the same allegations, waged a
successful campaign to transfer management of the National Forests from
the Interior Department to Pinchot's newly-established Forest Service. Here
it is worth observing that Pinchot assumes the federal land laws were
reasonable and fit the circumstances to which they applied. Yet pervasive
non-compliance is often a sign that a law is poorly designed, that it conflicts
with economic reality.

Interestingly, Pinchot later acknowledges (albeit in passing) that a 160-
acre limit on individual claims to federal coal fields made doing business
impossible: "It was a poor law, for the cost of development was such that
nobody could reasonably hope to work a single claim by himself and make
it pay" (396). Yet much the same could be said of the Homestead Act, the
Timber and Stone Act, the Desert Land Act, and other public land laws
Pinchot admired. A tract of 160 acres might sustain a prosperous farm on the
rich, moist soil of the Ohio valley. But in most of the West, even 640 acres
was too small for an economic farming or ranching operation. Indeed, in an
arid state like Arizona, a rancher might require 50,000 acres just to provide
forage for a small herd of 50 to 100 head of cattle. Similarly, strictly
enforcing the Timber and Stone Act's 160-acre rule would have prevented
efficient, economies-of-scale logging in the Pacific Northwest.[14] Pinchot
never considered the possibility that fraud and corruption might be a
consequence of the law itself.

Understandably, his critics would charge that Pinchot—and the laws he
was so zealous to enforce—were products of eastern snobbery and ignorance
of western conditions. No one had cried foul when the eastern states clear-
cut their forests to make room for civilization. Yet having now become rich
and comfortable, they wanted to deny western states the same opportunities.
As an Oregon newspaper editorialized, the settlers in the West needed the
land covered by the forests to grow "apples, pears, potatoes and other
products, vastly more useful and profitable than the growing of pine
cones."[15]

Conservation: Science and Politics

The chief political question facing Pinchot and his circle in the late
1880s—around the same time Roosevelt was forming the Boone and
Crocket Club—was how to put Forestry on the national agenda. In 1889,

Garden and Forest editor Charles Sargent came up with a "long-shot" plan—a special commission, appointed by the president, to investigate the condition of public lands and make recommendations for their improvement (86). *Garden and Forest* published the proposal, as did the American Forestry Association, the *Century Magazine*, and many newspapers. Nothing came of these efforts, however, until five years later. In December 1894, Pinchot produced the outline of a bill authorizing the president to appoint a commission to study public timberlands. On the same day (December 17), Pinchot and Robert Underwood Johnson of the *Century Magazine* presented the outline to a committee of the New York Chamber of Commerce, and on January 3, 1895, the Chamber passed a resolution recommending the commission plan to the U.S. Congress. A copy was sent to each representative and senator. Half a year later Pinchot gave a speech on "The National Timberlands" to the New York Board of Trade and Transportation, and obtained the board's endorsement of the plan (87).

Several points in this brief narrative are noteworthy. Pinchot was nothing if not persistent. He held the bit of the commission proposal in his teeth for over half a decade. Although still a private forester, he was adept at working with the press, interest groups, and business leaders. He knew how to bring outside pressure to bear on legislators. He appreciated how a seemingly neutral investigation could be used to advance a political agenda.

Furthermore, Pinchot had a lively sense of the prestige and moral authority of science. This was, after all, an age that practically worshiped science. So when Dr. Wolcott Gibbs, head of the National Academy of Sciences, suggested that the academy was the ideal body to conduct the investigation, Pinchot lost no time setting the wheels in motion. The trick was to get a department of the U.S. government to request an NAS study on forests. Pinchot got Edward Bowers, former Commissioner of Public Lands, to put Gibbs's proposal before Hoke Smith, Grover Cleveland's Secretary of Interior. In November 1895, Smith agreed to call upon the NAS for a report. Gibbs appointed seven men to serve on the National Forest Commission. All were members of the academy save one—Gifford Pinchot (89-92).

President Cleveland gave the Forest Commission strategic advice that its chairman, Charles Sargent, disregarded—much to Pinchot's chagrin. Pinchot made good use of it later in his career. Cleveland's counsel was as follows:

> Take up the organization of a forest service first and then the question of more [forest] reserves.

> Let the plan be one that looks small, and at first costs little, and yet has in it elements of growth; let it avoid points liable to attack by reaching its object, if possible, along other lines. To that end, the bills necessary to carry out the plan should be prepared in consultation with someone familiar with the temper of Congress. (94)

Loosely translated: Establish an institutional foothold first, pursue dominion later. Start small and inexpensively but lay the foundations of future expansion. Avoid frontal assaults and know the political lay of the land.

Sargent ignored Cleveland's advice and Pinchot's urging to make the establishment of a forest service the first objective, to recruit Congressional allies, and to complete the report before the president's annual message to Congress. Sargent also rejected Pinchot's pleas to stress conservation for use rather than preservation. With just ten days left in office, Cleveland, on February 22, 1897, approved the Commission's recommendations and created thirteen Forest Reserves—21.2 million acres in all. This ignited a "most remarkable storm" (108) of opposition, both because the commission had not consulted Congress and because, under existing legal definitions, reserves had to be withdrawn from use. A legislative battle ensued in which Congress voted to suspend Cleveland's proclamation and open all reserves to use under Federal administration. Pinchot considered this a great if unexpected victory. Congress had cleared the way for Forestry and the Forest Service on public lands (119).

Pinchot quarreled with those, like Sargent, who hoped to protect the forests by putting them beyond the reach of the woodman's ax. Preservationism was an understandable reaction to forest devastation. But Pinchot opposed it as bad economics and worse politics. America was a growing nation and had to have an expanding resource base to meet the needs of its people. Attempts to withdraw resources from use could only turn the logger, miner, farmer, settler, and grazer against Forestry and conservation. In a formula, Pinchot wanted to save the forests *for* use, preservationists wanted to save them *from* use. Pinchot's objective was "not to stop the ax but to regulate its use" (29).[16]

Pinchot was acquainted with the view that nature has a worth beyond its use-value for human production and consumption, but it had little appeal to him. In the 510 pages of his autobiography there are only two passages that bear any resemblance to the modern environmentalist sensibility.

> At Melville, outside the Sierra Forest Reserve, I ran into the
> gigantic and gigantically wasteful lumbering of the great
> Sequoias, many of whose trunks were so huge they had to be
> blown apart before they could be handled. I resented then, and I
> still resent, the practice of making vine stakes hardly bigger than
> walking sticks out of these greatest of living things. (102)

Pinchot and John Muir spent an "unforgettable day on the rim of a
prodigious chasm" of the San Bernardino mountains. "And when we came
across a tarantula, he wouldn't let me kill it. He said it had as much right
there as we did" (103). Pinchot does not draw any general conclusions from
these passages. Nor does he connect them in any thematic way even though
they appear on successive pages.

   To repeat, for Pinchot, conservation meant saving (and developing)
resources for use. One biographer says: "Other conservationists—naturalists,
park enthusiasts, wildlife groups—sometimes looked at Pinchot and his
practices with sincere shock."

> Proponents of parks, and persons especially concerned with 'the
> promotion of public beauty,' found it hard to understand Pin-
> chot's approval of the disfigurement of a portion of Yosemite
> National Park by the construction of the Hetch Hetchy dam to
> provide water for the city of San Francisco. And still others,
> appalled by his lukewarm concern for the preservation of
> wildlife, questioned his sincere interest in what they regarded as
> 'true' conservation.[17]

To Pinchot, however, the point of conservation was to help human beings
provide for their economic necessities: "The object of our forest policy is not
to preserve the forests because they are beautiful . . . or because they are
refuges for the wild creatures of the wilderness . . . but . . . the making of
prosperous homes. . . . Every other consideration becomes secondary."[18]

A Beachhead in Government

   As a member of the National Forest Commission, Pinchot met several
times with Secretary of Interior Cornelius Bliss. In June 1897, Bliss
appointed Pinchot Confidential Forest Agent of the Land Office. Pinchot's
job was to survey public timberlands and produce a plan for the
establishment of a Forest Service. Pinchot traveled far and wide, learning
much about forests but also about journalism and advocacy: "My contact

with newspapers like the St. Paul *Dispatch*, the Spokane *Spokesman Review*, Seattle *P. I.*, Portland *Oregonian*, San Francisco *Chronicle*, and Los Angeles *Times* gave me some inkling of how public opinion is created and directed." In Washington, he "met two Presidents in the White House on a working basis; became acquainted with the leaders of both the House and Senate; found out at least something about how legislation comes to pass, the bearing of public sentiment upon it, and the jargon in which it is written; and began drawing bills myself." He also sought contact with "older men, outside of politics, who not only knew the United States from one end to the other but whose experience in dealing with public men and public questions made their example a sort of terrestrial guiding star" (132). In short, Pinchot threw himself heart and soul into the business of mastering the political game.

In May 1898, Dr. Bernard Fernow left his position as head of the Agriculture Department's Forestry Division for a professorship at Cornell. Dr. Charles Walcott, director of the U.S. Geological Survey who had served with Pinchot on the National Forest Commission, recommended to Agriculture Secretary James Wilson that Pinchot be appointed to fill the vacancy. Five days after starting the new job, Wilson gave Pinchot the title "Forester," instead of chief of division. This pleased Pinchot greatly and we may infer that he suggested the title change to Wilson: "In Washington chiefs of division were as thick as leaves in Vallombrosa. Foresters were not" (137). A unique title confers distinction—an undeniable political asset.

The division over which Pinchot now presided had a "microscopic and mixed outfit" (137) of ten and almost no equipment. "There was not even a marking hatchet—clear proof that the Division wasn't thinking about practical Forestry, for with that tool the forester marks the trees to cut or leave standing." The budget was minuscule: "less than one cent to spend for every dollar available to the rest of the Department—no great war chest with which to open the campaign for saving a million or so square miles of unsaved forest" (139).

Pinchot wanted to start practicing Forestry on the public lands. There was just one problem. The government forests—43 million acres of reserves and several times more millions of unreserved public timberland—were under jurisdiction of the Interior Department. All the government foresters, namely Pinchot and his friend Harry Graves, were in the Department of Agriculture. The Forestry Division of the Department of Agriculture was mostly engaged in scientific and educational work; it did not actually practice Forestry. "Forests and foresters were in completely separate watertight compartments" (140).

But if the government forests were out of reach, "[p]rivately owned timberlands were not." About half a billion acres of woodlands were in private hands. Surely some of the owners might choose to practice Forestry if they knew about it. So Pinchot began advertising. In October 1898, he issued Circular 21, offering to help farmers, lumbermen, and other private timber owners apply Forestry to their holdings. The response was overwhelming: "Within four months after I took office, applications had been made for help in handling nearly a million acres in nineteen states" (141). Pinchot was building an agency clientele. "I'm from Washington and I'm here to help" was good politics then and still is today.

By June 30, 1899, some 123 lumbermen, farmers, and others had asked the division for help in starting Forestry on a million and a half acres of timberland in thirty-five states. At long last Forestry was making inroads into the lumber woods of America. The entire operation cost the Federal government a mere $4,133.35 in fiscal year 1898-99. Pinchot comments: "Large oaks from little acorns grow" (142). This was starting inexpensively and small, as President Cleveland had advised.

Decades before anyone had ever heard the phrase "direct mail campaign," Pinchot used targeted mailings to nurture and expand his division's support base. Within a year after the division began assisting private lumbermen, the mailing list grew "from 1,200 to 6,000 names, including 2,000 newspapers" (143). Pinchot spent many long hours rewriting, or showing the authors how to rewrite, letters prepared for his signature. As in a modern Congressional office, constituent mail was to be answered promptly. By the time Pinchot left the Forest Service in 1909, the mailing list "reached a total of 781,000 and was divided into such categories as: engineers, 16,000; lumbermen, 56,000; newspapermen, 22,000; farmers, 321,000; educators, 111,000, etc"[19]

Although the division was overloaded with requests for help, and several foresters from abroad applied for positions, Pinchot decided against hiring any foreigners.

> I was perfectly certain it would be worse than useless to fill the gap with imported Europeans, even if we had the money to import them, and in that I was perfectly right. To do the work we had to do, a man must know about forests, of course, but he must also know about how people think, and how things are done in America. In a very real sense, that came first. (147)

To establish Forestry, it was first necessary to sell it. The ability to market Forestry to a skeptical public was more important than technical expertise.

Besides, foreign accents might be off-putting to those who spend their lives in the woods.

To remedy the shortage of foresters, Pinchot used student assistants willing and able to undertake arduous physical labor during their summer breaks. This built a cadre of college-educated, old-boy-networked, forestry enthusiasts. Another device for alleviating the shortage was the appointment of "Collaborators"—experts of established reputation in forestry-related disciplines at universities, state agriculture colleges, and elsewhere (149). In 1900 there were fifteen Collaborators. Ten more were appointed in 1901, among them respected American scientists. Thus did Pinchot recruit allies among the nation's intellectual elite.

But to secure a permanent presence in higher learning, there must be a school of Forestry. In 1900, the Pinchot family donated $150,000 (later $300,000) to found the Yale Forest School. Pinchot's fellow alum, Henry Graves, left the division, to be the new school's first dean. So many of the school's graduates ended up working as federal foresters that the division (and, later, the Forest Service) was sometimes called "the Yale Club." In 1905, for example, twenty-four out of the fifty-five individuals who passed the civil service exam for the bureau were Yale graduates. Pinchot comments:

> The Yale Forest School did what was expected of it. It supplied
> the men we needed in the early days. It furnished many of the
> leaders of the United States Forest Service. From 1905 to 1940
> without a break, the heads of the Forest Service were founders or
> graduates of the Yale School. (153)[20]

Thus did Pinchot provide for his succession. More broadly, by writing the basic field manual (*A Primer of Forestry*), by setting the code of conduct for U.S. government foresters, by requiring regular rotations so Forest Service personnel would be more attached to the service than to any local interest, and by establishing a school to train future Forest Service leaders, Pinchot, the Founder, ensured the perpetuation of his handiwork.

The "inside-outside" strategies that play so prominent a role in Washington politics today would not have surprised Pinchot in the least. Indeed, in November 1890, Pinchot founded his own "outside" group—the Society of American Foresters—to assist and build support for the work of the division.[21] The first meeting was held in Pinchot's office. Subsequent weekly meetings were conducted in his home. "By and large the Society had no small share not only in educating our men, but also, and that was even more important, in establishing genuine respect for the profession of Forestry" (150). Prominent Americans in any field related to Forestry spoke at these meetings. Speakers included Agriculture Secretary James Wilson and, later on, President Theodore Roosevelt. As Pinchot notes, presidents "seldom, if ever, address meetings in private homes" (151).

The division had no coercive authority, but this made it easy to heed Cleveland's admonition against frontal assaults:

> We had no control over the forest property of the Government, or of anybody else, except by the voluntary action of the owner. We could say 'Please,' but we couldn't say 'Don't.' We could say 'come on,' but we could not say 'Get out.' (157)

Hence, the division was "not in the way of principalities or powers, and we exercised no check on wickedness in high places" (157). Pinchot and his staff were making friends without making enemies.

All of this meant a stronger hand in the annual appropriations process. But Pinchot wasn't leaving anything to chance. During the 1899-1900 fiscal year, he lectured "whenever and wherever" he could, and published articles. In September 1899, the division printed the first edition of Pinchot's *Primer of Forestry, Part I*, distributing 10,000 copies. "The book was well bound and well illustrated—a new thing in Department publications—and the Senate promptly ordered 35,000 copies more." Pinchot had, in effect, launched a book tour to promote the division. He had also taken great care to establish a good relationship with the newspapers. Pinchot explained: "They printed hundreds of millions of copies a year, and their items about our work reached a thousand readers to the bulletin's one" (156)[22] The results spoke for themselves. When Pinchot came to the division, its budget was $28,520. In the ten years that followed, "it multiplied more than a hundred times" (153).

Expanding the Bureaucratic Front

On July 1, 1901, the division became a bureau. It had advised private owners of some three million acres. About 177,000 acres had been put under management. But soon the greatest demand for its services came from the Interior Department, which wanted management plans for all the Forest Reserves. Pinchot had made a client of the very department whose authority over timberlands he wanted to seize.

Our war had many fronts. My first great purpose was to start practical Forestry going in the woods. My second, to get all Government forest work together in one place, was never out of my mind. We lost no time laying pipe for the transfer of the Forest Reserves to the Department of Agriculture, and we kept at it. In December 1898, the National Board of Trade passed resolutions recommending it. So did the American Forestry Association, that year, the next, and the next two. And so did a long succession of local and national associations until transfer came to pass in 1905. (160)

The war for transfer to Agriculture was in part a campaign against the Interior Department's sloth, corruption, and incompetence.

However lightly the Western men of those days may have held the land laws, they had high standards of personal courage and hardiness, and they were not lazy. Such men could have nothing but contempt for a service manned by the human rubbish which the Interior Department had cheerfully accepted out of Eastern and Western political scrap heaps and dumped in the Western Reserves. (167)

Pinchot had found the rhetoric capable of appealing to westerners who had no great respect for the land laws he hoped to enforce. In addition, he capitalized on their contempt for the complexity and rigidity of Interior Department regulations, which created interminable delays in harvesting and selling timber on the reserves (169).

Pinchot also acted on a classic maxim of bureaucratic infighting: Knowledge justifies control. If your bureau knows more about an issue than any other, it will gain jurisdiction over it. Innocent sounding studies lay the groundwork for future control. Here's how Pinchot set the ball in motion. He spoke to Hiram Jones, a former colleague on the National Forest Commission who was now with the General Land Office. Jones spoke to W. A. Richards, acting commissioner of the General Land Office. Richards advised Interior Secretary Ethan Allen Hitchcock to request that the Forestry Bureau make a comprehensive survey of the Forest Reserves. Hitchcock transmitted the request to Agriculture Secretary James Wilson, who was happy to oblige. "The play had been Pinchot to Jones to Richards to Hitchcock to Wilson to Pinchot" (173).

During these years Pinchot continued to build the bureau's clientele and make friends in high places. In 1900, the New York Forest, Fish, and Game

Commission asked the bureau for working plans for the State Forest Preserve. The commission hoped this would persuade the people of New York to modify the state's constitution to permit controlled cutting on the preserve. New York Governor Theodore Roosevelt championed the commission's plan in his annual message to the legislature. Although the plan never went anywhere, because public sentiment remained hostile, Pinchot became the working ally of the man who was to become America's first conservation president (182-84).

On September 14, 1901, President McKinley fell to an assassin's bullet. On the same day, Roosevelt was sworn in as President of the United States. Pinchot met frequently with "T.R." and drafted language on Forestry in Roosevelt's first message to Congress, delivered December 2, 1901. At one stroke, exults Pinchot, Forestry had become an issue of "continental consequence." Roosevelt stressed that forest protection is not an end in itself but a means to sustain and increase the resources of the country and industries that depend on them. "The Forest Reserves [said T.R.] will inevitably be of still greater use in the future than in the past. Additions should be made to them whenever practicable, and their usefulness should be increased by a thoroughly businesslike management." Then came what Pinchot calls "the heart and soul" of the message: "These various functions . . . should be united in a Bureau of Forestry, to which they properly belong" (190). In fine, the reserves should be expanded and put under Pinchot's jurisdiction.

Pinchot and Roosevelt lost no time finding a Congressional sponsor for this proposal. Rep. John F. Lacey of Iowa, chairman of the House Committee on Public Lands, introduced legislation to transfer certain reserves to the Department of Agriculture. However, House Appropriations Chairman Joe Cannon "threw his vast influence against the bill," and blocked its passage (198).

About a month later (January 2, 1902), Pinchot helped revise a bill introduced by Rep. Page Morris to create a Forest Reserve in Minnesota, and persuade the state's congressional delegation to back it. Although the land still belonged to the Interior Department, the bill gave Pinchot's bureau free rein to manage the reserve's rich pine forests. It was a step closer to the goal (205).

In time, Pinchot had his adversary surrounded. He had big clients in all parts of the country—a million acre Longleaf Pine forest in Texas ("owned jointly by the Kirby Lumber Company and the Houston Oil Company"); a 50,000 acre tract in South Carolina; a 62,000 forest in Georgia; Maine's Great Northern Paper Company; the Baltimore and Ohio Railroad in West

Virginia; the New York Central and Pennsylvania Railroads; and state government officials in Vermont, New York, Michigan, and California (236).

Nor is that all. The Yale Forest School, with its close ties to the bureau, had started a trend. The University of Michigan established a Forest School. Harvard was on the verge of doing so. The University of Nebraska instituted a Department of Forestry. The Mount Alto Forest Academy was founded in Pennsylvania. The University of Maine and several others began offering courses in Forestry (236-37).

In 1903, Pinchot proposed that T.R. appoint a Committee on the Organization of Government Scientific Work, ostensibly to eliminate duplication and inefficiency, but actually to delegitimize Interior's control over the national forests. The committee was chaired by Pinchot's friend, Dr. Charles D. Walcott, director of the Geological Survey. Pinchot served as secretary. The committee reviewed the scientific work of twenty-five bureaus in six departments, the ICC, and the Smithsonian Institution. It found a lack of "efficiency and coordination" in government scientific work (241), and proposed that all the elements necessary to the solution of a distinct scientific problem be placed within a single "administrative unit." Specifically, control of the Forest Reserves "should be transferred to the Bureau of Forestry in the Department of Agriculture" (242). Who should control millions of acres of valuable timberland, under which management practices, and for what purposes—all controversial policy questions—were to be resolved by appeal to the exigencies of scientific efficiency.

Although political opposition in Congress defeated this stratagem, the endeavor served Pinchot well. He learned about the executive branch as a whole and gained "priceless" experience for planning the Roosevelt commissions that were to follow. Through this exercise, Pinchot became (in T.R.'s words) the president's "counselor and assistant on most of the work connected with the internal affairs of the country" (243).

Pinchot quickly put this experience to work. In the same year, he asked T.R. to appoint a Public Lands Commission to investigate the condition, operation, and effect of the public land laws and to make recommendations for their improvement. Pinchot saw to it that the commission documented the waste, fraud, and corruption that the Interior Department had permitted on the lands entrusted to its care.

The American Forest Congress, held in Washington, in January 1905, under the auspices of the American Forestry Association, delivered the final blow. Pinchot admits, or rather crows, that his bureau "planned, organized, and conducted" the Congress for the specific purpose of obtaining transfer

(254). It was an impressive line up. The sponsors included the secretary of agriculture, who presided; the presidents of the Pennsylvania and Northern Pacific Railroads; the presidents of the National Lumber Manufacturers, Live Stock, and Irrigation Associations; the heads of the U. S. Geological Survey, the U. S. Reclamation Service, and the General Land Office; and a number of senators and congressmen. Newspapers, universities, and many other institutions were represented. "And so at length, thanks to the long struggle we had made for it, and thanks to the American Forest Congress, H.R. 8460, the Transfer Act, passed easily through both Houses of Congress" (256). T.R. signed the legislation on February 1, 1905, the day he received it.

A footnote to this tale further reveals Pinchot's political savvy. Section 5 of the Transfer Act provided that all money received from the sale of any products or use of any resources on the Forest Reserves should for five years be placed in a special fund for the "protection, administration, improvement, and extension of the Reserves." The bureau acquired a revenue stream independent of Congressional appropriations (257).

That Pinchot won the support of some of the very business interests he proposed to regulate is less paradoxical than it may seem. Dam building, flood control, irrigation, and navigation improvements—all part of the larger conservation agenda and all subsidized by tax revenue—were of direct benefit to farmers, timber men, and shippers. Cattle "barons" stood to gain from another policy championed by Pinchot—legalization of fence construction on public range lands. To Pinchot, fences were a necessity of rational management. To the cattlemen, fences were a way of restricting access to sheep men and homesteaders. Finally, regulation itself was a barrier to entry. Big Timber could bear the costs of the new rules far more easily than could smaller, independent operators:

> As additional tracts of forest land were set aside by the government and the prescribed procedures for cutting government timber became more difficult to meet, the advantages held by the large and established lumber companies seemed to increase. For these reasons giant lumbermen not infrequently marched in step with the Forest Service and proclaimed their support of its policies.[23]

On March 3, 1905, the bureau was renamed the Forest Service. This was fitting, as the agency now wielded new powers and authorities.

> Before the Forest Reserves came into our hands, all we could say
> to whoever controlled a forest, public or private, was 'Please' …
>   After the transfer the situation radically changed. While we
> could still say nothing but 'Please' to private forest owners, on
> the national Forest Reserves we could say, and we did say, 'Do
> this,' and 'Don't do that.' (258-59)

Pinchot had waged the transfer campaign for almost seven years. "Overnight he was transformed from a man with some foresters and no forests, into a man with 86 million acres of forest land."[24] We may also surmise that the bureau's new name added another notch of distinction to Pinchot's career. There were many bureaus in Washington, but only one Forest Service.

Selling the Public

Breaking New Ground tells the story of "how Forestry and Conservation came to America." We have seen how Forestry got started. What role did Pinchot play in founding the wider conservation movement?

Pinchot had immersed himself in government organization issues since the start of T.R.'s presidency. He was the driving force behind the Committee on the Organization of Government Scientific Work, the Public Lands Commission, and the "Keep" Committee on Government Business Methods (296). In 1905, when the Forest Service was created, Pinchot observed that various government organizations concerned with natural resources "were all in separate and distinct watertight compartments" (319). Three agencies dealt with mineral resources, four or five had to do with streams, half a dozen had authority over forests, and a dozen or so exercised some supervision over wildlife, soils, erosion, and other land issues. Each went off in its own direction, often with no knowledge of what the others were doing. "It was a mess." There was only one cure, only one way to "bring order out of this chaos," and that was to find the "common ground" on which each agency could take its place, and do its proper work, in coordination with the others (320). Conservation proved to be that common ground. Amazing though it may seem, for Pinchot, the idea of conservation grew out of an organizational imperative—a bureaucratic planner's imperative.

Pinchot reports that conservation came to him one afternoon while he was riding a horse named Jim in Rock Creek Park. Suddenly he realized that the natural resource responsibilities of the various bureaus were not "different, independent, and often antagonistic questions." Rather, there was "one

single question with many parts." The seemingly disparate questions made
up one great central problem: "the use of the earth for the good of man"
(322).

What Pinchot seems to be saying is that conservation is a master or ruling
discipline. Conservation is the science of managing natural resources for the
betterment of mankind. This management is to be accomplished by
government agencies working together under an integrated plan. "It took
time for me to appreciate that here were the makings of a new policy, not
merely nationwide but worldwide in scope—fundamentally important
because it involved not only the welfare but the very existence of men on the
earth" (323).

Although Pinchot does not say so in this passage, conservation also grew
out of a political imperative—the necessity for a unifying theme, vision, and
agenda to build a popular movement. Conservation as Pinchot conceived it
had enormous moral appeal. In Pinchot's rhetoric, natural resources are the
"common heritage" of the nation or even all mankind. Government's "first
duty" is to ensure that those resources—the material foundations of human
existence—are protected, not squandered, and managed for "the benefit of
all," not for "the use and profit of a few."[25]

At the end of *Breaking New Ground*, Pinchot makes explicit what
attentive readers will already have gathered: "Through all my working days,
a part of my job, in office and out, and a most essential part, has been to
estimate and understand public opinion, and to arouse, create, guide, and
apply it" (505). Pinchot contributed to founding the conservation movement
not by developing its theoretical underpinnings but by arousing, creating,
guiding, and applying public opinion. Let's watch him in action.

At Pinchot's suggestion, Roosevelt, in March 1907, established an Inland
Waterways Commission to investigate the condition of the nation's rivers
and suggest improvement. The next step was "to create a public demand that
would support the President." This was "easy," says Pinchot, because
business interests had already formed numerous associations to promote the
improvement of America's waterways (327-28). "The appointment of a
national commission would be water on their wheels, and the petitions for
it which they sent to the President were vigorous and effective" (328).

But endorsements were not enough. Getting what is today called "earned
media" was even more critical. As Pinchot explains, "Action is the best
advertisement. The most effective way to get your cause before the public
is to do something the papers will have to write about." So to grab national
attention, T.R. and the commission sailed down the Mississippi River in a
flotilla. Large crowds turned out to welcome the president at various stops

along the way. The trip was a "huge success"—not least because twelve governors joined the president's party at Keokuk, Iowa, and ten more at St. Louis (329). On the final day, Roosevelt spoke to a convention of the Lakes-To-The-Gulf Deep Waterway Association, and announced his intention to call a national conference on conservation. As we will see, under Pinchot's direction, each media event was a platform for unveiling another.

Impressive though the river trip was, the sequel was even more spectacular:

> In November [1907], T.R. invited the Governors, each with three advisors, to attend the Conference. All the Governors accepted. In December the great national organizations concerned with natural resources, some three score and ten in number, were asked to be represented by their presidents, and half a hundred general guests were added. Earlier invitations had been sent to all Senators and Representatives of the Sixtieth Congress, Justices of the Supreme Court, and members of the Cabinet. . .
>
> Five outstanding citizens were chosen to represent the people of the United States. They were William Jennings Bryan, thrice candidate for President; Andrew Carnegie, foremost steel magnate of his time; John Mitchell, foremost labor leader of his day; James J. Hill, builder of the Great Northern Railroad; and ex-President Cleveland, whom illness kept away. (345-46)

In short, the guest list included everybody who was anybody. Never before had all the governors or their chief lieutenants assembled in one place. Never had so many leading scientists and government officials attended the same event.[26] This was a Mega Conference, a PR extravaganza.

As to theme and message, nothing was left to chance. Pinchot and his associates carefully scripted all remarks.

> The four special guests were anxious for help in preparing their speeches. So were other speakers. We were equally anxious that they should say what needed to be said. Accordingly McGee[27] wrote how many speeches for how many speakers I can no longer recall. But it was an astonishing number, and every one of them clicked. (346)

Roosevelt gave the keynote, declaring (in addition to the remarks already highlighted in the previous chapter) that the various uses of natural resources are "so closely connected" that they should be "coordinated" in one "coherent plan" (347). The long-term good of the nation must take precedence over the short-term profit of the individual. Next to T.R.'s speech, the "high point" was the Declaration of the Governors, drafted, Pinchot says, by Governor Blanchard and McGee (350). It proposed federal regulation of private forest land: "We recognize that the private ownership of forest lands entails responsibilities in the interests of all the People, and we favor the enactment of laws looking to the protection and replacement of privately owned forests" (351).

Pinchot comments that the effect on the governors was profound. "The Governors especially came away with a conviction of national unity that had never dawned on most of them before" (352). Of course it hadn't dawned on them before! Pinchot and McGee had never put words in their mouths before. Hearing each other express identical views on the same topics must have created a strong impression of unity, indeed. The unity lay in the speech writing team rather than in a prior national consensus. However, this may be beside the point. Politicians don't like being out of step. If a governor didn't know what he thought about conservation before the conference, he likely did afterwards.

Furthermore, the conference was not a one shot affair. The Governors' Declaration affirmed the need for "similar Conferences on Conservation in the future" and proposed the creation of permanent state and national conservation commissions (351). Pinchot speculates that future historians may well look back upon the conference as a "turning point in human history" (352). The Conference "introduced to mankind the newly formulated policy of Conservation of Natural Resources, it exerted and continues to exert a vast influence on the United States, and on the Peoples of the whole earth" (352). From that moment on, conservation became "an inseparable part of the national policy of the United States" (353).

Honoring the obligation that Pinchot had written into the Governors' Declaration, T.R. in June 1908 created a National Conservation Commission. "It was a distinguished company, full of Senators and Representatives [and Governors], the heads of Government Bureaus and professional schools, and other leaders in their lines" (356). In all, forty-eight prominent individuals had now publicly committed themselves to T.R.'s conservation policy.

And yet this too proved to be a link in a chain. Roosevelt, on Pinchot's advice, convened a North American Conservation Conference. Pinchot chaired this one. It had three broad objectives. First, lock conservation in place on the home front by incorporating it into multilateral agreements or understandings. Second, pave the way for a similar conference for "all nations of the world" (361). Third, establish the framework for permanent multilateral consultation and cooperation on natural resource matters. The leitmotif of the conference was that conservation problems transcend national boundaries, and so require concerted action.[28]

In its declaration, the North American Conservation Conference called upon the president to sponsor a World Conservation Conference. Since Pinchot wrote the text with T.R.'s approval, it is hardly surprising that Roosevelt honored the duty that the declaration laid upon him. The world conference was to be held in the Netherlands. In September 1909, fifty-four nations were invited to meet at The Hague. Thirty had accepted when President William H. Taft, T.R.'s successor, killed the plan. However, Pinchot was later able to sell the idea to Presidents Franklin Roosevelt and Harry Truman. Truman proposed it to the United Nations Economic and Social Council a few days after Pinchot's death. In March 1947, the UN accepted the plan and put it on the agenda for 1948 (366-72).

At least one other of Pinchot's projects to shape public opinion deserves mention. As noted earlier, Pinchot founded a pressure group—the Society of American Foresters—while serving as a government official. In 1909, shortly before leaving the federal government, he created another such group, the National Conservation Association. Its first president was outgoing Harvard president, Charles W. Eliot, and its executive board included Henry L. Stimson (who would later serve as secretary of state as well as war). Upon leaving government service, Pinchot took over as president and served in that capacity from 1910 almost until the organization disbanded in the early 1920s. Pinchot largely bankrolled the association out of his own pocket. Although it never developed into the large membership organization he had hoped, it gave Pinchot a ready-made platform for speaking to the press and lobbying policy makers.

An Egalitarian Crusade

Historian Samuel P. Hays argues that the heart of the progressive conservation movement was a faith in the power of science to find objective answers to social problems, to develop methods for the rational management of public affairs. "Conservation," writes Hays, "above all was a scientific movement, and its role in history arises from the implications of science and technology in modern society." Hays continues:

> Conservation leaders sprang from such fields as hydrology, forestry, agrostology, geology, and anthropology. Vigorously

active in professional circles in the national capital, these leaders brought the ideals and practices of their crafts into federal resource policy. Loyalty to these professional ideals, not close association with the grass-roots public, set the tone of the Theodore Roosevelt conservation movement. Its essence was rational planning to promote efficient development and use of all natural resources. The idea of efficiency drew these federal scientists from one resources task to another, from specific programs to comprehensive concept. . . . It is from the vantage point of applied science, rather than of democratic protest, that one must understand the historic role of the conservation movement.[29]

As a description of Pinchot, this assessment has much to recommend it. Like the socialist movements of the same period, his conservation can be viewed as a form of *scientism*—the belief that scientific methods can replace prudence in the realm of politics and market signals in the realm of economics. Progressives like Pinchot believed that decisions about natural resource management should be made neither by vote-seeking politicians nor by profit-seeking businessmen but by scientific managers loyal only to the public interest and the highest standards of their professions. Pinchot undoubtedly believed in the desirability and feasibility of the rule of non-partisan experts. But he also appreciated the partisan advantage that the claim to scientific expertise could confer. And he understood how seemingly neutral considerations of efficiency could be used to disguise, and thus advance, a controversial agenda. Finally, he recognized that efficient management could not be achieved without relentless partisan action on its behalf. One reason he went on to help found a political party (the Bull Moose) was to safeguard the management practices he and Roosevelt had instituted.

The conservation movement did not "bubble up" from the grass roots. It was the creation of an intellectual elite. Efficiency, the eternal preoccupation of managers and planners, played a vital role in the birth of the conservation idea, as Pinchot himself suggests. Yet this cannot be the whole story. First, efficiency is about means, not ends. In itself, efficiency tells us nothing about the purposes scientific managers are supposed to serve. Second, although efficiency is generally deemed a good thing, it is not the stuff of which moral crusades are made. Pinchot and other intellectuals in his circle still honored the ideal of an America dedicated to liberty and justice for all. Progressives believed the rule of experts could bring the reality of American life closer to that ideal.

So after leaving government service, Pinchot in 1910, along with Robert La Follette and a handful of other anti-Taft Republicans, organized the National Progressive Republican League. In 1912, Pinchot and other Progressives founded the Bull Moose Party, with Theodore Roosevelt as its presidential candidate. The league and the Bull Moose Party proposed a host of egalitarian reforms: presidential primaries, direct election of senators, women's suffrage, child labor laws, corporate taxation, regulation of railroads, and regulation of public utilities.[30]

Pinchot was among the most egalitarian of the Progressive leaders. He supported a scheme of judicial "recall," whereby the people, through popular referenda, could overturn judicial decisions. He also favored nationalizing the railroads and other "natural" monopolies, although, believing such measures too radical for the times, he did not push for their inclusion in the Bull Moose platform.[31]

Thus, Pinchot's actions are of a piece from the moment he embarked on his career. There was no pre-existing demand for Forestry or conservation, but Pinchot was brilliant at assessing public opinion and appealing to the egalitarianism that has always been a powerful current in American public life. Pinchot sold conservation in America by presenting it as the scourge of monopoly—by defining the fight for conservation as the fight for equal opportunity and justice for the little man. The following passage, an excerpt from Pinchot's most widely published speech, conveys the gist and flavor of his rhetorical approach:

> There is no other question before us that begins to be so important, or that will be so difficult to straddle, as the great question between special interest and equal opportunity, between special privileges for the few and the rights of the many, between government by men for human welfare and government by money for profit, between the men who stand for the Roosevelt policies and the men who stand against them. This is the heart of the Conservation problem today. (444-45)

In the sequel, Pinchot nearly identifies conservation with the cause of morality itself:

> Is it fair that thousands of families should have less than they need in order that a few families should have swollen fortunes at their expense? Let him who dares to deny that there is wickedness in grinding the faces of the poor, or assert that these are not moral questions which strike the very homes of our

people. If these are not moral questions, there are no moral
questions. Too often we have seemed to forget that a man in
public life can no more serve both the special interests and the
people than he can serve God and Mammon. (445)

What exactly was the connection between conservation and the trust-busting
side of the Progressive agenda? Or, as Pinchot himself put it, why was
conservation "the heart" of the Progressive movement? He answers:

Because, for one thing, Conservation is the most effective
weapon against monopoly of natural resources, and monopoly of
resources is the basis for the concentration of wealth in the hands
of the few. In a democracy that is the fundamental evil. That is
what Progressives fight. (464)

The irony is that the Progressive policies allowed the Federal government to
become one of the largest monopoly landlords on the face of the earth. The
little man cannot own land in most of the western United States today,
because his government won't let him. Would Pinchot have been bothered
by this? Personally, I doubt it. Great concentrations of wealth in the hands
of government seldom trouble the self-appointed guardians of the people.
Men of princely ambition often find that kind of inequality exactly to their
liking.

Conservation and Sustainable Development

There are both obvious similarities and differences between the
Progressive conservation movement and today's environmentalism. The two
movements share a deep distrust of big business, as well as a strong faith in
the ability of government experts to manage economic affairs in the public
interest. The Progressives pioneered the industrial restructuring, economic
regulation, and government stewardship schemes that are central
components of the sustainable development agenda. Pinchot and his
colleagues mobilized public support by warning of timber famines, housing
shortages, and other hypothetical perils that bear more than a passing
resemblance to the overpopulation and resource-depletion scares promoted
by environmental groups. The environmental movement also clearly owes
much to the advocacy techniques (e.g., the use of international conferences
and treaties to shape domestic policy) that Pinchot was among the first to
develop.

The conservation agenda was narrower in scope than that of environmentalism. Progressive conservationists were almost exclusively concerned with natural resource questions. Although public health issues related to what we would call environmental quality were already on the public agenda, Pinchot did not address them, let alone any of the particular environmental risk issues (toxic waste, airborne particulate matter, climate change) that figure so prominently in today's policy debates. But let's suppose for a moment that Pinchot and his colleagues had been cognizant of such low-probability but potentially catastrophic risks as a cancer epidemic from trace pesticide residues on food or the collapse of the West Antarctic ice sheet from human-induced global warming. Would Progressives have approached risk issues with the same precautionary zeal as today's environmentalists? My guess is that Pinchot would have been cool toward any policy that threatened to shut down the engines of industrial progress. Recall that he had no use for preservationism. America was much poorer a century ago, and the hazards of over-regulation were more obvious. So perhaps the Progressives would have taken a more balanced approach to risk regulation.

In the final analysis, though, Pinchot's brand of conservation offers no clear and compelling alternative to sustainable development. First, both fail to recognize the law of unintended consequences and the limits of politics to change human behavior. Just as environmentalists hope to instill a new conservation ethic by forcing people to recycle, or by penalizing development of wildlife habitat, so Pinchot sought to promote good stewardship by rigorously enforcing impractical land laws. It may not be irrelevant to note here that Pinchot supported prohibition, and did so before prohibition became a politically popular cause.[32]

Second, conservation and sustainable development overestimate the ability of government to set sensible priorities. Pinchot, for example, once proposed that a "non-partisan scientific commission" be established to set tariffs for the United States—as if it were possible to take politics out of trade policy.[33] Government ownership and control insulates decision-makers from the costs of their decisions; for the costs of government intervention are not borne by politicians and bureaucrats but by consumers and taxpayers and the losers in interest-group conflict. There is no scientific method for determining whether a particular forest should be managed for timber production, livestock grazing, wildlife conservation, or recreation. But this much is clear: if bureaucrats manage the forest, they will do so without benefit of the discipline experienced by those who risk their own capital in the marketplace. Whatever balance those bureaucrats manage to strike among rival user groups will likely reflect the political balance of power rather than a balanced assessment of public priorities.[34]

Decades of experience should have taught us that "scientific" (non-political) management of public lands is a chimera,[35] that regulatory agencies are vulnerable to capture by special interests, and that the growth of bureaucratic power erodes personal initiative and private rights. Nonetheless, the flame that Pinchot and other Progressives lit a century ago still burns bright in our time. Environmentalists may repudiate Pinchot's love of industrial civilization. But they possess an even stronger faith in the wisdom and virtue of central planning, economic regulation, and government stewardship of natural resources.

Finally, conservation and sustainable development ignore the power of market institutions—property rights, freedom of contract, and common law liability rules—to create incentives for good stewardship. Most environmental problems are not the result of too much protection for property rights but too little, not the result of market failures but of a failure to incorporate specific parts of nature into the market order of protected properties. For over a century, policy makers have tried to avert various tragedies of the commons by regulating—and thus politicizing—the commons. A more promising approach, albeit one that cannot be elaborated here, is to let markets and technology evolve new ways of privatizing humanity's terrestrial surroundings.[36] Most people do not throw trash in their own back yard. The goal of policy should be to make more of the world someone's back yard, not expand the political sector. The conservation and sustainable development movements have been marching in the wrong direction.

Notes

1. James Sheehan, "Sustainable Development: The Green Road to Serfdom?" *The Greening of U.S. Foreign Policy* (Hoover Institution, forthcoming), 1-3.

2. As general assessments of global conditions, all these statements are false. See Ron Bailey, ed., *The True State of the Planet* (New York: The Free Press, 1995).

3. Gifford Pinchot, *Breaking New Ground* (Washington, D.C.: Island Press, 1998), 137. All quotations in the text are to this source.

4. The phrase is Niccolo Machiavelli's. It appears to mean new practices, laws, or moral codes and new organizations, institutions, or regimes.

5. Martin Nelson McGeary, *Gifford Pinchot: Forester-Politician* (Princeton: Princeton University Press, 1960), 111.

6. When in 1892 he first went to Biltmore to look at George W. Vanderbilt's estate, Pinchot met Laura Houghteling of Chicago, and soon fell in love. He hoped to marry Laura but her health was poor and she died in 1894. For twenty years he continued to make notes in his diary about his beloved. "His slow recovery from the shock undoubtedly helped to explain his continued bachelorhood until the age of 49." McGeary, *Gifford Pinchot*, 32-33. The depth of his grief may also partly explain the utter silence of *Breaking New Ground* about Pinchot's private life.

7. Gifford's father, James Pinchot, was a successful New York merchant who married Mary Eno, daughter of a wealthy and prominent family. James and Mary "counted among their acquaintances some of the most celebrated persons in the nation," including General William T. Sherman and President Benjamin Harrison. McGeary, *Gifford Pinchot*, 6.

8. McGeary, *Gifford Pinchot*, 15.

9. Robert H. Nelson, *Public Lands and Private Rights: The Failure of Scientific Management* (Lanham, Md.: Rowman & Littlefield Publishers, Inc., 1995), 68, 78.

10. Indur M. Goklany and Merrit W. Sprague, "Sustaining Development and Biodiversity: Productivity, Efficiency, and Conservation (Cato Institute Policy Analysis, No. 175, August 6, 1992), 11-15. Although government has heavily subsidized agricultural research and production, federal farm programs have often been detrimental to the efficiency and competitiveness of U.S. agriculture. See James Bovard, *The Farm Fiasco* (San Francisco: Institute for Contemporary Studies, 1988). Federal subsidies have also encouraged farmers to drain wetlands and clear forestland. In contrast, the conservation gains from technology have been experienced around the globe. If crop yields had remained at 1950 levels, today's farmers would have to plow an additional ten million acres of forest and wildlife habitat to produce the same amount of food for domestic and foreign consumption. See Dennis Avery, "Saving the Planet with Pesticides: Increasing Food Supplies While Preserving the Earth's Biodiversity," in Bailey, ed., *The True State of the Planet*, 50.

11. Later (120), Pinchot comments: "Government control of cutting on all timberland, private as well as public, is still today [1947], as it was then [1897], the one indispensable step toward assuring a supply of forest products for the future of the United States."

12. McGeary, *Gifford Pinchot*, 29.

13. Almost half a century later, the Forest Service studied the tree plantations started on Vanderbilt's estate. "Although commercially the plantations have not fulfilled the expectations of their founder [Pinchot]," noted the report, "they have set up for foresters a notable lesson of success and failure in forest planting." McGeary, *Gifford Pinchot*, 30.

14. Nelson, *Public Lands and Private Rights*, 29-30.

15. McGeary, *Gifford Pinchot*, 131.

16. On the distinction between saving for use and saving from use, see Ike Sugg and Urs Kreuter, *Elephants and Ivory: Lessons from the Trade Ban* (London: IEA Studies on the Environment, No. 2, 1995), 11.

17. McGeary, *Gifford Pinchot*, 87.

18. Quoted in Nelson, *Public Lands*, 28.

19. McGeary, *Gifford Pinchot*, 88.

20. McGeary, *Gifford Pinchot*, 49.

21. The older, American Forestry Association, supported Pinchot's policies. Gifford's father, James, had at one time been its vice president. Gifford served on the staff of its magazine, *The Forester*, and occasionally contributed articles. Impatient with the association's slow-growing membership, however, he eventually concluded it was "no use whatever" in lobbying Congress. McGeary, *Gifford Pinchot*, 62.

22. According to McGeary,*Gifford Pinchot*, 50: "No government agency had ever made such extensive use of handouts of stories for newspapers and magazines."

23. McGeary, *Gifford Pinchot*, 59-60, 70-71, 85.

24. McGeary, *Gifford Pinchot*, 61.

25. These sentiments appear frequently in Pinchot's writing. See especially "What It All Means," the final chapter of *Breaking New Ground*, and Pinchot's 1910 book, *The Fight for Conservation* (New York: Doubleday, Page, 1910). In the latter, Pinchot asserts that "The planned and orderly development and conservation of natural resources is the first duty of the United States."

26. McGeary, *Gifford Pinchot*, 96-97.

27. Pinchot's colleague, Dr. W.J. McGee, was "the scientific brains of the new movement. . . . It was McGee, for example, who defined the new policy as the use of natural resources for the greatest good of the greatest number for the longest time" (325-26).

28. McGeary, *Gifford Pinchot*, 108.

29. Samuel P. Hays, *Conservation and the Gospel of Efficiency: The Progressive Conservation Movement, 1890-1920* (Cambridge, Mass.: Harvard University Press, 1959), 2.

30. Martin L. Fausold, *Gifford Pinchot: Bull Moose Progressive* (Westport: Greenwood Press, 1961), 50, 56, 98, 101.

31. Fausold, *Pinchot: Bull Moose*, 82, 152-56, 191.

32. McGeary, *Gifford Pinchot*, 244.

33. Fausold, *Pinchot: Bull Moose*, 160.

34. For further discussion, see Paul Georgia, Fred L. Smith, Jr., and Randy Simmons, "The Tragedy of the Commons Revisited: Politics vs. Property," Competitive Enterprise Institute, October 1996.

35. Nelson, *Public Lands*, 3-146.

36. A superb introduction to this approach is Robert J. Smith, "Resolving the Tragedy of the Commons by Creating Private Property in Wildlife," Competitive Enterprise Institute, January 1996.

4

Aldo Leopold's Human Ecology

Larry Arnhart

Many environmentalist scholars argue for an *ecocentric* or *biocentric* view of nature as an alternative to the *anthropocentric* view taken in the conservationist tradition. While many conservationists believed that natural resources had value insofar as they satisfied human desires, environmentalists often insist that nonhuman nature has inherent worth regardless of whether it serves human desires. In making this argument, environmentalists claim to be following a path opened by Aldo Leopold (1887-1948).

They concede that Leopold was a traditional conservationist throughout much of his life. His early career in forestry and game management and his early writings—including *Game Management* (a book first published in 1933)—show his devotion to the principles of conservationism. Like Gifford Pinchot, Leopold believed through much of his life that natural resources should be conserved only insofar as they had some instrumental value for human beings, thus assuming an anthropocentric view of nature.

But to many environmentalists Leopold appeared to undergo a great change from the middle of the 1930s to his death in 1948, as he moved away from the purely utilitarian and human-centered perspective of conservationism. In *A Sand County Almanac*, which he finished writing shortly before his death, Leopold argued for a "land ethic" in which intrinsic moral worth resides not only in human beings but also in the biotic community to which they belong. He formulated this in a general statement at the end of the book: "A thing is right when it tends to preserve the integrity, stability, and beauty of the biotic community. It is wrong when it tends otherwise."[1] According to some of the leading textbooks on environmentalism, this land ethic provides the foundation for the ecocentric ethics of those environmentalists and conservation biologists who reject the conservationist tradition.[2] In

contrast to the conservationist claim that human beings should control nature
for the satisfaction of human desires, Leopold seems to deny the moral
supremacy of human desires, because he affirms the intrinsic value of nature
as the "land," Leopold's term for the interdependent community of soil,
water, plants, and animals.

Contemporary Misunderstandings of Leopold

Although this account of Leopold's position has become commonly
accepted by environmentalist scholars, I believe it is wrong. I agree with the
other contributors to this book that environmentalists have often been unfair
in their interpretations and assessments of conservationist thinkers, and I
think this is particularly clear in the failure of environmentalists to appreciate
the consistency and depth of Leopold's conservationism. Even some of the
proponents of the environmentalist account of Leopold admit its weakness.
For example, Donald Worster claims that Leopold experienced a "personal
conversion" in which he moved away from the economic or utilitarian view
of conservation towards "a biocentric, communitarian ethic that challenged
the dominant economic attitude toward land use." But then Worster says that
Leopold never really moved away from the conservationist view that human
beings should control nature for human benefit. "For all his disenchantment,
he never broke away altogether from the economic view of nature. In many
ways his land ethic was merely a more enlightened, long-range prudence: a
surer means to an infinite expansion of material wealth, as he promised in
'Natural History'."[3]

Worster is referring to the following passage in Leopold's essay on
"Natural History":

> Modern natural history deals only incidentally with the identity
> of plants and animals, and only incidentally with their habits and
> behaviors. It deals principally with their relations to each other,
> their relation to the soil and water in which they grow, and their
> relations to the human beings who sing about 'my country' but
> see little or nothing of its inner workings. This new science of
> relationships is called ecology, but what we call it matters
> nothing. The question is, does the educated citizen know he is
> only a cog in an ecological mechanism? That if he will work with
> that mechanism his mental wealth and his material wealth can
> expand indefinitely? But that if he refuses to work with it, it will
> ultimately grind him to dust? If education does not teach us these
> things, then what is education for?[4]

Leopold states here the fundamental idea of the land ethic—the dependence of human beings on the ecological community of the land as including soil, water, plants, and animals. But contrary to those environmentalist scholars who assume an ecocentric interpretation of the land ethic, Leopold's concern here, as Worster sees, is clearly anthropocentric, because his implicit argument is that human beings must understand and work with the biotic community to which they belong for the sake of increasing their mental wealth and material wealth. Of course, by including the desire for mental wealth along with the desire for material wealth, he goes beyond economic utility narrowly understood in a way that might have been quite familiar to Roosevelt. But still his ultimate standard of value is what satisfies human desires, and thus nonhuman nature has value only insofar as it somehow serves human desires.

The reluctance to accept the anthropocentric character of Leopold's reasoning is clear in the work of J. Baird Callicott, who is the foremost philosophic exponent of Leopold's land ethic. Callicott rightly claims that Leopold's reasoning is best understood as an extension of the moral-sense tradition of ethical philosophy as developed by Adam Smith and David Hume and then adopted by Charles Darwin. But this characterization hardly supports Callicott's conclusion that Leopold's position is ecocentric rather than anthropocentric. On the contrary, if ethics is ultimately rooted in human passions, sentiments, or desires, as the moral-sense philosophers believe, then it would seem that all moral standards are centered on the affective responses of human beings.

Callicott argues, however, that the Humean-Darwinian theory of the moral sense is "humanly grounded, though not humanly centered." Nonhuman natural entities "may not be valuable in themselves, but they may certainly be valued for themselves," because human beings are moved by their social sentiments to feel concern for other human beings, and this sentiment of humanity can become a general affiliative drive that encompasses even nonhuman organisms that are perceived to belong somehow to the biotic community that includes human beings. "Hence, to those who are ecologically well-informed, nonhuman natural entities are inherently valuable—as putative members of one extended family or society. And nature as a whole is inherently valuable—as the one great family or society to which we belong as members or citizens."[5]

Yet the idea of an "extended family or society" implies that human beings are at the center of the circle, and that the human attachment to oneself and those closest to oneself is stronger than that to the more distant members of the society. Callicott concedes this point when he speaks of the moral sentiments radiating out in concentric circles that represent a hierarchy of moral communities where those at the center take precedence over those at the perimeter. Typically, our strongest attachments are to immediate friends and family members. Our attachments to more distant groups—tribe, nation, country—are somewhat weaker. Our attachment to humanity as a whole is much weaker. And our attachment to the biotic community as including nonhuman entities is usually very weak. In this image of the ethical community, which Callicott draws from Leopold, the human attachment to oneself and one's own is literally at the "center" of things, while the biotic community belongs to the "perimeter."[6] It is hard to imagine a more anthropocentric view of ethics.

I disagree, therefore, with commentators like Worster and Callicott who try to show that Leopold's land ethic was ecocentric and therefore contrary to the anthropocentrism of conservationism. I will argue that Leopold, in both his career and his writings, always adhered to a conservationism that accepted human use of science to control nature for the satisfaction of human desires. Yet in his land ethic, Leopold deepened this idea by philosophically elaborating it as rooted in human ecology. Like Roosevelt, he tries to reconcile the utilitarian outlook towards nature of a Pinchot with a sense of obligation or stewardship. For the modern environmentalist, the teaching of ecological and evolutionary biology that all living things are interdependent refutes the anthropocentrism of conservationism, because such interdependence appears to deny the claim that human beings can or should control nature for human benefit. But I believe Leopold argues, in contrast, that the scientific understanding of the interdependence in biotic communities helps human beings to strive for a prudent management of nature to satisfy their intellectual, ethical, and aesthetic desires. Far from rejecting conservationism in developing the land ethic, Leopold showed that the goal of conservationism—the wise use of natural resources for the good of human life—could be served best by developing a science of human ecology that would explain the dependence of human beings on the ecological conditions that sustain human civilization. Leopold's land ethic as founded on human ecology is conservationism rightly understood.

To support this conclusion, I will begin with a survey of Leopold's career to show that his professional activity—as a forester, as a game manager, and as a professor of wildlife ecology—was always in the service of conservationism. I will then show that his arguments for the land ethic—as founded on his understanding of natural science, natural ethics, and natural aesthetics—began from and deepened the principles of the conservationist tradition.

Preservation and Conservation—A Great Divide?

In 1909, at age twenty-two, Leopold received his Master of Forestry degree from the Yale Forest School, which Gifford Pinchot's family had helped to establish. Just as Pinchot would have expected, he immediately joined Pinchot's United States Forest Service, and thus became one of the first professional foresters in the United States,[7] promoting the principles and policies of conservationism.

"Conservationism," according to Pinchot, "means the wise use of the earth and all its resources for the lasting good of men."[8] This general principle of the "wise use" of natural resources required four subsidiary principles.[9] First, natural resources should be developed for human use. Second, natural resources should not be wasted. Third, natural resources should be developed and conserved for the good of all people and not just for a powerful few. Finally, the scientific study of natural resources should help us to make the best use of those resources.[10] The combination of these principles constitutes Pinchot's conservationist position: the wise use of natural resources for the good of human life requires the development of those resources and the elimination of waste, guided by the scientific study of nature, to serve the common good of all human beings. Leopold's career was devoted to that conservationist position. But if, as Lewis argues, Pinchot was more interested in practice than in theory, Leopold in contrast struggled to define the key terms in this position. What is meant by "wise use," "development," "elimination of waste," the "common good," and "natural science"? The history of conservationism is largely a history of the controversy in defining the meaning of these terms both in theory and in practice.

In the early 1890s, the founders of the conservationist movement seemed to agree on the meaning of these terms. For example, when the editor of *The Century Magazine* asked conservationist leaders in 1895 to comment on "the general need of a thorough, scientific, and permanent system of forest management," conservationists such as Theodore Roosevelt, Gifford Pinchot, and John Muir responded with articles suggesting general agreement on this goal. Muir agreed that forests should be managed both for the preservation of wilderness and the economic development of forest products. "It is impossible, in the nature of things," he insisted, "to stop at preservation. The forests must be, and will be, not only preserved, but used; and the experience of all civilized countries that have faced and solved the question shows that . . . the forests, like perennial fountains, may be made to yield a sure harvest of timber, while at the same time all their far-reaching beneficent uses may be maintained unimpaired."[11]

Within a few years, however, the conservationist movement seemed to be split between preservationists like Muir and utilitarians like Pinchot, or at least that is the common view of those scholars like Samuel Hays who have written on the history of conservationism.[12] According to this view, the "preservationists" believed that conservationism meant the protection of nature in its wild state so that it would remain unspoiled by human alteration, while the "utilitarians" believed that conservationism meant the development of nature for human uses to sustain the growth of civilization. When political leaders in San Francisco proposed to overcome their shortage of water by building a dam for a reservoir in the wild Hetch Hetchy Valley in Yosemite National Park, utilitarian conservationists supported it, while preservationist conservationists opposed it. Pinchot thought the benefits to San Francisco from using the valley as a reservoir outweighed the loss of wilderness, but Muir saw this as a desecration of a natural wonder by people corrupted by their sordid materialism.[13]

As some of the authors of this book suggest, this assumption by Hays and other scholars of a deep conflict in conservationism between preservationists and utilitarians ignores the common ground shared by Muir and Pinchot. Muir did not want to preserve all wilderness, and Pinchot recognized aesthetic and cultural value in wilderness beyond purely material interests. Muir and Pinchot could agreed on the principles of conservationism, and yet disagree about the application of those principles to the particular case of Hetch Hetchy. Leopold's life and writings are valuable because they show the intellectual and practical struggle required to understand the common principles of conservationism and to understand their applications to contexted cases (as Roosevelt saw would be so important).

Curt Meine's meticulous and comprehensive biography of Leopold shows that he strove throughout his life to combine utilitarian and preservationist views of nature and thus preserve the unity of the conservationist movement. "In part because he held both a Muir-like appreciation of nature and a Pinchot-like intent to use nature wisely," Meine observes, "Leopold was destined to lead a life of conflicting desires, constant questioning, and unending effort to better define the meaning of conservation."[14] Eventually, Leopold came to define the meaning of conservation as founded on the insight of human ecology that the success or failure of civilization depends on the ability of human beings to find prudent ways to satisfy their desires as members of a complex biotic community that includes soil, water, plants, and other animals. He thus deepened and elaborated the common ground between Muir and Pinchot.

Wilderness Policy and Human Nature

As a young boy growing up in Iowa, Leopold enjoyed hunting and fishing. As a forester assigned to national forests in Arizona and New Mexico, he developed a taste for hunting and fishing trips through wild country. But when he saw that the few remaining areas of wilderness in the United States would be soon lost as a result of economic development and motorized tourism, he began to argue in the early 1920s that the Forest Service should preserve some wilderness areas in their wild state. He proposed defining such an area as "a continuous stretch of country preserved in its natural state, open to lawful hunting and fishing, big enough to absorb a two weeks' pack trip, and kept devoid of roads, artificial trails, cottages, or other works of man."[15] Although contemporary ecocentric environmentalists might see this as showing Leopold's move away from the anthropocentric view of conservationism, it is clear that Leopold measured the value of wilderness by its service to human recreational desires for hunting, fishing, and camping in wild country.

Leopold's proposed wilderness policy would seem to follow from Muir's preservationist position, and yet Leopold defended this policy as conforming to Pinchot's doctrine of "development" for "wise use," indicating Leopold's assumption of a common ground of conservationist principles that unites Muir and Pinchot. Leopold agreed that in most cases the proper use for natural resources was commercial or industrial development. But he argued that in some cases the best use for a wild forest would be preserving it as wilderness for human recreation. He specified three conditions. First, designated wilderness areas should be only a small part of the total area managed by the Forest Service. Second, they should be areas where normal economic development would be difficult. And, finally, they should be areas that have some distinctive recreational value. Where these stringent criteria were satisfied, the loss in withholding such areas from economic development would be small compared with the large gain for those people who desire a chance to see a wilderness.

Leopold conceded that only a minority of people would enjoy traveling through such a wilderness. Most people would not want to forgo the conveniences of motorized recreation. Yet Leopold argued that "our recreational development policy" should serve the desires of the minority as well as those of the majority. The variability in human nature creates a wide range of desires, so that some human beings yearn for contacts with wild nature that most human beings would find distasteful. Protecting some wilderness areas could satisfy the desires of those few who love wild things without unduly frustrating the desires of the many who do not. The "wise use" of natural resources must be a varied use to reflect the variability in human desires.[16]

Hays and other scholars see a split in the conservationist movement between the preservationists and the utilitarians, because they assume that the human desires for wilderness life were opposed to the human desires for civilized life. But, as is shown by other chapters in this book, Muir and Roosevelt deny this assumption; and I would say that the same is true for Leopold. In his proposal for preserving wilderness, he argued that the success of civilization in controlling nature for human benefit should allow human beings to satisfy the full range of human desires—including the "instinctive craving for the wilderness life."

> The measure of civilization is in its contrasts. A modern city is a national asset, not because the citizen has planted his iron heel on the breast of nature, but because of the different kinds of man his control over nature has enabled him to be. Saturday morning he stands like a god, directing the wheels of industry that have dominion over the earth. Saturday afternoon he is playing golf on a kindly greensward. Saturday evening he may till a homely garden or he may turn a button and direct the mysteries of the firmament to bring him the words and songs and deeds of all the nations. And if, once in a while, he has the opportunity to flee the city, throw a diamond hitch upon a packmule, and disappear into the wilderness of the Covered Wagon Days, he is just that much more civilized than he would be without the opportunity. It makes him one more kind of man—a pioneer.[17]

So I disagree with Meine's claim that Leopold's idea of wilderness preservation "signaled a departure from the Pinchot path."[18] Leopold was clear in endorsing Pinchot's idea that the human control over nature permits us to use natural resources in sustaining a civilized life. But Leopold argued for expanding this principle. Preserving some land as wilderness could be seen as a prudent use of the land for enlarging the range of human experience to include recreational contacts with wild life. "The question of wilderness playgrounds," he insisted, "is a question in self-control of environment." "Good use is largely a matter of good balance—of wise adjustment between opposing tendencies."[19]

In arguing for preserving wilderness areas as part of a general policy for managing forests for human use, Leopold was developing a view of conservationism that transcended the false dichotomies that would later lead environmental historians to see a split between the preservationists and the utilitarians. Insofar as the love of wild nature is a natural human desire diversely expressed in individuals, human beings should use their control of nature to satisfy that desire in ways that are balanced with other desires. Preservationists would be wrong if they thought the human love of nature requires giving up all the benefits of civilized life. After all, John Muir's writings manifested one of the prime achievements of a civilized society—the cultivated perception of nature by an educated mind. On the other hand, the utilitarians would be wrong if they thought the human love of comfort requires an utterly artificial world where there is no need for exertion. After all, the success of Gifford Pinchot's conservationist policies depended not only on bureaucratic infighting, but also on the popular appeal of Teddy Roosevelt's devotion to the "strenuous life" of hunting, fishing, and camping in wilderness areas. Leopold shows that conservationism rightly understood transcends the false dilemma of choosing between the preservation of wild nature and the cultivation of civilized life.

That Leopold could not be happy with a narrowly utilitarian conservationism became evident when he was transferred in 1924 to the United States Forest Products Laboratory in Madison, Wisconsin. This facility was the primary research laboratory for the Forest Service in studying the industrial uses of forest products. Leopold agreed that it was important to promote economic efficiency in the production and consumption of lumber.[20] But he wondered whether the national forests could be properly managed according to only one simple formula: "land + forestry = boards." Even if this formula captured "the current ideals of the majority," he doubted that this would satisfy the needs of that minority of people who sought recreational benefits from the forests that could not be measured in narrowly economic terms.[21]

The Science of Game Management

In 1928, Leopold left the Forest Products Laboratory and the Forest Service to survey game wildlife in nine midwestern states for the Sporting Arms and Ammunition Manufacturers' Institute. He began to develop a science of game management, which led to the publication in 1933 of *Game Management*, the first textbook on the subject. Also in 1933, he was appointed to a new chair of game management at the University of Wisconsin in Madison, where he would remain until his death in 1948. In

1939, he became chairman of a new Department of Wildlife Management at the university, and he began teaching an introductory course on wildlife ecology for students in the liberal arts as well as students in wildlife management.

Game Management summarizes all the major themes of Leopold's conservatism as developed over his professional career as a forester and game manager. Some of the themes of the book—particularly, the ethical and aesthetic principles of conservatism—are more fully elaborated later in *A Sand County Almanac*. Contrary to the common view of many environmentalist scholars, there is no radical break in Leopold's thinking after 1933 to indicate a move away from the conservationism of his early career.

In *Game Management*, Leopold defines the new science of game management as "the art of making land produce sustained annual crops of wild game for recreational use." The "central thesis" of game management is that "game can be restored by the *creative use* of the same tools which have heretofore destroyed it—axe, plow, cow, fire, and gun." Leopold explains this as an application to one kind of natural resource of Theodore Roosevelt's teaching that natural resources should be conserved by wise use as guided by scientific knowledge. In general, conservationism is concerned with "how wild life and civilization should be adjusted to each other" through the scientific control of nature.[22] Game management contributes to this adjustment by using the science of wildlife ecology to control nature in moderate ways that allow civilized human beings to hunt wild animals for recreational purposes.

In the first part of *Game Management*, Leopold develops a scientific theory of the biological mechanism that determines game populations. In the second part, he surveys the methods by which game managers can control that mechanism. In the last part, he reflects on the human desires—the economic, aesthetic, and ethical motivations—that justify and sustain game management as an effort to understand and control populations of wild game animals.

Leopold believes game management is "applied ecology," because ecology explains the biological mechanism that determines animal populations, and game management seeks to control that mechanism.[23] Every animal population has an intrinsic natural rate of increase that is reduced by environmental conditions. Environmental "factors" such as predators, disease, and the availability of food, water, and coverts act directly on the game's rate of survival and reproduction. Environmental "influences" such as weather, fire, and agricultural activity act indirectly on the population of game by influencing a factor. For example, intensive agricultural cultivation can reduce the population of quail by depriving them of food and coverts.

Leopold's theory of how environmental conditions determine the population of an animal species has been confirmed and elaborated in modern ecological research. And like some contemporary ecologists, Leopold believes that human beings are similar to other animals in that their survival and reproduction depend on environmental circumstances.[24] Every animal society—both human and nonhuman—is a competitive and cooperative struggle to find the best places to feed, hide, rest, sleep, play, and breed. Any human settlement must include all such places required for the human animal within the daily cruising radius.[25]

For Leopold, therefore, conservation ecology depends on animal ecology, and animal ecology includes human ecology.

> We are depicting here the fundamental behavior of all aggregations of living things. Game management is only one of a thousand human activities, including sociology itself, directed toward the interpretation and government of that behavior. Civilization is, in its essence, the will to interpret and govern it.[26]

To some degree, all animals change their environments to make them more hospitable to their survival and reproduction. Human beings are unique only in the greater degree of control that they can have over their environment. Leopold views game management as one of many ways that human beings strive to understand and control their natural environment to satisfy their desires.

The human desire for hunting could not be satisfied for long in the modern world without some control of nature to prevent the depletion of the supply of game animals. Leopold devotes the second part of his book to the many techniques of game management for controlling the supply of game. The fundamental concept in those techniques is that "hunting is the harvesting of a man-made crop, which would soon cease to exist if somebody somewhere had not, intentionally or unintentionally, come to nature's aid in its production."[27]

Ethics and Aesthetics of Game Management

Many people—including many who would consider themselves preservationists in the conservationist movement—would object that hunting is an atavistic activity that is both unnecessary and wasteful in the modern world. But Leopold defends hunting as satisfying an aesthetic desire for recreational sport. Hunting is a natural instinct that manifests "the biological basis of human nature."[28] Physical combat between human beings and beasts was an economic necessity throughout most of human evolutionary history. Now hunting is no longer necessary for survival for most modern people in the industrialized societies. But the hunting instinct remains so strong, for at least some people, that it now seeks expression as a sport rather than as an economic need. A similar transformation explains the desire for athletic sports; physical combat between human beings was originally an economic activity, but now it has become an aesthetic activity to satisfy an instinct for physical combat that was shaped by natural selection in evolutionary history.

To satisfy the natural desire for hunting as an aesthetic activity rooted in primordial instinct, the game manager must see that "the recreational value of game is inverse to the artificiality of its origin, and hence in a broad way to the degree of control exercised in its production."[29] In the modern world, some human control over nature is required to preserve opportunities for hunting, but control that is too intensive deprives the hunter of the pleasure that comes from the feeling of confronting wild nature. Using highly mechanized weapons to kill artificially reared animals introduced into an artificially controlled hunting area gives little satisfaction to the hunter.

For Leopold this point illustrates a general principle that should govern all conservation, a principle that he calls "naturalism." "It is an effort to avoid artificiality in the manipulation of natural processes for conservation purposes." "We return to an approximation of nature. We still manipulate, but in a nearly natural instead of a largely artificial manner."[30] Through a moderate control of nature that approximates wild nature, game management strives for that prudent adjustment of wilderness and civilization that is the ultimate end of all conservation.

In doing this, game management should serve not only the aesthetic desires of the hunter but also ethical and intellectual desires. Leopold finds the ethical roots of game management in ancient tribal taboos that restricted hunting to preserve the supply of game for all members of the tribe. The idea of conservation as developed by Theodore Roosevelt extends this ethical concern to include a moral responsibility for preserving wildlife.[31] A code of sportsmanship imposes an individual ethics on the hunter that restricts what and how he kills. Hunting with bow and arrow, for example, which Leopold enjoyed, is a self-imposed moral restraint on hunters who take proud satisfaction in exercising the skill that comes from killing wild game with primitive weapons.[32]

Wildlife and Liberal Education

The deepest human pleasures derived from game management, however, are intellectual. Since the development of Darwinian biology, Leopold believes, human beings have been able to interpret the "Great Book" of nature to an extent that was impossible before Darwin's work. In applying ecology to read the book of the land, game management is ultimately justified by "its enrichment of the human faculty for observation." The highest calling of the game manager is the highest calling of any human being—to observe the drama of nature and discern the invisible causes that explain its visible order.[33]

Believing that the ultimate success of conservationism depended upon the ability of citizens to find intellectual pleasure in understanding nature, Leopold transformed his undergraduate course on wildlife ecology at the University of Wisconsin into a course that would contribute to the liberal education of citizens. The purpose of "liberal education in wildlife," he argued in 1942, is "to teach the student to see the land, to understand what he sees, and enjoy what he understands."[34] The last time he taught his wildlife ecology course, in the spring semester of 1947, he explained to his students that the object of the course was "to teach you how to read land," and he confessed that his "ulterior motive" in doing this was to promote conservationism.

> If the individual has a warm personal understanding of land, he will perceive of his own accord that it is something more than a breadbasket. He will see land as a community of which he is only a member, albeit now the dominant one. He will see the beauty, as well as the utility, of the whole, and know the two cannot be separated. We love (and make intelligent use of) what we have learned to understand.
> . . . Once you learn to read the land, I have no fear of what you will do to it, or with it. And I know many pleasant things it will do to you.[35]

Leopold could give his students examples of "reading the land" from his own experience as a landowner. In 1935, he purchased an abandoned farm in southwestern Wisconsin. The only structure still standing on the property was a chicken coop. Leopold and his family converted this into a house they called "the shack." Whenever possible, Leopold's family spent their weekends and summer months at the shack. Leopold began keeping journals of his observations at the shack, which would eventually provide material for his book, *A Sand County Almanac*.

In writing *A Sand County Almanac*, which was published shortly after his death, Leopold wanted to do for his readers what he had done for his students. The book would provide a "liberal education in wildlife" in a pleasing literary form that would engage a popular audience, and it would thus promote in the public mind the only dependable motivation for conservation—"a warm personal understanding of land."

Environmentalist scholars insist that this book, more clearly than any other of Leopold's writings, shows his move away from an anthropocentric conservationism towards an ecocentric environmentalism. But my reading of this book suggests that it elaborates the same conservationist position that Leopold defended early in his career.

The continuity with his earlier writing is evident in the opening lines of the "Foreword":

> There are some who can live without wild things, and some who cannot. These essays are the delights and dilemmas of one who cannot.
>
> Like winds and sunsets, wild things were taken for granted until progress began to do away with them. Now we face the question whether a still higher 'standard of living' is worth its cost in things natural, wild, and free. For us of the minority, the opportunity to see geese is more important than television, and the chance to find a pasque-flower is a right as inalienable as free speech.
>
> These wild things, I admit, had little human value until mechanization assured us of a good breakfast, and until science disclosed the drama of where they come from and how they live. The whole conflict thus boils down to a question of degree. We of the minority see a law of diminishing returns in progress; our opponents do not.[36]

As in his earlier defense of wilderness areas, which he first stated in 1921, Leopold defends the claims of that minority of people who desire contact with wild nature. His disagreement with those who think they can live without wild things is, however, only "a question of degree." He agrees with them about the importance of economic and technological development, because this ensures a "good breakfast" for the lovers of wild nature and provides the conditions for the scientific inquiry that reveals the wonderfully beautiful order of that wild nature. As in his earlier writings, he believes that human beings can exercise a prudent control over nature that accommodates both wilderness and civilization. His position in this book is still as human-centered as in his earlier writings, because he continues to argue that wild things have "human value" insofar as they serve human desires.

At the end of the "Foreword," Leopold summarizes the three ideas that run throughout the book.

> We abuse land because we regard it as a commodity belonging to us. When we see land as a community to which we belong, we may begin to use it with love and respect. There is no other way for land to survive the impact of mechanized man, nor for us to reap from it the esthetic harvest it is capable, under science, of contributing to culture.
>
> That land is a community is the basic concept of ecology, but that land is to be loved and respected is an extension of ethics. That land yields a cultural harvest is a fact long known, but latterly often forgotten.
>
> These essays attempt to weld these three concepts.[37]

These three concepts correspond to three human desires. Because of their intellectual desire for understanding, human beings can take pleasure in perceiving the land as a complex mechanism. Because of their ethical desire for community, human beings can take pleasure in respecting the land to which they are tied by a biotic web of relationships. And because of their esthetic desire for beauty, human beings can take pleasure in marveling at the land as a cosmic drama. I will take up each of these three kinds of desire as supporting Leopold's conservationist position.

Natural Philosophy

In their use of tools for controlling nature, Leopold observes, human beings exert a God-like power for creating and destroying living things. With a shovel, a human being can plant a tree and thus give life. With an axe, he can chop it down and thus take life. All other tools are ultimately either variations on or instrumental to this original pair of tools. All human vocations are ultimately devoted to either using or managing these tools. "But there is one vocation—philosophy—which knows that all men, by what they think about and wish for, in effect wield all tools. It knows that men thus determine, by their manner of thinking and wishing, whether it is worth while to wield any."[38] Leopold writes as a philosopher in *A Sand County Almanac*, because he knows that the success or failure of conservationism depends upon what people think about and wish for as they wield their shovels and axes. He writes to bring about an intellectual change in how people think about nature, which will then bring about an emotional change in how they feel about nature. "As a land-user thinketh, so is he."[39]

He writes to change the thinking of his readers so that they can finally accept the formulation of the land ethic that he offers in the closing pages of the book.

> Quit thinking about decent land-use as solely an economic problem. Examine each question in terms of what is ethically and esthetically right, as well as what is economically expedient. A thing is right when it tends to preserve the integrity, stability, and beauty of the biotic community. It is wrong when it tends otherwise.[40]

This land ethic presupposes "some mental image of land as a biotic mechanism," because "we can be ethical only in relation to something we can see, feel, understand, love, or otherwise have faith in."[41] How we use the land is always an economic problem, because economic feasibility always limits what we can do with the land. But if we learn from evolutionary and ecological science to think about the land as a biotic community to which we belong and on which we depend for our survival and happiness, then our care of the land will be guided not only by economic desires for what is profitable but also by ethical desires for what is right and esthetic desires for what is beautiful.

The only way to fully appreciate the power of Leopold's writing in changing the thinking of his readers through the "mental image of land as a biotic mechanism" is to read *A Sand County Almanac*. But as an illustration of Leopold's technique that indicates why so many readers have been deeply moved by the book, we can look at the first sketch in the book. This begins the first third of the book, which consists of essays arranged chronologically as an "almanac" from January to December. This first essay is entitled "January Thaw."

> Each year, after the midwinter blizzards, there comes a night of thaw when the tinkle of dripping water is heard in the land. It brings strange stirring, not only to creatures abed for the night, but to some who have been asleep for the winter. The hibernating skunk, curled up in his deep den, uncurls himself and ventures forth to prowl the wet world, dragging his belly in the snow. His track marks one of the earliest datable events in that cycle of beginnings and ceasings which we call a year.

The track is likely to display an indifference to mundane affairs uncommon at other seasons; it leads straight across-country, as if its maker had hitched his wagon to a star and dropped the reins. I follow, curious to deduce his state of mind and appetite, and destination if any.

* * *

The months of the year, from January up to June, are a geometric progression in the abundance of distractions. In January one may follow a skunk track, or search for bands on the chickadees, or see what young pines the deer have browsed, or what muskrat houses the mink have dug, with only an occasional and mild digression into other doings. January can be almost as simple and peaceful as snow, and almost as continuous as cold. There is time not only to see who has done what, but to speculate why.

* * *

A meadow mouse, startled by my approach, darts damply across the skunk track. Why is he abroad in daylight? Probably because he feels grieved about the thaw. Today his maze of secret tunnels, laboriously chewed through the matted grass under the snow, are tunnels no more, but only paths exposed to public view and ridicule. Indeed the thawing sun has mocked the basic premises of the microtine economic system!

The mouse is a sober citizen who knows that grass grows in order that mice may store it as underground haystacks, and that snow falls in order that mice may build subways from stack to stack: supply, demand, and transport all neatly organized. To the mouse, snow means freedom from want and fear.

* * *

A rough-legged hawk comes sailing over the meadow ahead. Now he stops, hovers like a kingfisher, and then drops like a feathered bomb into the marsh. He does not rise again, so I am sure he has caught, and is now eating, some worried mouse-engineer who could not wait until night to inspect the damage to this well-ordered world.

The rough-leg has no opinion why grass grows, but he is well aware that snow melts in order that hawks may again catch mice. He came down out of the Arctic in the hope of thaws, for to him a thaw means freedom from want and fear.

* * *

The skunk track enters the woods, and crosses a glade where the rabbits have packed down the snow with their tracks, and mottled it with pinkish urinations. Newly exposed oak seedlings have paid for the thaw with their newly barked stems. Tufts of rabbit-hair bespeak the year's first battles among the amorous bucks.

Further on I find a bloody spot, encircled by a wide-sweeping arc of owl's wings. To this rabbit the thaw brought freedom from want, but also a reckless abandonment of fear. The owl has reminded him that thoughts of spring are no substitute for caution.

* * *

The skunk track leads on, showing no interest in possible food, and no concern over the rompings or retributions of his neighbors. I wonder what he has on his mind; what got him out of bed? Can one impute romantic motives to this corpulent fellow, dragging his ample beltline through the slush? Finally the track enters a pile of driftwood, and does not emerge. I hear the tinkle of dripping water among the logs, and I fancy the skunk hears it too. I turn homeward, still wondering.[42]

"January Thaw" appears to be merely a collection of animal stories told in a charming style. (Some readers have the same reaction to Teddy Roosevelt's nature writings.) There is no explicit reasoning that suggests the formal logic of a scientific or philosophic argument. And yet these stories quietly introduce the readers to all the themes that Leopold elaborates later in the book as he works toward the abstract formulation of the land ethic at the end. He thus draws his readers into the book through his engaging stories about his life at the shack, but those stories are artfully contrived so that when the readers reach the end of the book, they can accept the abstract conclusions of the land ethic as their own conclusions from their observations of nature in reading the book. The attentive readers of *A Sand County Almanac* will thus engage in the very activity that Leopold wants to promote: his readers learn to see the mechanism of the biotic community at work in the natural world around them, and as they find pleasure in understanding wild things, they develop an ethical and aesthetic appreciation for wild nature. Only through the proper appreciation of such stories can "the land" become a vivid and rich reality of human experience rather than a mere abstraction.

In "January Thaw," Leopold follows a skunk track in the snow because he is curious to explain the animal's movements by deducing "his state of mind and appetite, and destination if any." Later in the book, as we have seen, he speaks of human beings as moved by their "thinking and wishing."[43] So it seems that human beings are not the only animals whose movements are determined by reason and desire: all animals, to some degree, display "mind and appetite" in that they gather information in their environment relevant to their desires and then act according to their assessment of that information to satisfy their desires.[44]

Of course, poets who tell animal stories often enliven their stories by attributing human characteristics to their animals. This technique engages our interest because we feel more concern for animals that we imagine to be like us. Leopold is doing the same thing, but he would like eventually to persuade us that the new sciences of evolution and ecology show us that other animals really are like us in their intellectual and emotional powers, and therefore our concern for animals that seem to be like us can be grounded on scientific fact as well as poetic fiction. Moreover, this view depicts our role as human beings in our biotic communities. The complex character of our mind and desires defines our uniqueness as human beings, and yet we can extend our human-centered concern to encompass other living beings insofar as they share or support our intellectual and emotional dispositions.

Even if the difference in "mind and appetite" between human beings and other animals is only a difference in degree, not a difference in kind, it is still true that the difference in degree is very great. The greatness of that difference is evident in "January Thaw," because the curiosity and wonder that move Leopold to follow the skunk track show an intellectual desire for understanding that goes beyond the mind of the skunk or any other animal. The peak of that uniquely human intellectual desire is science or philosophy—the attempt to explain the rational order of the whole through the rigorous analysis of logic and experience.

Leopold's work as an ecological scientist is indicated casually in "January Thaw" when he mentions searching for bands on chickadees as one of his possible activities in January. Later in the book, he explains that banding chickadees trapped at his feeding station is part of his scientific study of this animal's home range. Some of his neighbors feed chickadees, but only he bands them and records their daily and seasonal movements so that he can draw scientific inferences about home range. This allows Leopold to show his readers how a farmer who enjoys feeding and watching chickadees manifests the human inclination that leads to the scientific study of nature. "Every farm is a textbook on animal ecology; woodmanship is the translation of the book."[45]

Much of that textbook is devoted to the study of the land as a complex system of food chains and energy circuits. In "January Thaw," Leopold helps his readers infer from evidence in the snow that an owl has eaten a rabbit that previously had eaten an oak seedling. In the next essay of the book—"Good Oak"—Leopold explains that an oak tree captures and holds the energy of the sun. This energy is released for human use when human beings wield axe and saw to appropriate the oak for firewood. Later Leopold explains how an oak might belong to biotic communities organized by the flow of energy through the land pyramid—from soil and water to plants and then to animals stacked in a food pyramid from small prey to large predators. This food chain is altered by human activity. So, for example, "soil-oak-deer-Indian" was the predominant chain earlier in American history that has recently been converted to "soil-corn-cow-farmer."[46] Leopold thereby conveys in a vivid manner for a popular audience Charles Elton's ecological theory of the animal community as tied together by food chains, which Leopold regarded as the most important contribution wildlife ecology could make to the liberal education of citizens.[47]

In "January Thaw" we see the original disposition from which science or philosophy emerges—the ordinary curiosity of a human being looking at the natural world around him. Leopold would seem to agree with Aristotle that "all men by nature desire to understand," and that intellectual desire can lead men to find the deepest pleasure in studying animals and other living things.[48] Even if most of Leopold's readers will never become scientists or philosophers, he can appeal to that naturally human sense of wonder in all of his readers.

By eliciting his readers' natural desire to understand the natural world, Leopold leads them from animal stories to animal ecology. "To promote perception," Leopold believes, "is the only truly creative part of recreational engineering." In *A Sand County Almanac*, he promotes in his readers "the perception of the natural processes by which the land and the living things upon it have achieved their characteristic forms (evolution), and by which they maintain their existence (ecology)."[49] By the end of the book, he has so developed their perception that they have a "mental image of land as a biotic mechanism." He believes that once he has led them to understand themselves as members of a biotic community that includes soil, water, plants, and animals, his readers will desire to conserve the wild things that belong to their community.

Natural Ethics

According to Aristotle, "the good is not the same for all animals, but is different in the case of each."[50] In "January Thaw," Leopold seems to agree, because the animals have conflicting interests, and each has its own teleological view of nature as centered on its own cares. The mouse is sure "that grass grows in order that mice may store it as underground haystacks, and that snow falls in order that mice may build subways from stack to stack." The hawk, on the other hand, "has no opinion why grass grows, but

he is well aware that snow melts in order that hawks may again catch mice."
So while the mouse sees freedom from want and fear in snow, the hawk sees
freedom from want and fear in the thawing of the snow.

By speaking of mice, hawks, and rabbits as desiring freedom from want
and fear, Leopold parodies the sentiments of Franklin Roosevelt's "four
freedoms" speech, suggesting that all animals worry about economic crises.
The mouse's maze of tunnels under the snow is a complex economic system,
and its collapse in a winter thaw is just as catastrophic for the mouse as the
collapse of a human economic system is for human beings.

If the good differs for each animal, then human ethics is necessarily
anthropocentric, because just as all animals must assume, in their actions if
not in their thoughts, that the good is what is good for them, human beings
must judge the human good as what is good for human beings. Early in *A
Sand County Almanac*, Leopold captures this human-centered perspective
of human conduct by quoting a line from Walt Whitman: "Man brings all
things to the test of himself."[51]

Leopold always defended the conservation of natural resources as
necessary for the satisfaction of human desires. To his students at the
University of Wisconsin, he explained: "I am interested in the thing called
'conservation.' For this I have two reasons: (1) without it, our economy will
ultimately fall apart; (2) without it many plants, animals, and places of
entrancing interest to me as an explorer will cease to exist. I do not like to
think of economic bankruptcy, nor do I see much object in continuing the
human enterprise in a habitat stripped of what interests me most."[52]
Conserving the land is good because the land satisfies both the economic and
the aesthetic desires of the human beings who live on the land.

It follows, therefore, for Leopold that individual landowners rather than
governmental bureaucrats are in the best position to practice conservation,
because landowners benefit directly from the utility and beauty of their land.
Criticizing the tendency of conservationists to rely on governmental
regulation, Leopold insisted that the success of conservation would depend
on the voluntary practice of conservation by private landowners.[53] *A Sand
County Almanac* was part of Leopold's effort to promote such conservation
by instilling a land ethic in private landowners so that they would have the
personal incentives to properly manage their land.

The original idea for "January Thaw" can be found in an article from
1940 that Leopold wrote for the *Wisconsin Agriculturist and Farmer*.[54] He
suggested that farmers adopt his practice of strolling over his land in January
to track animals and thus to notice how many animals were missing because
of bad farming practices such as cutting down woodlots and draining

marshes. In January, Leopold implies, Wisconsin farmers derive little pleasure from their land unless they have preserved suitable habitats for wild animals that they can hunt or observe. "We seek contacts with nature," Leopold believes, "because we derive pleasure from them." In sketches like "January Thaw," Leopold shows that farmers and other landowners with any knowledge of ecology discover that "there is pleasure to be had in raising wild crops as well as tame ones."[55]

When we learn to take pleasure in observing and understanding wild nature, we feel an obligation to preserve wild things, and we lament their disappearance as a loss. In "January Thaw," the meadow mouse feels grieved about the thaw, because this threatens his economic survival. When human beings feel grieved by economic loss, they are not fundamentally different from the mouse. But we can imagine that a man like Leopold, who enjoys observing mice, skunks, hawks, and rabbits on his farm in January, would grieve at the disappearance of those animals. When some ornithologists erected a monument to the passenger pigeon, because it had become extinct in Wisconsin, Leopold observed that "for one species to mourn the death of another is a new thing under the sun," and he saw this as "objective evidence of our superiority over the beasts." He explained this ethical superiority as based on an intellectual superiority. We can comprehend Darwin's theory of evolution as teaching us "that men are only fellow-voyagers with other creatures in the odyssey of evolution," and this new knowledge can give us "a sense of kinship with fellow-creatures; a wish to live and let live; a sense of wonder over the magnitude and duration of the biotic enterprise."[56]

Perceiving nature as a biotic community promotes an intellectual appreciation of nature as an object of wonder and an ethical appreciation of nature as an object of respect. That is the key to his argument for the land ethic near the end of *Sand County Almanac.* Leopold points out that such an "extension of ethics" has happened before when, for example, we abolished slavery. He intends by such an analogy not to extend rights or any other specific moral category to the land, but to bring it within the domain of our respect as an element of the biotic community we share.

Natural Aesthetics

Such thinking also promotes an aesthetic appreciation of nature as an object of beauty. "Our ability to perceive quality in nature begins, as in art, with the pretty. It expands through successive stages of the beautiful to values as yet uncaptured by language."[57] Those "successive stages of the beautiful" correspond both to different stages in the development of an individual and to different temperaments among individuals.

While hunting and fishing were originally economic activities pursued for the sake of survival, they are now also aesthetic activities pursued for the dramatic pleasure of doing for amusement what was previously done by necessity. The aesthetic pleasure in hunting is like the pleasure in opera or any other dramatic art that satisfies a natural human desire for imitating actions through artful illusion. And in hunting as in other arts, the pleasure is more refined as the art of the illusion is so carefully concealed that it appears to be natural. The game captured by the hunter is a trophy that certifies the skill of the hunter, and the more artificial the management of the game—as, for example, in the artificial breeding of game for killing by highly mechanized weapons—the less valuable the trophy.[58] It seems that Leopold would agree with Aristotle that the best art imitates nature and thus satisfies the natural human desire for imitation.[59]

People who dislike the imitative arts of hunting and fishing may find aesthetic pleasure in nature in different ways. Some see beauty in the indirect trophies of photographs of natural scenes or checklists of birds. Others seek natural environments for the feeling of isolation or release from the daily routine of urban life. These and other forms of the recreational appreciation of nature are accepted by Leopold as esthetic expressions of the diversity of human desires in seeking pleasurable contacts with nature.[60]

Clearly, however, Leopold believes (distantly echoing Emerson) that of the "successive stages of beauty," the highest is attained by the scientist who perceives the beauty of nature's order as revealed by evolutionary and ecological science.

> Recreation . . . is not the outdoors, but our reaction to it. Daniel Boone's reaction depended not only on the quality of what he saw, but on the quality of the mental eye with which he saw it. Ecological science has wrought a change in the mental eye. It has disclosed origins and functions for what to Boone were only facts. . . . The incredible intricacies of the plant and animal community—the intrinsic beauty of the organism called America, then in the full bloom of her maidenhood—were as invisible and incomprehensible to Daniel Boone as they are today to Mr. Babbitt. The only true development in American recreational resources is the development of the perceptive faculty in Americans.[61]

Many Americans will seek aesthetic satisfaction from reading books about nature. And when they read a book like *A Sand County Almanac*—a book about nature written to convey the lessons of ecological science in a poetically appealing style—they will develop their perceptive faculty.

As this suggests, Leopold would not accept the sharp dichotomy that many environmental scholars make between "intrinsic value" and "instrumental value."[62] According to the conservationist, they claim, only human beings have "intrinsic value," while the rest of nature has only "instrumental value" as serving human needs. By contrast, they advocate an ecocentric ethics that recognizes the "intrinsic value" of nonhuman nature. Leopold claims, however, that although nature does have "intrinsic beauty," the perception of that beauty depends on the intellectual and emotional reactions of human beings. Even if the land has an inherent worth as a biotic community that cannot be fully mastered by human beings, that natural worth becomes visible to the "mental eye" of human beings only insofar as it satisfies their intellectual, ethical, and aesthetic desires.

Human Ecology

It is often said that Leopold's great achievement was his rooting of conservationism in the newly emerging science of ecology. It would be more precise to say that he showed how conservationism could be understood as *human* ecology. "Conservation," he once stated, "is our attempt to put human ecology on a permanent footing."[63] As far as I know, this is the only time he used the term "human ecology," but the idea behind the term is common in his writings.[64]

Human ecology would fuse the natural and social sciences through Leopold's concept of the land as a biotic community. The land is the community of soils, water, plants, and animals (including human animals). Human ecology would be the science of the land, because it would unite the sciences of the human community (such as sociology, economics, and history) with the sciences of the plant and animal community (such as geology, botany, and zoology).

In an essay published in 1942, "The Role of Wildlife in a Liberal Education," Leopold shows how wildlife ecology as the study of the land community could contribute to a liberal education.[65] To illustrate his point, he offers a diagram of the "Lines of Dependency (Food Chains) in a Community," which could be regarded as a chart of the range of human ecology as including all the intellectual disciplines that study the land. To understand lines of dependency such as "student-lawyer-grocer-farmer," we must study social sciences such as economics and sociology. To understand "farmer-cow-alfalfa-soil-rock," we must study sciences such as animal husbandry, agronomy, botany, and geology. Such lines of dependency, which are fundamental to modern civilization, are so embedded in complex biotic webs that one cannot fully understand these human relationships without combining knowledge from all the arts and sciences of nature and human life.

The character and duration of civilization are determined by the reaction of the land to human activity. For example, as a general rule, the resilience of an ecosystem in resisting human abuse varies inversely to its aridity. Consequently, the durability of civilization in northeastern Europe has been largely shaped by the biotic stability of the land in that wet climate, while the vulnerability of civilization in the Middle East manifests the fragility of the land in that arid climate. Similarly, in the United States, the wet climates of the eastern regions allowed for heavy human settlement with little deterioration in the land, but the dry climate of the American Southwest could not sustain the same level of human settlement without extensive deterioration of the land.

Recently, the unprecedented power of human technology and the growth in human population have strained the biotic mechanism that supports modern civilization. Insofar as civilization depends upon the human effort to understand and control human interactions with the land, human ecology could become the architectonic science of civilization. Although human ecology has still not emerged as a fully mature science, some ecological biologists and ecological historians have begun to develop such a science.[66]

Leopold's conservationism as human ecology would support many of the current lines of research in conservation biology. For example, when Edward O. Wilson in 1984 first coined the term "biophilia" to denote the natural human love for living beings, he saw this natural affinity for life as supporting Leopold's conservation ethic.[67] As products of natural selection, human beings have a natural instinct to explore and affiliate with living environments like those that were typical of human evolutionary history. Therefore, Wilson argued, Leopold was correct in seeing that the success of conservationism would depend on stimulating and extending the human desires for contact with wild nature.

Another recent extension of Leopold's conservationism is the development of ecological economics.[68] Economists and ecologists have cooperated in estimating the economic value of the services provided by natural ecosystems. Robert Costanza and his colleagues have recently estimated the annual economic value of seventeen ecosystem services for sixteen biomes encompassing the entire biosphere. The total value of $33 trillion annually is almost twice the annual global gross national product of $18 trillion. Of the seventeen ecosystem services, the most valuable is nutrient cycling (such as nitrogen fixation); but the second most valuable ecosystem service is the cultural value of natural products and processes that provide aesthetic, artistic, educational, or scientific values. Of course, assigning monetary values to ecosystem services for which there are no market prices is highly speculative and controversial. For example, one factor in measuring the monetary value of the aesthetic pleasures derived from oceans is the willingness of people in California to pay more for land on or near an ocean coastline. But even if such monetary measurements give us only rough approximations of the value of nature's services for human beings, it supports Leopold's view of conservationism as human ecology in at least two general ways. It draws attention to the cultural value of nature in satisfying aesthetic, ethical, and intellectual desires. And it emphasizes the anthropocentric basis of conservationism by showing how natural ecosystems gain value by serving human desires.[69]

This view of natural ecosystems as instrumental to human welfare would support a claim by Aristotle that is often dismissed by modern readers as an absurd statement of anthropocentric teleology. "Plants are for the sake of animals," Aristotle declares, "and animals are for the sake of men. Domesticated animals are for use and for food, and wild animals, at least most if not all, for food and for comfort, such as clothing and other instruments. Accordingly, since nature makes nothing imperfect or in vain, she must have made all other things for the sake of men."[70] From the point of view of human ecology, we could say that human beings have been adapted by natural selection in evolutionary history with the ability to manipulate natural ecosystems for human benefit. The success of that human manipulation of nature, however, requires a prudent adjustment of human desires to the natural environment.

By rooting conservationism in human ecology, Leopold shows that conservationism rightly understood requires a stable accommodation between nature as wild nature and nature as human nature. By nature, the land is the flow of energy through a circuit of soil, water, plants, and animals. By nature, human beings strive to satisfy their desires for the vital goods of body and mind. Conservationism as human ecology would prescribe a prudent control over nature to achieve harmony between the natural energy of the land and the natural desires of human beings.

Notes

1. Aldo Leopold, *A Sand County Almanac, and Sketches Here and There* (New York: Oxford University Press, 1949), 224-25.

2. See J. Baird Callicott, *In Defense of the Land Ethic: Essays in Environmental Philosophy* (Albany: State University of New York Press, 1989); Callicott, "Conservation Values and Ethics," in Gary K. Meffe and C. Ronald Carroll, eds., *Principles of Conservation Biology* (Sunderland, MA: Sinauer and Associates, 1994), 24-49; Joseph Des Jardins, *Environmental Ethics: An Introduction to Environmental Philosophy* (Belmont, CA: Wadsworth Publishing, 1993); Gary K. Meffe and C. Ronald Carroll, "What is Conservation Biology?," in Gary K. Meffe and C. Ronald Carroll, eds., *Principles of Conservation Biology* (Sunderland, MA: Sinauer Associates, 1994), 3-23; Roderick Nash, *Wilderness and the American Mind*, 3rd ed. (New Haven: Yale University Press, 1982).

3. Donald Worster, *Nature's Economy: A History of Ecological Ideas* (Cambridge: Cambridge University Press, 1985), 284-90.

4. Aldo Leopold, *Round River: From the Journals of Aldo Leopold,* ed. Luna Leopold (New York: Oxford University Press, 1953), 63-64.

5. Callicott, *In Defense,* 151-52, 162-63.

6. Callicott, *In Defense,* 93-94; Callicott, "Conservation Values," 44-47.

7. See Curt Meine, *Aldo Leopold: His Life and Work* (Madison: University of Wisconsin Press, 1988).

8. Gifford Pinchot, *Breaking New Ground* (New York: Harcourt, Brace, 1947), 505.

9. Gifford Pinchot, *The Fight for Conservation* (New York: Doubleday, 1910), 40-52.

10. Pinchot, *Breaking New Ground,* 306-13.

11. John Muir, "A Plan to Save the Forests," *The Century Magazine* 49 (1895): 630-31.

12. See Nash, *Wilderness,* 122-81; and Samuel P. Hays, *Conservation and the Gospel of Efficiency: The Progressive Conservation Movement, 1890-1920* (Cambridge: Harvard University Press, 1959), 122-98.

13. John Muir, *The Yosemite* (New York: The Century Company, 1912), 249-62.

14. Meine, *Aldo Leopold,* 78.

15. Aldo Leopold, The *River of the Mother of God and Other Essays,* ed. Susan L. Flader and J. Baird Callicott (Madison: University of Wisconsin Press, 1991), 79.

16. Leopold, *River of the Mother of God,* 78-81.

17. Leopold, *River of the Mother of God*, 129.

18. Meine, *Aldo Leopold*, 198.

19. Leopold, *River of the Mother of God*, 126, 133-42.

20. Leopold, *River of the Mother of God*, 143-47.

21. Meine, *Aldo Leopold*, 257.

22. Aldo Leopold, *Game Management* (New York: Charles Scribner's Sons, 1933), xxxi, 3, 19.

23. Leopold, *Game Management*, 38-39.

24. Compare H. G. Andrewartha and L. C. Birch, *The Ecological Web* (Chicago: University of Chicago Press, 1984).

25. Leopold, *Game Management*, 125, 128.

26. Leopold, *Game Management*, 45.

27. Leopold, *Game Management*, 210.

28. Leopold, *Game Management*, 391.

29. Leopold, *Game Management*, 4.

30. Leopold, *Game Management*, 396.

31. Leopold, *Game Management*, 5-21.

32. Leopold, *Game Management*, 110, 209, 217, 225, 227.

33. Leopold, *Game Management*, 38, 45, 71-72, 123, 194, 252, 275, 303, 322-25, 385-88.

34. Leopold, *River of the Mother of God*, 302.

35. Leopold, *River of the Mother of God*, 336-37.

36. Leopold, *Sand County Almanac*, vii.

37. Leopold, *Sand County Almanac*, viii-ix.

38. Leopold, *Sand County Almanac*, 68.

39. Leopold, *Sand County Almanac*, 225.

40. Leopold, *Sand County Almanac*, 224-25.

41. Leopold, *Sand County Almanac*, 214.

42. Leopold, *Sand County Almanac*, 3-5.

43. Leopold, *Sand County Almanac*, 68.

44. In *Darwinian Natural Right: The Biological Ethics of Human Nature* (Albany: State University of New York Press, 1997), I develop this thought in arguing for a Darwinian ethics founded on the idea that the good is the desirable.

45. Arnhart, *Darwinian Natural Right*, 78-81, 87-92.

46. Arnhart, *Darwinian Natural Right*, 104-108, 214-20.

47. See Leopold, *River of the Mother of God*, 301-305; and Charles Elton, *Animal Ecology* (New York: Macmillan, 1927).

48. Aristotle, *Metaphysics*, 980a20; Aristotle, *Parts of Animals*, 644b23-45a37.

49. Leopold, *Sand County Almanac*, 173.

50. Aristotle, *Nicomachean Ethics*, 1141a31-32.

51. Leopold, *River of the Mother of God*, 196; Leopold, *Sand County Almanac*, 8.

52. Leopold, *River of the Mother of God*, 336-37.

53. Leopold, *Sand County Almanac*, 175, 212-14, 225; Leopold, *River of the Mother of God*, 193-202, 216, 255-65, 298-300, 317-19; Leopold, *Game Management*, 21, 209-10, 226-27, 386-88, 395-407.

54. Leopold, *River of the Mother of God*, 274-75.

55. Leopold, *Sand County Almanac*, 168; Leopold, *Round River*, 58.

56. Leopold, *Sand County Almanac*, 109-10.

57. Leopold, *Sand County Almanac*, 96.

58. Leopold, *Game Management*, 391-405; *Sand County Almanac*, 168-72, 192-94; *River of the Mother of God*, 158-63, 169-72, 190-91, 212-17, 226-29; *Round River*, 166-73.

59. Aristotle, *Poetics*, 1448b4-24.

60. Leopold, *Sand County Almanac*, 165-87.

61. Leopold, *Sand County Almanac*, 174.

62. See Callicott, "Conservation Values"; and Des Jardins, *Environmental Ethics.*

63. Leopold, *River of the Mother of God*, 298.

64. See Leopold, *Game Management*, xxxi, 25, 39, 45, 47, 49, 125, 128, 254, 260, 304-5, 324-25, 343-46, 387, 391-405, 421-22; *River of the Mother of God*, 71-77, 91-97, 109, 115, 157, 181-92, 209-17, 237, 270-73, 281-86, 298, 300, 301-305, 310-19; *Round River*, 158-65; *Sand County Almanac*, 186-87, 196, 204-7.

65. Leopold, *River of the Mother of God*, 301-5.

66. See H. G. Andrewartha and L. C. Birch, *The Ecological Web* (Chicago: University of Chicago Press, 1984); Stephen Boyden, *Western Civilization in Biological Perspective: Patterns in Biohistory* (Oxford: Oxford University Press, 1987); and William Cronon, *Nature's Metropolis: Chicago and the Great West* (New York: Norton, 1991).

67. See Edward O. Wilson, *Biophilia* (Cambridge: Harvard University Press, 1984), 119-40.

68. See Richard B. Norgaard, "Ecology, Politics, and Economics: Finding the Common Ground for Decision Making in Conservation," in Gary K. Meffe and C. Ronald Carroll, eds., *Principles of Conservation Biology* (Sunderland, MA: Sinauer Associates, 1994), 439-65; Gretchen C. Daily, ed., *Nature's Services: Societal Dependence on Natural Ecosystems* (Washington, D.C.: Island Press, 1997); Robert Costanza et al., "The Value

of the World's Ecosystem Services and Natural Capital," *Nature* 387 (1997): 253-60; and Stuart L. Pimm, "The Value of Everything," *Nature* 387 (1997): 231-32.

69. See Lawrence H. Goulder and Donald Kennedy, "Valuing Ecosystem Services: Philosophical Bases and Empirical Methods," in Gretchen Daily, ed., *Nature's Services*, 23-47.

70. Aristotle, *Politics* 1256b16-22.

Part Two
Precursors

5

Was John Muir a Darwinian?

James G. Lennox

Contemporary environmentalism has been slow to learn the lessons of the branches of biology known as ecology and evolution. The rhetoric of much of its literature leaves its readers with the distinct impression of the earth as one vast, delicately balanced system, the slightest change in which will lead to global destruction,[1] and of species extinction not as a natural process, but as a terrible aberration to be prevented at all costs.[2] The Endangered Species Act mandates species preservation regardless of whether the cause of a decline in a population is human activity.[3] Human readers are typically enjoined not to think of themselves as one more natural product of the evolutionary process, but as nature's worst nightmare.[4] Our exponential population increase is not to be viewed as one more example of the force that, as Darwin taught us, has ever driven evolutionary change, but as somehow different from the identical process found in all other species.[5] Our exploitation of the natural world for our own ends is morally suspect, rather than another example of a biologically universal phenomenon.

The following discussion explores the historical roots of this ambivalence, by exploring John Muir's exposure to, and attitude toward, the ideas of Charles Darwin (1809-1882). As previous chapters have shown, conservationist thinkers like Roosevelt and Leopold clearly accepted Darwin's insights.[6] I shall make the case that, unlike them, Muir refused to embrace Darwinism, a refusal rooted in profound differences between Muir's philosophy of nature and Darwin's. To the extent that it is Muir's philosophy of nature that continues to inspire and animate the environmental movement today, its ambivalence is not the least bit surprising.

Parallel Lives, Intersecting Paths

On April 21, 1838, as John Muir was entering the world in Dunbar, Scotland, Charles Darwin was attending a dinner party at the home of one Sarah Williams. From his account of the event in a letter to his sister Susan, there is no hint that six months later he would be engaged to marry his cousin, Emma Wedgwood:

> On Saturday last, I dined with Sarah Williams, who sent me the most charming little note, that ever man received.—it was worth the penance of half a dozen dinner parties to receive such a note.— We had there sundry people, —a charming widow, all in black, young & pretty, —she took the line of looking charming & saying little.—Old Hopkinson,—rather a buffoon & a little vulgar.—he was, however, by the aid of his own witty sayings & those borrowed from Theodore Hook rather amusing. I sat by Mr. Alexander, who edified the company by repeating all the witty & unwitty things, which sundry lords and dukes had lately uttered.[7]

Nor from the lighthearted character of this letter would one gather that Darwin was daily feverishly making entries in *Species Notebook* C, as we now call it, on the "Species Question," taking notes on the works of animal and plant breeders and hybridizers, explorer/naturalists, and taxonomists, a full-blown "transformist" (i.e., evolutionist) but as yet completely at sea regarding the mechanisms of evolutionary change.

John Muir would have had difficulty imagining the comfortable life into which Charles Darwin was born. The son of Daniel Muir, a poor but enterprising evangelical Christian, he spent his early years toiling long and hard. Reading anything other than the Bible was suspect, and it was virtually impossible to live a day piously enough to avoid a beating from his father. Ever in search of a purer Christian faith, Daniel moved his family to Wisconsin in 1849 to be part of a Campbellite sect settled there. By this time John and his brother had learned to escape their father's wrath by spending their free time roaming the hills of Scotland and then Wisconsin, even if, as Pencek argues, John did not entirely escape his father's religiosity.

Yet, in spite of their very different circumstances, there were many remarkable parallels in the lives of Muir and Darwin. And not only parallels, but intersections—for *On the Origin of Species* was published when Muir was but twenty-one. Indeed, he may have been one of its very first American readers.[8] Darwin's *Beagle* journal was already available around the time that

Alexander von Humboldt's *Personal Narrative*, upon which it was modeled, was enthralling the young Muir.[9] Muir's famous "Thousand Mile Walk" was inspired by reading Humboldt, just as were Darwin's plans to explore the Canary Islands with some of his Cambridge mates, plans overshadowed by the invitation to pilgrimage to Mecca—i.e., to Humboldt's South America!—on Her Majesty's Ship *Beagle*, as gentleman naturalist. Though I know of no evidence that Darwin knew of Muir, Muir came to be friends with many of Darwin's American followers, most notably Harvard's Asa Gray, America's foremost botanist and spokesman for Darwinism (and, like Muir's father, a Calvinist).

Like Charles Darwin's, Muir's scientific reputation (such as it was) was built on early publications in the field of geology rather than natural history. More than that, these publications defended a "uniformitarian" understanding of the shaping of the Yosemite region by means of glacial action against a then-dominant "catastrophic" upheaval hypothesis, just the sort of geology defended by Darwin, who had been convinced of this approach by Charles Lyell's *Principles of Geology* while on the *Beagle*.[10] Finally, both had a passion for botany. Muir credits a fellow student at the University of Wisconsin named Griswold for his entré into the study of plants, and after mentioning geology and botany among his course of studies, he notes that he "wandered away on a glorious botanical and geological excursion, which has lasted nearly fifty years and is not yet completed."[11] Darwin wrote six books and more than a dozen articles on botanical topics in his later years, but his *Beagle* botanical collection was extensive,[12] and the *Origin* shows him to be as thoroughly at home with botanical as with zoological material.

With all of this by way of shared influences, interests, and beliefs, Muir's many enthusiastic biographers may be forgiven for assuming that Muir was a Darwinian, through and through.

And so many of them do. Take the following remarks, from James M. Clarke, as representative:

> Darwin's *Origin of Species* had been published in 1859—only two years before John entered the university—but the ideas spread with the speed of an earth tremor, and the western world felt the after-shocks for a long time. To the many who had committed their faith to a literal interpretation of the Biblical story of earth's creation and man's fall, 'Darwinism' was at best dangerous radicalism and, at worst, deadly sin.
>
> John Muir, who had never accepted his father's fundamentalist beliefs, had no trouble in adopting the Darwinian

conception of evolution. And he was wide open to an equally controversial theory concerning the history of the earth itself, which was then outraging the orthodox, including many scientists who had spent their professional lives in trying to reconcile observed phenomena with a six-day creation and Noah's flood.[13]

And he rejected the 'survival-of-the-fittest' interpretation of organic evolution, which was often summoned to support the laissez faire doctrine. He had found more mutual benefit occurring among species and varieties growing together in pure wildness than to believe that competition is the primary, overriding law. He saw in nature more harmony than lethal strife—except for the destructive intervention of man.[14]

These two passages display a remarkable inconsistency. If Darwin's theory does have the idea of a competition among the members of a species at its core, then how could Muir at once have no trouble accepting Darwin's concept of evolution and yet reject its competitive core?

More fundamentally, they give the distinct impression that if a competition for (relatively) scarce resources is at the theory's core, then the idea of mutual cooperation within or among species cannot be. Yet the *Origin* emphasizes the mutual cooperation among and within species—Darwin wrote entire books on such topics as the marvelous mutual adaptations of insect and insect-pollinated plants. Darwin, however, sought not merely to stand back and admire such things, but to explain them, and he believed that such cooperation was perfected by (for example) orchids "competing" with one another to attract insects and insects "competing" for the energy provided by orchids.

These two passages also paint an historically inaccurate picture that makes Muir seem far more radical than he was. Though the distinct impression is left that Muir knew of Darwin's ideas in his college years, as I noted earlier, there is no concrete evidence that he did. Nor would any serious geologist in the 1860s (and very few in the 1760s, in fact) attempt to defend a geology consistent with a literal reading of Genesis. The debate in the early to mid-nineteenth century between so-called "uniformitarians" and "catastrophists" was not about this at all. It was a subtle debate over the legitimacy of explaining observed geological formations by postulating different and more powerful causes in the prehistoric past than have been observed in historic times.[15]

Louis Agassiz is, in fact, a case study in the subtlety of this debate. The Harvard geology professor was also America's most celebrated opponent of

Darwinism, and John Muir's geological inspiration. He is usually identified as a "catastrophist," and it is, strictly speaking, true that no human observer has recorded a global ice sheet sliding down over the temperate regions of earth, with all the incredible changes this brings. On the other hand there are glaciers all over the globe, and we can observe how they change from year to year, and the effects of those changes. So does the extrapolation of ice ages to explain geological formations make one a "uniformitarian" or a "catastrophist"? In fact what makes the label of "catastrophism" stick on Agassiz is that he sought to explain everything he saw by this hypothesis, even when there was virtually no evidence for it.[16]

With Muir a staunch disciple of Agassiz, on the one hand, and an eventual close friend of Asa Gray, on the other, he must have regularly heard both sides of the debate over Darwinism in the latter half of the nineteenth century. But to know what he heard, we need to get beyond stereotypes and confusions about this debate. A first step toward considering Muir's probable reaction to Darwinism is a brief account of the Darwinism to which he would have been exposed. For to accept Darwinism in the last half of the nineteenth century meant accepting a radical and unfamiliar way of looking at the world.

The Scientific Heart of Darwinian Nature

Darwin began the work that was to distinguish him by trying to solve two puzzles that transcend any particular kind of organism, puzzles that, no matter what corner of the natural world in which you look, look back at you. These puzzles were on every naturalist's mind in the early nineteenth century, forced there by a rapidly expanding mass of fossil evidence for an inconceivably long history of species creations and extinctions, and an equally rapidly expanding understanding of the biogeographic distribution of existing species.[17] The classic statement both of the evidence and of the puzzles was Charles Lyell's *Principles of Geology*, the first volume of which was published just months before Charles Darwin took a copy with him on H. M. S. *Beagle*. Darwin was so taken by it that he had the second and third volumes shipped to him on route, to be picked up in Montevideo and the Falkland Islands. That he read these volumes while exploring the South American mainland and its surrounding islands goes a long way toward explaining the shape of his inquiry into the origin of species.

The first, *geological*, puzzle arises from studying the patterns of similarity and difference between the organisms living in the world today and those that the fossil record suggests lived in the world in previous eras. To cite two questions of this sort that first puzzled Darwin: Why are the fossils of mammals found near the surface in South America on the one hand clearly similar to mammals living in South America today, and yet, on the other, different enough to be classified as different species? And why are the fossilized shells of ocean dwelling mollusks *generically* similar to ones now living in the Atlantic, found many hundreds, and sometimes even thousands, of feet away from (and often above) the nearest salt water? This is the puzzle of the systematic similarities and differences between the fossil and living representatives of different regions—why the similarities, and why the increase in differences as one moves away from the surface (i.e., back in time)?

The other major universal puzzle had to do with the patterns to be found in the *current distribution* of animals and plants around the world. The world's flora and fauna are regional. One doesn't find the same species in all the world's rainforests; there are rainforest flora and fauna distinctive to South America, Australasia, and Africa. Similarly, the species inhabiting islands near a certain continent belong to the same *families* as the species on that continent, yet are typically different species. These regional "family resemblances" often make no sense from a purely "design" standpoint—the "arboreal mammal" niche in a region of Australia, for example, is filled by a kangaroo not especially well-suited to living in trees, and the Galapagos archipelago, though filled with species that would be excellent mammalian prey, has no native mammalian predators! Surely an omnipotent creator could do better!

Overlaid on these puzzling historical and regional patterns is the pervasive fact of adaptation. As Darwin noted in the introduction to *On the Origin of Species*,

> . . . it is quite conceivable that a naturalist, reflecting on the mutual affinities of organic beings, on their embryological relations, their geographical distribution, geological succession, and other such facts, might come to the conclusion that each species had not been independently created, but had descended, like varieties, from other species. Nevertheless, such a conclusion, even if well founded, would be unsatisfactory, until it could be shown how the innumerable species inhabiting this world have been modified, so as to acquire that perfection of structure and coadaptation which most justly excites our admiration.[18]

The mechanism that explains patterns of resemblance in place and time must also explain adaptation. Solving *that* problem took Darwin two or three years of hard cognitive labor, a struggle we can vicariously partake in by reading his "Species Notebooks," now superbly edited and published.[19] The struggle ended triumphantly.

Very briefly: the scientific core of Darwinism is an extremely wide-ranging theory which postulates a constant "struggle for existence"[20] among individuals who vary slightly with respect to every feature. This struggle is a consequence of a clash between a tendency to reproduce at an exponential rate and a limited and hostile environment. This "struggle" favors individuals with variations that provide some slight advantage relative to other members of their species, giving them a greater chance of surviving and their offspring a greater chance of inheriting those advantageous variations. In this way, populations will constantly adapt to their environments. But in constantly *fluctuating* environments, such as Earth's, this process of "adaptation" results in a tendency for the mean values of these variations to change over time, and given enough time, this change produces new species.

Extinction, as Darwin stresses, is an inevitable consequence of this struggle: "it follows that as each selected and favoured form increases in number, so will the less favoured forms decrease and become rare. Rarity, as geology tells us, is the precursor to extinction."[21] As a population decreases in numbers, any severe fluctuation in climate or increase in the number of predators will greatly increase the likelihood of extinction, and decrease the chances that a favorable variation will appear, or, if it does, that it will make any difference.

Most of Darwin's life work as a scientist can be seen as the gathering and organizing of evidence for this theory, including its continuous application to unusual, and preferably apparently inexplicable, phenomena. Thus late in his life we find, along with the books on the *Expression of Emotions* and the *Descent of Man*, others on climbing and insectivorous plants, and on their powers of movement, and on the incredible variety of mechanisms for fertilization in orchids. Similarly, the four-volume work of the classification of the Barnacles (Cirripidae), published prior to *On the Origin of Species,* provided him with a specialist's knowledge of anatomical, physiological, and developmental variation in an extensive and worldwide invertebrate order. The confident control over these subjects in the *Origin* was a product of this painstaking ten-year project.

In the *Origin*, Darwin acknowledges that it is easy to miss the struggle to survive that is at the core of all biological explanation.

> We behold the face of nature bright with gladness, we often see
> superabundance of food; we do not see, or we forget, that the
> birds which are idly singing round us mostly live on insects or
> seeds, and are thus constantly destroying life; or we forget how
> largely these songsters, or their eggs, or their nestlings, are
> destroyed by birds and beasts of prey; we do not always bear in
> mind, that though food may be now superabundant, it is not so at
> all seasons of each recurring year.[22]

But if we miss it, we miss the fundamental fact of life—that is his message.

The Philosophical Heart of Darwinism

Philosophically, Darwin became, during the *Beagle* voyage and under the
influence of Charles Lyell and John Herschel,[23] deeply committed to a form
of "causal realism" associated by these nineteenth-century natural
philosophers (whether accurately or not) with Isaac Newton. Science was the
search for empirically verifiable causal theories, and empirical verification
came in two forms: direct evidence for the operation of the cause and its
production of the effect (e.g., observing a lava flow laying down layers of
igneous rock and altering the chemical nature of surrounding minerals), and
the ability of the causal theory to account for an extensive and apparently
unconnected set of unexplained correlations (e.g., the ability to explain many
distinct geological formations by showing them all to be the effect of a lava
flow).

Darwin's *Origin* is organized in strict accordance with these philosophical
commitments. The first four chapters provide direct evidence for each
condition of his causal theory: wide-ranging intra-specific *variation*, its
heritability, the *struggle for existence* consequent on the tendency toward
exponential population growth, and (the best he could do) domestic selection
of favored variations, producing more and more divergent varieties as time
passed. After three transitional chapters fending off expected objections, the
final five chapters show how evolution by natural selection explains a vast
range of empirical generalizations in geology, biogeography, comparative
anatomy, embryology and systematics—how, that is, it solves the puzzles of
geological succession, geographic regionalism, and pervasive adaptation that
struck him so vividly while on the *Beagle*.

Darwin claims to have begun the *Beagle* voyage a full-blown Christian,
yet it is clear he is approaching agnosticism in his early notebooks, written
shortly after his return to England. Given his family background, it is
unlikely his Christianity was ever very *deep*, however full-blown. His

grandfather Dr. Erasmus, a member, with Joseph Priestly[24] and Josiah Wedgwood,[25] of Birmingham's radical Lunar Society, advocate of the ideals of the French Revolution, author of nature poetry that vaguely presented a progressive, evolutionary (and sexually charged) view of the botanical world, apparently accepted Unitarianism as about as far as he was willing to go theologically; and the family circle of Darwins and Wedgwoods was full of members who vacillated between Unitarianism and outright agnosticism. Darwin's first school was Unitarian, established at the behest of his mother, a Wedgwood, who encouraged a Mr. George Case to set up a Unitarian congregation and school for her children in Schrewsbury. This vague deism fit well with the natural philosophy of Lyell and Herschel, which saw science as the unbounded search for secondary causes, leaving questions of a first cause to the theologians.[26]

Darwin's early notebooks (1837-1838) include, besides four (B-E) dealing with "the Species Question," two (M, N) he described as "full of Metaphysics on Morals and Speculations on Expression," and another that argues page by page with John Macculloch's *Proofs and Illustrations of the Attributes of God*. In these latter we find Darwin's earliest systematic thinking about man's place in nature and about natural theology.

Man is to be viewed as one more product of the natural causal process of evolutionary change. Physically, the evidence for this claim was not new.[27] In the late seventeenth century, the anatomist Edward Tyson had, at the request of the Royal Society, dissected a chimpanzee, concluding his report to the society by comparing it to a species of monkey and to humans. He noted that it closely resembled humans in forty-eight characteristics, and the monkey in twenty-seven. Similarly, the systematist Carl Linneaus, in the *Systema Naturae* of 1758, put humans and chimps in the order *Anthropomorpha*. Preceding the publication of Darwin's *Descent of Man* by nearly ten years, Thomas Huxley's *Man's Place in Nature* explicitly used comparative anatomy and embryology to make the case for a common evolutionary ancestry of ape and human.

The chief problem facing Darwin was explaining, by evolutionary means, those features of human behavior that traditionally were associated with an immaterial and immortal soul: reason, free will, a moral sense, and the emotions associated with moral behavior in particular. He gradually works out a strategy for dealing with these questions: Find, among recently evolved mammals, behaviors that evidence such things as the making of inferences and choices, social instincts promoting care for others or loyalty, and emotions such as joy, sadness, or remorse. One needed to convince skeptics that our distinguishing features were not so radically different from those of our most closely related fellows that they could not have evolved from features of a common ancestor. As he puts it:

> If no organic being excepting man had possessed any mental power, or if his powers had been of a wholly different nature from those of the lower animals, then we should never have been able to convince ourselves that our higher faculties had gradually developed. But it can be clearly shown that there is no fundamental difference in kind.[28]

The Darwin that Muir would have encountered and heard heated discussions about in the 1870s, thus represents not just a narrowly constrained biological theory, but views on the nature of man, his place in nature, the nature of science, and the relationship between a scientific and a theological understanding of nature. Needless to say, these were all questions upon which John Muir thought deeply.

Common Themes in Darwin and Muir

We have very little to go on if we want to answer the historical question of the actual influence of Darwin's writings on Muir—his references to Darwin are few, typically vague, and sometimes downright puzzling.[29] But if we want to ask a more complicated question about compatibility or incompatibility of Muir's ideas with Darwin's Darwinism, I believe materials are available sufficient to answer the question. And this consideration may allow us to make some plausible conjectures about why, with the constant exposure to Darwinism through his friendship with Asa Gray and other channels, there appears to be virtually no genuine attempt to grapple with what was arguably the most important philosophical and scientific idea of the late nineteenth century, and one with major, and obvious, implications for our understanding of the natural world and our place in it.

Both Darwin and Muir reject orthodox Christianity, and both did so during their first prolonged intensive exploration of the natural world: Darwin on the *Beagle* voyage and Muir during his 1000-mile walk to the Gulf.[30] And in at least one respect, there is a common basis for this rejection, namely, the questioning of man's immaterial soul as distinguishing man from other organisms, and the related notions that man is thus special in the eyes of God, created in God's image, with the rest of his creation intended for human use. Muir notes, "They tell us that plants are not like man immortal, but are perishable—soul-less. I think this is something we know exactly nothing about."[31] For all we know the Creator has an equal interest in all animals.

> Doubtless these [alligators] are happy and fill the place assigned them by the great Creator of us all. Fierce and cruel they appear to us, but beautiful in the eyes of God. . . . How narrow we selfish, conceited creatures are in our sympathies! how blind to the rights of all the rest of creation![32]

He is thus contemptuous of the idea that the rest of nature was created solely for man's use. "The world we are told was made for man, a presumption that is totally unsupported by facts."[33] A morning hunt for venison in Florida provoked the following outburst.

> To me it appeared as 'damnedest' work to slaughter God's cattle for sport. 'They were made for us,' say these self-approving preachers; 'for our food, our recreation, or other uses not yet discovered.' As truthfully we might say on behalf of a bear, when he deals successfully with an unfortunate hunter, 'Men and other bipeds were made for bears, and thanks be to God for claws and teeth so long.'[34]

From here it is but a short (though logically illicit) step to actually taking sides with the beasts, as he almost does in the next paragraph: "if a war of races should occur between the wild beasts and Lord Man I would be tempted to sympathize with the bears."[35]

As Pencek rightly argues, however, quite particular rejection of orthodox Christian doctrine regarding the Creation and man's place in it seems not to have brought with it any doubt about the Creator. Rather, in these and many other passages the anthropocentricity of orthodox Christianity is replaced by a Creationist egalitarianism.

> Now it never seems to occur to these farseeing teachers that Nature's object in making animals and plants might possibly be first of all the happiness of each one of them not the creation of all for the happiness of one. Why ought man to value himself as more than an infinitely small composing unit of the one great unit of creation? . . . The universe would be incomplete without man; but it would also be incomplete without the smallest transmicroscopic creature that dwells beyond our conceitful eyes and knowledge.[36]

Darwin's rejection of Christianity, on the other hand, is a consequence of his gradual acceptance of the idea that man has descended from a common ancestor with the other great apes, and thus that his attributes must be continuous with theirs.[37] As a result, like Muir, Darwin from the start of his *Species Notebooks* is a critic of anthropocentric thinking:

> It is absurd to talk of one animal being higher than another. We consider those, where the cerebral structure, intellectual faculties, most developed, as highest.—A bee doubtless would [consider those] where the instincts were.[38]

What leads Darwin to this position, however, is a thoroughly materialistic attitude toward human cognition. Besides the radical dissenting nature of his family, Charles Darwin received early exposure to materialist theories of mind when a teenaged medical student at Edinburgh University. His mentor there, Dr. Robert Grant, was a Lamarckian with materialist sympathies. He sponsored Darwin into the Plinian Society, where Darwin heard papers presented in 1827 by W. A. Browne and a Mr. Grey defending the view that "mind" was simply the functional output of the human brain.[39] These ideas surface explicitly in his own thinking in the *Species Notebook* C.

> Thought being hereditary it is difficult to imagine it anything but structure of brain. Love of the deity effect of organization, oh you materialist! . . . Why is thought being a secretion of brain, more wonderful than gravity a property of matter? It is our arrogance, our admiration of ourselves.[40]

Both Muir and Darwin reject the idea that Man has a special place in the Creation; but for Darwin this doesn't lead to a deification of nature, nor to ascribing immortal souls to other organisms. In fact, Darwin's naturalism is more far-reaching than Muir's. John Muir rather quickly moves from the idea that humans have no special, divinely ordained, place in nature, to the conclusion that "Lord Man" stand in opposition to nature. The deification of man is replaced by the deification of nature. It is one thing to compare man's hunting of the deer with the bear's hunting of man, a comparison Darwin might have approved of—it is quite another to side with the bear!

John Muir's attitude toward natural science is well-summarized by Harry Fielding Reid:

> To me Muir was a poet rather than a scientific man . . . he loved
> Nature and spent his life observing her works; but his
> observations were the observations of a poet, of a lover, and not
> the systematic observations of the man of science.[41]

Variation: Chance or Design?

From Muir's very few comments on Darwin and Darwinism, Stephen Fox
attempts to reconstruct his attitude toward Darwin's ideas. He notes Muir's
reference to Gray and Darwin as "great progressive, unlimited" men, and his
praise of Darwin's "noble character" as a "devout and indefatigable seeker
after truth."[42] Yet this does not add up to his "veering toward" Darwinism,
as Fox suggests, since these are comments about Darwin's character, not an
endorsement of his theory. On the other hand, Fox fixes on Muir's use of the
adjective "ungodly" to modify Darwin's idea of a "struggle for existence."
But the passage from which this quote is taken is more interestingly
ambiguous:

> There are ten flowering plants of large size that go above all of
> the pinched blinking dwarfs *which almost justify Darwin's
> ungodly word 'struggle,'* and burst into bloom of purple and
> yellow as rich and abundant as ever responded to the thick
> creamy sun-gold of the plain.[43]

This remark is one of a very few in Muir that suggest a careful reading,
or at least familiarity with, the doctrines of the *Origin*, and in particular of
its third chapter, on the struggle for existence. Examples such as Muir here
so vividly describes are precisely those to which Darwin appeals to explain
that he is using the word "struggle" in a "large and metaphorical" sense.[44]
Here we have taller plants "struggling" for the sunlight, and preventing the
"pinched blinking dwarfs" from receiving it. In this, and in the various other
passages noted by Fox, we see an important clue to the role of Muir's
friendship with Asa Gray in his uncomfortable relationship with Darwinism.

Gray, recall, was both a Harvard professor of botany and an orthodox
Calvinist. He was one of the first people to whom Darwin outlined his
theory, in correspondence.[45] Gray easily came to see natural selection as a
valid deduction from natural (i.e. ,"secondary" or "intermediate") laws, and
one that beautifully accounted for adaptations. Since natural law was viewed
by him (as by Herschel and Lyell) as the product of divine creation, he at
first saw no conflict between Darwin's ideas and his Christian beliefs.
Gradually, however, he fully absorbed the importance of chance variation as

providing the material for selection in Darwin's theory, and this became the source of a never-to-be-resolved disagreement between the two men.

> So long as gradatory, orderly, and adapted forms in Nature argue design, and at least while the physical cause of variation is utterly unknown and mysterious, we should advise Mr. Darwin to assume, in the philosophy of his hypothesis, that variation has been led along certain beneficial lines.[46]

Darwin replied:

> However much we may wish it, we can hardly follow Professor Asa Gray in his belief that 'variation has been led along certain beneficial lines,' like a stream 'along definite and useful lines of irrigation.' If we assume that each particular variation was from the beginning of all time preordained, then that plasticity of organisation, which leads to many injurious deviations of structure, as well as the redundant power of reproduction which inevitably leads to a struggle for existence, and as a consequence, to the natural selection or survival of the fittest, must appear to us superfluous laws of nature.[47]

For Darwin, giving up chance variation was giving up any role for natural selection, which Darwin saw as an inevitable consequence of the fact that *most* of the organisms that are born fail to survive due to their lacking beneficial variations. It is the very guts of his theory, the heart of Darwinism, that Gray was rejecting. Notice the absolutely central role of the struggle for existence in Darwin's reply, and its rejection of the Divine preordination in the idea that "variation has been led along certain beneficial lines." Gray's was a Darwinism for those who do not see, or forget the life and death struggle at its heart—for someone like John Muir.

Take, as an instance, the opening lines of Chapter X of *Our National Parks*. In some sense, it is an "evolutionary" narrative of the emergence of America's forests—but it is decidedly *not* a Darwinian narrative.

> The forests of America, however slighted by man, must have been a great delight to God; for they were the best He ever planted. The whole continent was a garden, and from the beginning it seemed to be favored above all the other wild parks and gardens of the globe. To prepare the ground, it was rolled and sifted in seas with infinite loving deliberation and forethought, lifted into the light, submerged and warmed over

and over again, pressed and crumpled into folds and ridges, mountains, and hills, subsoiled with heaving volcanic fires, ploughed and ground and sculptured into scenery and soil with glaciers and rivers,—every feature growing and changing from beauty to beauty, higher and higher. And in the fullness of time it was planted in groves, and belts, and broad, exuberant, mantling forests, with the largest, most varied, most fruitful, and most beautiful trees in the world.[48]

Asa Gray's "Darwinism" would not seem so obviously to conflict with this tale of a divinely preordained preparation of America for the world's most beautiful trees—Darwin's Darwinism quite obviously would.

In a letter, Darwin described Gray, using a botanist's metaphor he would have appreciated, as a "complex cross of lawyer, poet, naturalist and theologian." The academic naturalist Asa Gray found the logic of Darwin's argument and richness of its empirical support compelling. But the natural theologian and poet Asa Gray must have been equally attracted to the author of the following words:

Benevolent, solemn, fateful, pervaded with divine light, every landscape glows like a countenance hallowed in eternal repose; and every one of its living creatures, clad in flesh and leaves, and every crystal of its rocks, whether on the surface shining in the sun or buried miles deep in what we call darkness, is throbbing and pulsing with the heartbeats of God. All the world lies warm in one heart, yet the Sierra seems to get more light than other mountains.[49]

Muir's greatness is as a poet/naturalist—seeing every detail of a concrete scene and being able to convey that scene in a way that makes you feel either as if you are yourself seeing it or wished you were. Yet scattered throughout these vivid prose-poems on nature are constant references to nature's divinity, to its "throbbing and pulsing with the heartbeat of God." There is a deep and abiding faith that everything that happens, even the most violent and apparently meaningless death, is part of a divine scheme. Only one creature is left out of this picture, only one creature's actions are not so judged—those of Muir's fellow human beings.[50]

All of these ideas are expressed in Muir's notes from his 1000-mile walk, and are there unaltered in his latest essays. Later in life, they may have contributed to his disagreements with those in the conservation movement who have a more Darwinian attitude to man and his place in nature, and seek a way to use the sciences of evolutionary biology and ecology to aid in wildlife conservation.

Conservationists such as Theodore Roosevelt and Aldo Leopold saw the natural world in explicitly Darwinian terms, and saw the sciences of evolutionary biology and ecology as potential sources of insight into the proper management of natural resources. The post-1960 environmental movement sees the natural world not as the object of scientifically informed management, but as the object of an almost religious awe and as a source of spiritual inspiration. I have explored the historical roots of this attitude, focusing on whether Darwin's way of understanding the natural world and man's place in it had any significant impact on John Muir.[51] Despite the paucity of references to Darwin in Muir's writings, there can be little doubt of his familiarity with Darwinism, visited as he was on numerous occasions by Asa Gray and on one occasion by both Gray and his British counterpart, Darwin's close friend and ally, Sir Joseph Hooker—not to mention Roosevelt, Agassiz, and many others.

Given these and other shared influences, it is initially surprising that there is no apparent attempt to engage Darwinism on Muir's part. Yet when their philosophies of nature are compared, some of that initial surprise dissipates. One can identify in Muir four deeply held philosophical beliefs that were formed early in his thinking about nature, and which would make him strongly disinclined to follow Darwin.

1. First, Muir's essays are imbued with a rhetoric of nature as eternal, stable, harmonious, unified, and so on. Darwin's work, on the contrary, stresses the transitory, unstable, and conflict-ridden nature of organic existence.

2. Both Muir and Darwin see that the living world is crucially structured by the fundamental fact of death—yet Darwin would never have expressed this basic premise in terms of "the sympathy, the friendly union, of life and death so apparent in nature . . . the beautiful blendings and communions of death and life, their joyous inseparable unity."[52] Indeed, this reverie on life and death leads Muir to conclude "All is divine harmony." For Darwin, of course, natural selection, the motor behind adaptation and evolutionary change, is not merely the survival of the fitter, but the (more common) death of the less fit. But beautiful and joyous he did not find it, nor could he find divine harmony in it at all.

3. Muir's cognitive attitude toward nature is one of aesthetic, perhaps even mystical, contemplation, not critical inquiry. By contrast Darwin, from his early teenaged years as beetle collector on, was excited by the idea of scientific inquiry and, by the time of his first published works, was firmly in

the grip of the empirical realism that infused British science in the Victorian era. Thus every glance at a natural phenomenon seemed to raise for Darwin a question or problem requiring explanation, and every proposed explanation required critical scrutiny and empirical support and testing. Open any page of his *Journal of Researches*, his popular account of the *Beagle* voyage, and you see him constantly drawn away from the pure emotive response to Nature to a question or puzzle. Here for example is Darwin telling us about an evening spent listening to the noises of tropics:

> Nature, in these climes, chooses her vocalists from more humble performers than in Europe. A small frog, of the genus Hyla, sits on a blade of grass about an inch above the surface of the water, and sends forth a pleasing chirp: when several are together they sing in harmony on different notes. I had some difficulty in catching a specimen of this frog. The genus Hyla has its toes terminated by small suckers; and I found this animal could crawl up a pane of glass, when placed absolutely perpendicular.[53]

On page after page, sensory awareness creates a need to investigate.

4. Finally, there is the question of man and his place in nature. This was a critical issue among Darwin's followers as well as for Darwin. Herbert Spencer thought, much as contemporary sociobiologists do, that Darwin's theory should be extended to account for the entire range of human social and political behavior. Huxley, in direct response, argued that there were precisely zero moral or political conclusions to be drawn from Darwin's theory. But all did agree that humans should be viewed as one recent product of an evolutionary process, and it became a test of one's Darwinian faith whether you insisted on keeping the human soul beyond the scope of natural selection, treating man as somehow outside of nature.

It is on this point that John Muir's "philosophy," if we wish to call it that, finds its greatest tension with Darwin's. For all his rejection of orthodox Christian doctrine on man's special place in the creation, Muir tends simply to turn that doctrine on its head. Nature is now divine and special, but human beings are still apart, and constantly viewed as bent on destroying the perfection, beauty, and harmony of the divine natural world. The experience of wildness about which he so passionately evangelizes is rooted in man's need for redemption. The idea that nature was created for man's use is replaced by the idea that, unlike every other creature on earth, humans are to be morally condemned for their exploitation of other living things. All other cases of devouring and being devoured are part of a harmonious unity of life and death. Only man is not allowed into the game.

Notes

1. The *science* of ecology, on the other hand, has trouble formulating any generalizations about what will happen when a "community" undergoes a significant environmental change, since different organisms in the community will react differently depending on a large number of variables represented in those organisms: variables such as reproductive rate, population size, genetic variability, predator population size, prey population size, food web dimensions, and food chain length, to name a few. (A good survey of the issues is Stuart L. Pimm, *The Balance of Nature? Ecological Issues in the Conservation of Species and Communities* [Chicago: University of Chicago Press, 1991].) Notice how quickly the rhetoric of environmentalism would become ineffective if all of this "messiness" were stressed.

2. E.g., Rachel Carson: "Who has made the decision that sets in motion these chains of poisonings, this ever-widening wave of death that spreads out, like ripples when a pebble is dropped into a still pond?" *Silent Spring: Twenty-fifth Anniversary Edition* (Boston: Houghton Mifflin, 1987), 127. For a valuable and readable antidote to this way of thinking about ecosystems, again a good place to start is Pimm, *Balance of Nature*.

3. Chapter 35, section 1533 of the Endangered Species Act enjoins the secretary of the interior to take protective action if a species is endangered or threatened "because of the following factors:

(A) the present or threatened destruction, modification, or curtailment of its habitat or range;

(B) overutilization for commercial, recreational, scientific, or educational purposes;

(C) disease or predation;

(D) the inadequacy of existing regulatory mechanisms: or

(E) other natural or manmade factors affecting its continued existence."

It is clear that (A), (C), and (E) all mandate that Federal agencies prevent species extinction even when they are due to perfectly "natural" causes.

4. E.g., "The war against nature, which began just a few hundred years ago with such confidence and enthusiasm, with such bravado, has been lost." Jeremy Rifkin, *Biosphere Politics* (New York: HarperCollins, 1992), 81. "Today we enthusiastically participate in what is in essence a massive and unprecedented experiment with the natural system of the global environment, with little regard for the moral consequences. But for the separation of science and religion, we might not be pumping so much

gaseous chemical waste into the atmosphere and threatening the destruction of the earth's climate balance." Al Gore, *Earth in the Balance* (New York: Penguin Books, 1993), 275.

5. For example: "The penalty for frantic attempts to feed burgeoning populations in the next decade may be a lowering of the carrying capacity of the entire planet to a level far below that of 1968." Paul Ehrlich, "The Coming Famine," *Natural History* 77 (May 1968): 11. For telling criticisms of the use of "carrying capacity" in this essay, see Charles Rubin, *The Green Crusade: Rethinking the Roots of Environmentalism* (Lanham, MD: Rowman & Littlefield, 1998), 84.

6. Though not discussed in Lewis's treatment of Pinchot, the forestry practices he advocated, learned in Europe, are based on the Darwinian concepts of a competition for resources, genetic variation, selection, and adaptation that were, by the 1920s, taken for granted in ecology.

7. F. Burkhardt, S. Smith, eds., *The Correspondence of Charles Darwin: Vol. 2, 1837-43* (Cambridge: Cambridge University Press, 1986), 83.

8. The evidence that Muir read the *Origin* at this point in his life is in fact weak and indirect. During his years at the University of Wisconsin, he befriended Ezra and Jeanne Carr. Both were philosophically allied with Ralph Waldo Emerson. Ezra Carr taught natural sciences at Madison, and his library would likely have a copy of the *Origin* in it when Muir was a regular guest there. But there is no mention of any familiarity with Darwin in Muir's own account of his university years (John Muir, *My Boyhood and Youth* [Boston: Houghton Mifflin, 1916], 208-28), and it is more likely that he read it during his Yosemite years. In a letter to Jeanne Carr dated September 8, 1871, Muir mentions that John Runkle, then president of MIT, was "going to send me Darwin." We don't know which Darwin, but this is a year before his first visit from Darwin's leading American advocate, Asa Gray. The lack of "connect" between Emerson and Muir discussed below by Charles Rubin (156-57) may in part be due to the fact that Muir's "Emerson" was structured more by Jeanne Carr's memories of him from her years in New England than by familiarity with his thought.

9. Compare Stephen Fox, *John Muir and His Legacy* (Boston: Little Brown, 1981), 47 (and 84 on Muir's passion for Humboldt). Compare also Pencek, 5-6.

10. Charles Lyell, *Principles of Geology*, 3 vols. (London: John Murray, 1830-33). Again, there is no direct evidence of the influence of Lyell's *Principles* on Muir, but the probability here is very strong. He studied geology with Carr at Wisconsin, and in the 1850s and '60s Lyell would almost certainly been required reading—unlike the early 1830s, when

Darwin was reading it, and when it would have been radical and controversial for its stress on theory and causal explanation, and when its "uniformitarian" stress on limiting theorizing to processes of a kind and intensity actually observed would have been controversial.

11. John Muir, *My Boyhood and Youth*, 223-228. Thus I am entirely in accord with Pencek's stress on the importancc of the encounter with "Griswold," 5-6 and note 3.

12. See Duncan M. Porter, ed., "Darwin Notes on *Beagle* Plants," *Bulletin of the British Museum* (Natural History), Historical Series, Vol. 14, No. 2, 26 November 1987.

13. James M. Clarke's *The Life and Adventures of John Muir* (San Francisco: Sierra Club, 1980), 34.

14. Clarke, *Life and Adventures*, 52.

15. A clear and accurate presentation of this debate is Martin Rudwick's introduction to the recent reprint of Lyell's *Principles of Geology* (Chicago: University of Chicago Press, 1990), vii-lviii.

16. See Edward Lurie, *Louis Agassiz: A Life in Science* (Chicago: University of Chicago Press, 1960), 351-60.

17. By the end of the seventeenth century, most European "voyages of exploration" included someone whose job it was to record information about the flora, fauna, and mineralogy of the places visited, information usually published and consulted by naturalists. The *Beagle* library included, by my count, forty such "narratives" and "travels" (cf. F. Burkhardt, S. Smith, eds., *The Correspondence of Charles Darwin: Vol. 1, 1821-1836* (Cambridge: Cambridge University Press, 1985), 553-66.

18. Charles Darwin, *On the Origin of Species by means of Natural Selection* (London: John Murray, 1859), 3.

19. Paul H. Barrett et al., eds., *Charles Darwin's Notebooks: 1836-1844* (Ithaca, NY: Cornell University Press, 1987).

20. When Darwin introduces this concept in chapter 3 of the *Origin*, he notes that he is using it in "a large and metaphorical sense," and develops a series of examples to indicate what he intends. They range from an outright battle "between two canines at a time of dearth," at one extreme, to mistletoe which "may metaphorically be said to struggle with other fruit-bearing plants, in order to tempt birds to devour and thus disseminate its seeds rather than those of other plants," at the other (Darwin, *Origin of Species*, 62-63). Again, this is a subtlety lost on most commentators.

21. Darwin, *Origin of Species*, 109.

22. Darwin, *Origin of Species*, 62.

23. For its classic defense, cf. J. W. F. Herschel, *A Preliminary Discourse on the Study of Natural Philosophy* (London: D. Lardner's Cabinet Cyclopaedia, 1831). A letter from Darwin to his cousin and fellow beetle collector William Darwin Fox, dated February 15, 1831, concludes: "If you have not read Herschel in Lardners Cyclo—read it directly" (*Correspondence* Vol. 1, 118). In his autobiography Darwin claims that it was this work, along with Humboldt's *Personal Narrative* that "stirred up in me a burning zeal to add even the most humble contribution to the noble structure of Natural Science" (Francis Darwin, ed., *The Autobiography of Charles Darwin and Selected Letters* [New York: Dover Publications, 1958], 68).

24. Priestly arrived in Birmingham in 1780 expressly to minister to the Unitarian congregation there. For good surveys of the religious mores of the Darwin/Wedgwood clan, see Adrian Desmond and James Moore, *Darwin: The Life of a Tormented Evolutionist* (New York: Norton, 1991), 5-20; Janet Browne, *Charles Darwin: Voyaging* (Princeton: Princeton University Press, 1995), 3-64.

25. Founder of the Etruria Pottery works in Stoke-on-Trent, and Charles Darwin's maternal grandfather. From the friendship of Josiah Wedgwood and Erasmus Darwin emerges a dynasty of sorts. Josiah II, Darwin's uncle, talked his brother-in-law Dr. Robert Darwin into allowing Charles to sail on the *Beagle*. Caroline Darwin, Charles's older sister, married Josiah Wedgwood III. Charles married Emma Wedgwood, his first cousin—but not, perhaps, his first choice among cousins. In a letter to Fox date February 9, 1831 (*Correspondence Vol. 1*, 115-16), he apologizes that "I could not write a long letter even to Charlotte Wedgwood or Fanny Owen, so must excuse this short one." At the time, Fanny Owen was certainly his passion, so this reference to Charlotte is likely also romantic.

26. Perhaps the most interesting exchange on this topic is to be found in the letter of February 1836 to Charles Lyell from John Herschel on the question of a natural cause for species. The letter was printed in Charles Babbage's *Ninth Bridgewater Treatise: A Fragment* (London: John Murray, 1838), 225-27, where Darwin encountered it for the first time (see *Species Notebook* E, 59, in Barrett et al., *Notebooks 1836-44*, 413, and note 59-2). In the introduction to *On the Origin of Species*, there is a veiled reference to the letter, when he notes that a great philosopher has referred to the question of species origins as "the mystery of mysteries." What pleased Darwin the most in the letter ("Hurrah.—intermediate causes," he writes in his notebook) was Herschel's insistence that "we are led by all analogy to suppose that he [the Creator] operates through a series of intermediate

causes, and that in consequence the origination of fresh species, could it ever come under our cognizance, would be found to be a natural in contradistinction to a miraculous process." And of course he is praising Lyell, who in his second volume takes just this approach. This letter was written five months before Darwin visited Herschel in Capetown, South Africa, on the last leg of the *Beagle* voyage—Herschel was there constructing a "star map" for the Southern Hemisphere, to complete a project of his father's, the astronomer William Herschel.

27. The case at this time (1838-1871) had to be made essentially in the absence of any fossil evidence for human evolution. The first Neanderthal remains were discovered just prior to the publication of the *Descent*, but most Neanderthal and all pre-Neanderthal evidence is from the period 1890-present, accelerating from the 1950s due to the extensive work of the Leakeys, Walker, Johannsen, and others.

28. Charles Darwin, *The Descent of Man and Evolution in Relation to Sex (*London: John Murray, 1871), 35.

29. An undated notebook entry reads: "It is my faith that every flower enjoys the air it breathes. Wordsworth, Professors Wagner, French and Darwin claim that plants have minds, are conscious of their existence, feel pain, and have memories" (Linnie Marsh Wolfe, ed., *John of the Mountains: The Unpublished Journals of John Muir* [Boston: Houghton Mifflin, 1938], 436-37). Were the reference to Erasmus Darwin's *The Botanic Garden*, Muir might well have reasonably drawn this conclusion. Since neither Charles nor Erasmus were ever professors, it is just possible this is who he had in mind.

30. Fox, *John Muir*, 50-51.

31. *The Writings of John Muir, I: My Boyhood and Youth* and *A Thousand Mile Walk to the Gulf* (Boston and New York: Houghton Mifflin, 1916), 319.

32. *Writings of Muir, I*, 324.

33. Fox, *John Muir*, 52. As Fox notes (391, note to 52), this unpublished wording is revised in the published version to read "The world we are told was made especially for man—a presumption not supported by all the facts" (*Writings of Muir, I*, 354).

34. *Writings of Muir, I*, 343.

35. *Writings of Muir, I*, 343.

36. *Writings of Muir, I*, 356-57; and more generally 354-59.

37. An early expression of this notion is found in *Species Notebook* C: "I will never allow that because there is a chasm between man . . . and animals that man has different origin" (C223).

38. Barrett et al., *Notebooks 1836-44*, 74 (from September 1837).

39. Cf. Howard Gruber, *Darwin on Man: A Psychological Study of Scientific Creativity* (New York: E. P. Dutton, 1974), 39.

40. Barrett et al., *Notebooks 1836-44*, 166.

41. Quoted in Fox, *John Muir*, 81.

42. In an unpublished letter to Bidwell, quoted in Fox, *John Muir*, 81-82.

43. Wolfe, *John of the Mountains*, 118; from a letter dated Feb. 23, 1873; italics added.

44. Darwin, *Origin*, 62; see note 12, above.

45. In fact Darwin used the outline of his theory in this letter to Gray as his contribution to the co-presentation, with Alfred Russell Wallace, of the theory to the Linnean Society in 1858. Darwin had, in fact, written a fairly full account of his theory and the evidence in its favor in 1844.

46. Asa Gray, *Darwiniana* (New York: Appleton, 1876), 121-22.

47. Charles Darwin, *The Variation of Animals and Plants under Domestication* (London: John Murray, 1868), Vol. II, 7-28.

48. *Writings of Muir, VI: Our National Parks*, 357.

49. *Writings of Muir, VI*, 84.

50. As Pencek argues, Muir's work is "consistent with the mystical tradition of biblical religion" but not with "our century's claim that nature . . . is the product of chance interactions" (Pencek, 4).

51. Much the same can be said of George Perkins Marsh, another source often cited as a founding father of environmentalism, though completely overlooked by Stephen Fox in *John Muir and His Legacy*. Like Muir, Marsh refers to Darwin in a way that leaves little doubt he read him, yet virtually every reference is negative. And one can see why, when one reads passages such as the following: "Nature, left undisturbed, so fashions her territory as to give it almost unchanging permanence of form, outline and proportion, except when shattered by geologic convulsions; and in these comparatively rare cases of derangement, she sets herself at once to repair the superficial damage, and to restore, as nearly as practicable, the former aspect of her dominion." George Perkins Marsh, *Man and Nature or Physical Geography Modified by Human Action* (Cambridge, MA: Harvard University Press, 1965), 29.

52. *Writings of Muir, I*, 302-03.

53. Charles Darwin, *Journal of Researches* (London: John Murray, 1845), 42.

6

The Mystery of Nature and Culture:
Ralph Waldo Emerson

Charles T. Rubin

It is one of the truisms of our time that modern culture stands irrevocably opposed to nature. The opposition may rarely be presented—see J.S. Mill, for example[1]—as a vindication of modern culture. But in the environmental forms we are more accustomed to hearing, the opposition stands as a decisive criticism. The reasons adduced for believing in these irreconcilable differences vary widely in quality, ranging as they do from sophisticated accounts of modernity's practical and conceptual treatment of nature to emotional outpourings against roadside trash. From such reasons may be deduced "hyper modern" projects for the complete mastery of nature (as seen in notions of "managing planet earth") or to the "postmodern" longings for the primal and autochthonous that are to be found in "deep ecology."

Although the question of the relationship between nature and culture may be raised with a special urgency today, with the fate of the earth presumed to hang in the balance, it is in fact not new to our time. It is a topic for one of the most seminal thinkers in American intellectual history: Ralph Waldo Emerson (1803-1882). Emersonian transcendentalism has had an under-appreciated impact on the way in which American's have viewed their relationship with nature.

The most obvious route from transcendentalism to conservationism passes through Henry David Thoreau. Yet in Roderick Nash's charting of that course in *Wilderness and the American Mind,* as in other discussions of the conservation movement, Ralph Waldo Emerson keeps cropping up, as well he might. For it was Emerson who, in his first published work, *Nature* (1836), laid out most of the arguments upon which transcendentalism would build. He did so in a manner directly relevant to conservationism, for *Nature* is all about the relationship between the human and the natural world.

For Nash, that relationship, as described by transcendentalism, is straightforward. Nature reflects "universal spiritual truths" far more clearly than does human culture. Hence, wilderness is morally preferable to cities. Furthermore, technology and "the pursuit of progress" bring with them a materialism that draws us away from "a higher reality than the physical" that is our proper calling. These spiritual truths were to be achieved not through reason, but via "intuition and imagination."[2]

Hans Huth agrees that Emerson represents the beginnings of a sea change in how Americans looked at nature, and would not quarrel with Nash to the extent that the "new eyes" opened by Emerson looked at nature with a determination "to draw moral implications," particularly focused on "the beginning conflict between the traditional way of life and industrialism." Yet for Huth, Emerson began a reaction against a "romantic sentimentalism" that focused on "worn-out classifications such as sublimity, grandeur and picturesqueness," pointing instead to "a more rational and more substantial basis" for appreciating nature.[3]

If Nash and Huth are not in direct conflict about the basis upon which Emerson believed a proper relationship between man and nature was to be established, there is at least some tension between them on the question of reason versus intuition or imagination. The picture can be made more complicated still. Along with other scholars, Michael Lopez has argued that "Emerson's first book is conceived not only out of love of nature but also out of fear of it." *Nature* is "actually a central text in the history of that escalating rivalry that preoccupied so much of the nineteenth century: the struggle between human and natural powers." Lopez argues that Emerson sided with humanity from a fear that, were nature not under control by the mind, its power would prove overwhelming.[4]

Uncertainty about the character of Emerson's understanding of nature, and his contribution to conservationism, is not new. There is, after all, the famous story of John Muir's meeting with Emerson in 1871. Muir evidently felt he was about to meet a great soul mate, but was clearly disappointed at least to the extent that the sixty-eight-year-old Emerson proved unwilling to spend the night in the woods with him. He charitably blamed this lapse on Emerson's age and the pressure of his companions. For his part, Emerson in subsequent correspondence was happy to invite Muir to stay with him in Concord, once he had grown tired of his life in the wild—as Emerson seemed to expect (or even urge) him to do.[5]

There are wonderful possibilities for misunderstanding all around in this story. What was the influence exercised by Emerson over Muir? His copies of Emerson's writings are punctuated by critical annotations and questions.

Clearly Muir was no slavish disciple, but what aspect of his own appreciation of nature he expected to see also in Emerson is not immediately clear. Did Emerson fail to live up to expectations created by his work? Should a real Emersonian have leapt at the chance to spend time in the wild with Muir? Or did Muir misunderstand Emerson in thinking he would be as enamored of Yosemite as Muir himself was? Emerson's invitation to Muir to join him in Concord suggests that as far as Emerson was concerned, Muir had indeed only picked up on part of his teaching.

Such stories remind us of how difficult establishing the historical relations between one thinker or school of thought and another can be. Scholars can disagree about what the source said, how those it influenced understood it, and the substance of the position held by the individual or movement on whom the influence is supposed to have been exercised. In the face of such complications, the effort here to reconstruct Emerson's own thinking about nature and culture on its own terms may seem naive. However, such an effort is justified for three reasons. First, it provides a benchmark against which we can go on to make judgements about how well or poorly anyone who claims influence from the source might have understood what it was all about. We can only know what is original or derivative about conservationist authors if we understand the contribution of those who are supposed to have influenced them.

Second, Emerson's thought is notoriously difficult to understand. For a writer of such tremendous popularity, his prose is complex and nuanced to an extent that impressed even his contemporaries, who were accustomed to complexity and nuance far beyond what would be acceptable today for any literary production speaking to more than a highly specialized audience.

Finally, coming to grips with Emerson is useful for understanding conservationism because his thinking on nature and culture outlines the basic intellectual horizons that have come to be seen as containing the divergence within the movement between a "preservationist" like Muir and a "conservationist" like Pinchot. This particular disagreement, which seems like mere common sense, has its origins not only in Emerson. But the two attitudes Emerson attempted to join, by giving an account of what was important about nature on its own terms and the human use of nature in creating culture, is precisely what his descendants, direct and indirect, pulled asunder. In that context, understanding Emerson helps in deciding whether the marriage or the divorce was better grounded.

The Limits of Romanticism

Reading Emerson as a joyous proponent of encountering the beauties and wonders of the natural world in its apparently pristine state is not hard. Early portions of both *Nature* and the essay "Nature," published eight years later as one of his *Essays: Second Series*, are filled with paeans to the benefits of a good brisk walk in the woods and meadows:

> There are days which occur in this climate, at almost any season of the year, wherein the world reaches its perfection. . . . At the gates of the forest, the surprised man of the world is forced to leave his city estimates of great and small, wise and foolish. . . . Here is sanctity which shames our religions, and reality which discredits our heros. Here we find nature to be the circumstance which dwarfs every other circumstance, and judges like a god all men that come to her.[6] (541)

Encountering nature in this way has the immediate benefit of allowing us to shed the cares of the adult and civilized world; we can return to the happy wonder of a childlike state. Indeed, in one of his most infamous passages, Emerson extols the virtues of an even more fundamental self-forgetting that can be achieved by the appreciation of nature:

> Standing on the bare ground,—my head bathed by the blithe air, and uplifted into infinite space,—all mean egotism vanishes. I become a transparent eye-ball; I am nothing; I see all; the currents of the Universal Being circulate through me; I am part or particle of God.[7] (10)

Coming as they do early on in his accounts of nature, such idyllic pictures are likely to color the reader's perception of the arguments that follow—if the reader even makes it to those arguments. It takes a good deal of will to read Emerson through to the end these days, and the temptation to dip in and pull out the striking passages, shorn of their less aphoristic context, is one that even serious writers on Emerson apparently find hard to resist.[8] It might strengthen one's resolve to know that some Emerson scholars have observed that Emerson adopts other voices than his own when he writes, without broadcasting that fact. He is known to start an essay not from his own point of view, but from where he believes the reader is likely to start.[9] Both these attributes mean that it is dangerous to interpret the whole of an Emerson essay in the light of only one noteworthy part.

For his accounts of nature specifically, there are indications even early on that the childlike encounter with nature is not the whole story.

> Yet it is certain that the power to produce this delight, does not reside in nature, but in man, or in a harmony of both. It is necessary to use these pleasures with great temperance. For, nature is not always tricked in holiday attire, but the same scene which yesterday breathed perfume and glittered as for the frolic of nymphs, is overspread with melancholy today. Nature always wears the colors of spirit. (11)

Emerson thus starts to remind us that however much we might aspire to be transparent eyeballs in relation to nature, in fact our experience of it is not and cannot be immediate. We see nature through the lenses of our moods, feelings, or passions. But in a deeper way, nature is mediate to human purposes in a manner far transcending the use to which it is put by any other living being.

Emerson's first, and likely least controversial, example of this fact in *Nature* is the way in which human beings liberate the usefulness of nature through science and technology. This "green ball that floats in space" is designed in such a way as to make "[a]ll the parts incessantly work into each other's hands for the profit of man" (12). From this point of view,

> . . . how is the face of the world changed, from the era of Noah to that of Napoleon! The private poor man hath cities, ships, canals, bridges, built for him. He goes to the post-office, and the human race run on his errands; to the book-shop, and the human race read and write of all that happens, for him; to the court-house, and nations repair his wrongs. (13)

Of course, it comes as no surprise to us, heirs of a yet longer and more impressive era of technological development than Emerson could know, to think that nature is "exploitable" for human purposes. Two of the poles between which contemporary opinions about nature vacillate are defined by those who defend this use and those who lament it. But it seems fair to say that these outlooks share a sense that in so acting upon nature, human beings are impressing a stamp on it that is entirely their own. Emerson's outlook is different precisely on this point. For Emerson, it is nature that suggests to us the possibilities for its use by us.

> Nature, in its ministry to man, is not only the material, but is also the process and the result. All the parts incessantly work into

each other's hands for the profit of man . . . and thus the endless
circulations of the divine charity nourish man.
    The useful arts are reproductions or new combinations by the
wit of man, of the same natural benefactors. (12)

Given this postulated harmony between nature and human purposes, it is
not surprising that Emerson should begin by extolling the creative capacities
of human action. Still, he quietly introduces more jarring notes. Viewing
nature from the point of view of what it can do for us materially, it may seem
mysterious that we are not yet more comfortable in the world than we are.
He moves from asserting that the "misery of man appears like childish
petulance" to admitting that poverty, wrongdoing, and like ills continue even
given the cooperation of nature with human efforts at the amelioration of our
condition (12-13). By bracketing the transformed world between the eras of
Noah and Napoleon (for the sake of alliteration alone he might have said
Adam to Adams, or Methuselah to Madison), Emerson reminds us of what
stands in the way of our comfort. The human condition includes sin and
warfare. By reference to Noah he even reminds us of powers beyond our
own, be they considered Divine or natural, against which Napoleon,
considered either as creator or destroyer, appears little enough.[10]
    Should our obvious failure to achieve what nature seems to promise lead
us only to redouble our efforts, or need we re-examine the promise itself?
Emerson seems to have doubts about mere satisfaction of material needs. As
it turns out, the difficulty of satisfying them stems from the fact that they
extend beyond the merely bodily requirements that the interaction of nature
and technology can satisfy. "A man is fed, not that he may be fed, but that
he may work" (13).

Nature and the Work of Man

The bulk of *Nature* may be said to be about the "work" of human beings.
It should not for a moment be thought that for Emerson this work is any less
intimately bound up with nature than the satisfaction of material desires.
Emerson uses the possibility that the order of nature is consistent with the
satisfaction of our material needs as a springboard for suggesting that it is
equally consonant with the satisfaction of higher needs as well. In seeking
to suggest *that* the whole of human culture is imbued with nature, he will
slowly move to attempting to explain also *how* that is possible.
    As he moves beyond nature's ability to satisfy our material needs,
Emerson begins with the relatively noncontroversial topic of natural beauty.
We take "delight" in "the simple perceptions of natural forms" (14). There

is a sufficient "fit" between nature and our perceptions to allow nature to be aesthetically normative. The delight that Emerson speaks of hardly has to be explained in our age of Sierra Club books and eco-tourism. Yet once again Emerson turns the topic in a way that is likely to confound our expectations. The love of the wild—of nature thought to be untouched by man—that many today would take to be an expression of a love for natural beauty is not primarily what Emerson has in mind. "Go out of your house to see the moon, and 't is mere tinsel; it will not please as when it shines upon your necessary journey" (16). Nature "in combination with human will" does not compromise natural beauty, but comprises it (16).

Human action dignifies and beautifies the landscape in which it takes place. Emerson provides a striking pair of lists of five examples each of what he has in mind by this point. In the first case, he mentions the Spartans at Thermopylae, Arnold Winkelried throwing himself on Austrian spears in the Alps, Columbus in the new world, Harry Vane going to his execution on Tower-hill, and Lord Russel being taken to his execution through the streets of London. In the second instance, he mentions with greater brevity how fitly "Homer, Pindar, Socrates, Phocion associate themselves . . . in our memory with the geography and climate of Greece. The visible heavens and earth sympathize with Jesus" (17).

One point of the examples is clear enough; a "virtuous man is in unison with her [nature's] works, and makes the central figure of the visible sphere" (17). Still, why these specific cases? In these examples, we move from an instance in which the landscape is decisive (the pass at Thermopylae), to one in which it is constraining (the Alps), through one in which the particulars of the landscape are accidental only (Columbus could have landed anywhere in the new world) to one in which "common sense" nature appears only incidentally (Tower-hill) to one in which no natural landscape (in the common sense meaning) appears at all (the streets of London). Emerson is suggesting how the natural beauty of the actions in question persists even as the mere beauty of the landscape per se vanishes. At the same time, with the exception of the case of Columbus, what is at stake in the scene becomes progressively more abstract. The Spartans died in order to be good Spartans. Lord Russel, it has been argued, was among "the first martyrs for the sake of Party."[11] Beauty comes to reside not in the place, and not in the actors, but in an idea. Hence the second list. With the exception of Phocion, these are hardly men of action in the manner of those on the first list. Emerson reminds us that those who undertake virtuous action in the manner of the Spartans or Vane do so within a horizon they have not themselves created;

there is another kind of creative, active beauty in the virtue of poets, philosophers, and prophets.

In his later essay "Nature" this line of thought is expressed with radical clarity: "the beauty of nature must always seem unreal and mocking, until the landscape has human figures, that are as good as itself. If there were good men, there would never be this rapture in nature. If the king is in the palace, nobody looks at the walls" (545). The world satisfies the desire for beauty no less, indeed somewhat more, than it satisfies our need for material goods; there is a deep coherence between nature and virtue.

By this route, Emerson comes to a crucial point: nature is a source of moral norms. "Every natural fact is a symbol of some spiritual fact. . . . An enraged man is a lion, a cunning man is a fox, a firm man is a rock" (20). Nature is open to and suggests such correspondence no less than it suggests how it might be used to our material benefit. Just as the log does not warm us without human intervention, yet is well suited to that purpose, so a metaphor has to be thought, but we are equally supplied with suitable material. This openness is to be found in a "universal soul within or behind" our individual lives; we call this shared soul whose property we are "Reason" (21). What is Reason in relationship to us we call "Spirit" in relationship to nature. It is the creative power "man in all ages and countries" calls "FATHER" (21).

This attempt is Emerson's first directly to describe the "universal soul," a notion central to his intentions in this essay. It is Emerson's way of talking about the creative power that makes both natural and human creativity possible. After all, humans did not create themselves as creative beings. Emerson can thus draw a likeness between the universal soul and God with the metaphor of fatherhood. But the spiritual fact for which "FATHER" is the corresponding natural fact is ultimately not the same as the God of either Bible. "Spirit is the Creator" (21), Emerson says, but the universal soul is not a Creator who stands apart from His creation. As is already hinted here, and as Emerson will develop subsequently, the universal soul emerges in the human world through language/Reason. It thus sets the stage for creative possibilities beyond what can be achieved as Spirit, acting as it must through nature.

Natural Ethics

It is on this basis that, in a Copernican universe, Emerson can still assert that man is "placed at the centre of beings." All the bare facts of natural history such as science searches out are without meaning or interest without a marriage "to human history" (21). The rotation of the earth and its orbit around the sun are not merely matters of variable levels of light and heat. "[I]s there no intent of an analogy between man's life and the seasons? And do the seasons gain no grandeur or pathos from that analogy?" (21-22).

If we find such an argument about the moral significance of nature implausible, Emerson presents us with one possible explanation. Language becomes corrupted by "secondary desires" as for wealth, or reputation. Likewise, only a few great authors in a nation may "hold primarily on nature," while the rest will simply adopt their language mediated by the example of others. To this extent the "poet, the orator, bred in the woods" and thereby possessed of a more unmediated sense of the significance of language is likely to be of more use "amidst agitation and terror in national councils—in the hour of revolution" (23). Thus "nature" is not found by avoiding cultural artifacts like technology or "the roar of cities" or even the "broil of politics" (23). What is "nature" in the orator depends on yet still transcends his point of origin and reaches its height in the "agitation and terror in national councils." As Emerson noted earlier in the essay, the stars appear great "seen in the streets of cities" (9), not from the countryside.

It is not just the word tokens that we use to express particular moral facts that derive from nature. Morally speaking, the "world is emblematic. Parts of speech are metaphors, because the whole of nature is a metaphor of the human mind. The laws of moral nature answer to those of matter as face to face in a glass" (24). "This relation between mind and matter is not fancied by some poet, but stands in the will of God, and so is free to be known by all men" (24). Yet not all men in fact know it; indeed, its perception is the "standing problem" that is the object of genius throughout the ages (25). We may need the "abstruse" language of mysticism to express how this correspondence could be, but that it happens is evident to "a life in harmony with nature, the love of truth and of virtue" (25).

Obviously such a suggestion is going to be difficult for the contemporary reader to approve. We are accustomed to thinking that nature is open to our efforts at commodious self-preservation, and that understanding natural laws will aid in this effort. Emerson is suggesting that nature is no less constitutive of our moral world. However, if nature is open to our efforts for commodious living, why not also to our efforts to be good human beings? If study of nature suggests the possibilities and limits of the one, why not the other just as strongly? Is it any more remarkable that the world as it is should offer opportunities and guidance for our moral development than it should offer them for our physical comfort and well being?

Emerson's conception of a morally normative nature gives a "new interest" in the world around us, as we realize that everything in it can unlock "'a new faculty of the soul'" (25). Nature as a thorough-going educator of the practical understanding, teaching "necessary lessons of difference, of likeness, of order, of being and seeming, of progressive arrangement; of ascent from particular to general; of combination to one end of manifold forces" (26). Among these are the lessons of "Property and its filial systems of debit and credit" which, even unto grinding poverty, teach lessons "needed most by those who suffer from it most" (27). Nature "pardons no mistakes" (27); it is furthermore an inveterate teacher of difference, separation, and gradation. The wise understand this; the "foolish have no range in their scale, but suppose every man is as every other man. What is not good they call the worst, and what is not hateful they call the best" (27).

To this point, Emerson stresses the disciplining power of nature; "Her yea is yea and her nay, nay" (27). The high point of this argument is reached when Emerson asserts that every part of nature "shall hint or thunder to man the laws of right and wrong, and echo the Ten Commandments," making nature an ally to "the religious sentiment" (28). While Emerson here, as throughout his discussion of the discipline of nature, uses conventional Biblical and theistic language, the meaning attached to it is unconventional. It is important to remember that echoes become faint and are often more or less distorted. Nature does not simply teach the Decalogue; being allied to the "religious sentiment" is quite different from being allied to the doctrines of a religion. Indeed, "nature is thoroughly mediate. It is made to serve. It receives the dominion of man as meekly as the ass on which the Savior rode" (28). At last, the world becomes "only a realized will,—the double of the man" (28). Nature is the discipliner that it may be disciplined. Human beings can create culture, and its dominion over nature, because nature prepares us for that task.

The Mystery of Nature and Culture

The boundary between nature and culture becomes increasingly hard to identify, given Emerson's understanding. The more we come to see how the world around us is "realized will," the more we may begin to wonder about the status of nature, as something independent of human creativity. Emerson suggests that "motion, poetry, physical and intellectual science, and religion, all tend to affect our convictions of the reality of the external world" (38). Culture, in short, leads us to idealism, even to the point of being able to express a Cartesian-like doubt about the reality of the external world. However, Emerson draws back from "expanding too curiously the particulars of the general proposition, that all culture tends to imbue us with idealism" (38). To do so would be "ungrateful" to nature; "I do not wish to fling stones at my beautiful mother, nor soil my gentle nest" (38).

Emerson asserts that the "advantage" of the ideal theory is "that it presents the world in precisely the view which is most desirable to the mind" (39). Were we only mind, that would obviously be a decisive argument.[12] Even given we are not only mind, it holds a great weight; it is the perspective of "reason, both speculative and practical, that is, [of] philosophy and virtue" (39). Idealism is the "true position of nature in regard to man"; it is the goal of "right education" (38). It leaves us capable of seeing "the world in God" (39), of seeing the world and history as "one vast picture, which God paints on the instant eternity, for the contemplation of the soul" which thus becomes a "watcher more than a doer, and it is a doer, only that it may the better watch" (39).

Emerson is not entirely happy with this conclusion. We are not only mind; if we do not eat only to eat but to work, the fact remains that we must eat. It may be that only children "believe in the external world" (38-39), but Emerson has not completely rejected that point of view. Having used intimations of idealism to critique materialistic progressivism, Emerson now uses that materialism to keep idealism within bounds. The creative process that results in idealism would, if the ideal understanding were the last word, end creativity. That outcome is exemplified by the complaint of Xenophanes, who in old age lamented that "look where he would, all things hastened back to Unity. He was weary of seeing the same entity in the tedious variety of forms" (29). Yet Emerson holds to the possibility of "our own works and laws and worship" (7); he wants to restore the possibility of "new activity to the torpid spirit" (45).[13]

In a famous letter to his brother, Emerson spoke of a "crack" in *Nature* "not easy to be soldered or welded." This crack is usually, for some good reasons having to do with Emerson's original outline for the book, taken to be a reference to a change in plans about the way he would write the work.[14] But Emerson said, "There is, *as always*, a crack" (emphasis added). He may have been referring to something more than a literary problem. The crack may instead refer to Emerson's inability to accept the truth of idealism simply. Hence he would be left with "crack" between the educated and the childish, the contemplative and the actively creative, the good of the soul and the needs of the body.

The world is not perfect, but as we shall see, its imperfection makes possible the tensions that are the defining elements of the highest human possibilities. Broadly speaking, the crack makes a kind of life possible that is neither simply the satisfaction of bodily needs (the pure materialism of the animal world) nor the individual achievement of contemplative rest (unmediated idealism), the alternatives that Emerson finds inadequate when isolated one from the other. If we can be neither disembodied minds nor satisfied animals, we might have to conclude that to some extent we will never be as "at home" in the world as our imaginations might wishfully conceive. (The very possibility of such creative imagining might be the best indicator of the full extent of our *unheimlich* condition.) Yet the fact that there is "as always" a crack makes striving and effort possible, and so opens the door to a particular kind of progress. There is always a temptation upon seeing a crack to attempt to fill it in. That the world is not perfect for us ready made opens the door to hopes that it can be made perfect for us, or that we can perfect it for ourselves. Messianism and/or resurrection, for example, are traditional ways of filling this crack. If we take the world to be thus broken, then faith in the end of days allows us to foresee when it will be healed. Political utopianism develops plans to fill the crack ourselves. And indeed Emerson wishes to maintain the possibility of "somewhat progressive." But it cannot be our destiny to achieve a state of final perfection since such perfection would seem to be what a perennially existing crack precludes.

Emerson takes the existence of a "crack" to suggest a fundamental mystery about the world, a mystery that leaves it open to ongoing creative efforts. "To the intelligent, nature converts itself into a vast promise, and will not be rashly explained. Her secret is untold" (554). To the extent, then, that idealism transforms nature into "a perpetual effect . . . a great shadow pointing always to the sun behind us" (40), it cannot stand unqualified. Further criticisms of idealism point in a similar direction. Emerson says, "the views already presented do not include the whole circumference of man" (40). What has been left out? The ideal theory, as we have already seen, leads us to deny "that consanguinity" with our mother nature that we would otherwise acknowledge. In a similar vein, it denies the reality of our erotic attachments; it "balks the affections in denying substantive being to men and women" (41). Emerson also claims that though it allows us to see the "world in God" it "leaves God out of me" (41). We should perhaps read this statement as "It leaves God out of *me*," i.e., out of an embodied, particular being. For these reasons, Emerson wants the ideal theory "in the present state of our knowledge" to stand "as a useful introductory hypothesis."

Seeing its limits reminds "us of the eternal distinction between the soul and the world" (41) that we would otherwise be tempted to overlook if idealism told the whole story.

That distinction opens the door at least to change, and (as Emerson sees it) to progress. We should not look for this progress primarily in the realm of technology. "We anticipate a new era from the invention of a locomotive, or a balloon; the new engine brings with it the old checks" (554). Neither is the ongoing acquisition of scientific knowledge what Emerson has in mind; "the problems to be solved are precisely those which the physiologist and the naturalist omit to state" (43). Instead, we are to start from the "mystery" that man "finds something of himself in every great and small thing" (44). Emerson notes that this mystery is the impulse that leads many into science in the first place—the quest for understanding the world around them, and man's place in it, as a whole. But "the end is lost sight of in attention to the means" (45).

In short, Emerson does not seem to expect the discovery of final answers; a mystery at the heart of things must persist if we seek "somewhat progressive." A "wise writer" will concentrate on "announcing undiscovered regions of thought, and so communicating, through hope, new activity to the torpid spirit" (45). In fact, then, it is hope that drives us onward, hope for that which can only be seen dimly, at best. Emerson points out the "gleams of a better light," a world where we employ "reason as well as understanding," (46) to be found in:

> the traditions of miracles in the earliest antiquity of all nations; the history of Jesus Christ; the achievements of a principle, as in religious and political revolutions, and in the abolition of the Slave-trade; the miracles of enthusiasm, as those reported by Swedenborg, Hohenlohe, and the Shakers; many obscure and yet contested facts, now arranged under the name of Animal Magnetism; prayer; eloquence; self-healing; and the wisdom of children. These are examples of Reason's momentary grasp of the sceptre; the exertions of a power which exists not in time and space, but in an instantaneous in-streaming causing power. (46-47)

These remarkable instances make an important point. If we were spirit only, such events would not be exceptional. Jesus Christ would have no history, because our element would be eternity. On the other hand, if we were animals only, such exceptional events would not be possible for us.[15] The wonders to which Emerson calls attention are intended to open the door

neither to Ripley's Believe It or Not nor the credulous spirituality corresponding thereunto, but rather to our condition as embodied souls, and hence
to the power of "the redemption of the soul" (47).[16] Even the most materialistic can bear witness to this power as they pay homage to "drive," "energy,"
"dedication," etc. Emerson does not foresee the final victory of soul over
body or body over soul, but an ongoing relationship that admits the
possibilities and limits of both.

The "redemption of the soul" will show us the "miraculous in the
common" (47). We come to see how in the ordinary course of events, in the
experiences we share most with others, there is a remarkable combination of
spirit and matter. "Whilst the abstract question occupies your intellect,
nature brings it in the concrete to be solved by your hands" (48). When we
"look at the world with new eyes" we see it prepared to submit to the
creative abilities of the "educated Will" (48).

The Virtue of Creativity

Reason (which, recall, is none other than the universal spirit in its
relationship to us) makes progress when it comes to a present limit and seeks
to push beyond it into what is at the moment unexplored territory. Neither
does it seem that such new territory can be exhausted. It must be unbounded
to allow us to rise to the highest possibility of human life as Emerson
presents it: to "[b]uild . . . your own world."

As Emerson presents it, such creation is what great poets, philosophers
and leaders do. He puts the point quite directly in his well-known essay
"Self-Reliance":

> An institution is the lengthened shadow of one man; as
> Monarchism, of the Hermit Antony; the Reformation, of Luther;
> Quakerism, of Fox; Methodism, of Wesley; Abolition, of
> Clarkson. Scipio, Milton called 'the height of Rome'; and all
> history resolves itself very easily into the biography of a few
> stout and earnest persons. (267)

In many of these cases, of course, the individuals and movements in question
would have in their early days been looked at askance in the same way that
we may react to *Nature's* list of instances where reason comes to the fore.
Emerson's eclectic examples suggest that reason does not lead all great
thinkers and actors to the same understanding of the world. Whatever the
promises made by the creator, neither does the operation of reason produce
a state of perfection, an "end of history," at which moment all contradictions

are reconciled. Indeed, Emerson seems far less concerned with the *content* of such creative endeavors than with the fact that they are possible at all; to be too fastidious about *what* they contain might be the vice of our "retrospective" age, while Emerson is always on the lookout for "new lands, new men, new thoughts" (7).

The "prospects" possible for us under this view have with reason been called "apocalyptic" by one commentator, in the sense of the achievement of a completely new order of things.[17] What else, when we are promised that "disagreeable appearances, swine, spiders, snakes, pests, madhouses, prisons, enemies, vanish; they are temporary and shall be no more" (48)? And yet, when we understand "build your own world" properly, as an exhortation to the highest *individual* excellence, a passage like this takes on its proper meaning. If Emerson is not and could not be promising a utopian reconstruction of the order of things, then this promise reminds us of the single-minded ability of the creative genius already to see the world in the reconstructed state of his dreams, and in that sense to be elevated beyond the prosaic concerns of the moment.

Emerson claims that such creativity is as possible for a scholar, a cobbler, or a farmer as it is for a Caesar, who makes his own world in a very literal way. He seems open to the possibility that, despite his own more spectacular examples, we can eventually come to see the mysteries of life as readily in the prosaic and day to day as in extraordinary events. In achieving "the kingdom of man over nature . . . a dominion such as now is beyond his dream of God" we gain association with "beautiful faces, warm hearts, wise discourse, and heroic acts" (49). What is "beyond" our dream of God, what is beside, or in addition to it, but how we construct our life in the here and now? Whether spectacular or prosaic, such emphasis on human creativity and rebuilding the world is what makes scholars like Lopez conclude that there is a strong anti-natural strain in Emerson. However, their conception of "nature" is obviously much narrower than Emerson's to begin with. They forget that human creativity is not a product of human creativity. We are taught and disciplined by nature such that creativity becomes possible for us, and we act in harmony with this nature whether we build a new world in the wilderness or in Manhattan. The basis for this relationship between man and nature is to be found in the fact that it is the same creative power that we call reason in relation to us and Spirit in relation to nature. It is the same mysterious power through which nature and human culture emerge. In a more pious age, he might have spoken in more conventionally religious terms than he does of God. In a more secular age, he might have written about Being.

For Emerson, the apotheosis of reason is its recognition of the mystery inherent in the world and then its push into it; to be the wisest man is not to have a completed system, but to be aware of ever new and distant prospects. The creative possibilities of human action within nature do not culminate in encyclopedic knowledge or some final state of human life. The route to salvation is for each individual to become a "creator in the finite." There is a tragic side to this possibility, for it is at the moment that one *lives* in the world one creates, that one turns away from further "prospects," that one fails to achieve the kind of life most in accord with our nature. The point comes out clearly in "Self-Reliance":

> Life only avails, not the having lived. Power ceases in the
> instant of repose; it resides in the moment of transition from a
> past to a new state, in the shooting of the gulf, in the darting to an
> aim. This one fact the world hates, that the soul *becomes*; for that
> for ever degrades the past, turns all riches to poverty, all
> reputation to a shame, confounds the saint with the rogue, shoves
> Jesus and Judas equally aside. (271)

Any established mode or way of life (better or worse), any culture, obscures the universal soul emerging through nature and man. We fall as soon as we take a stand.

Emerson and Conservation

If we begin to assess Emerson's attempt to find a synthesis of nature and culture by examining it in relation to the conservation movement, we would not conclude that his effort was highly successful. His thinking seems to prefigure two strands of that movement generally taken to be at odds with one another. The rhapsodic Emerson, who writes paeans to the moral uplift that is to be achieved by encountering nature, points toward the "preservationism" of a figure like Muir. Yet Emerson writing about nature as thoroughly mediate to human purposes is suggestive of the "gospel of efficiency" that Samuel Hays ascribes to Pinchot and his followers.[18]

Likewise, it is not a good sign for the success of Emerson's enterprise that a similar sounding dichotomy is often ascribed to contemporary environmentalism. Deep ecologists argue that there is a "shallow" or "reform" environmentalism that simply wishes to find ways by which human beings can continue to exploit and transform nature that have fewer unintended consequences or bad side effects. Over against this, deep ecology teaches an "anti-anthropocentric" lesson. Human beings should not assume our purposes are foremost in the order of things. We should accept an "ecocentric" outlook that starts from the equality of needs of all life (and non-life) on the planet.

If the foregoing attempt to position Emerson within conservationism were the last word, there would be no end of good reasons to accept his marginal status to our present concerns about our relationship to nature. His attempt to explain the unity of nature and culture was not compelling enough to withstand the tensions that grew up within the conservation movement as the elements of his two-sided argument were drawn apart under the pressure of divergent judgements of particular instances in the world of practice. (Indeed, were it not for the fact that lower explanations are likely sufficient, one could even ascribe such divergences to Emersonian exhortations to build one's *own* world, as the truest disciple of Emerson would be his severest critic as well.) It may also be argued that if the reconciliation he offered takes place only on the basis of some mysterious notion of "universal soul" creativity, then the kind of murky spirituality that points to is best left at the fringes of thinking about our relationship to nature. What Emerson attempted to join is better sundered also because the separation provides a pragmatic clarity to our debates. It is easy and compelling to call for leaving nature alone. It is easy and compelling to call for the proper and thoughtful use of natural resources, i.e., "sustainable development" or "managing planet earth." Yet what follows from being exhorted to "build your own world"?

Still, knowing (for example) that even Muir and Pinchot were not always at loggerheads, we may wonder whether the now hoary dichotomies though which we understand various possibilities of our relationship to nature are as well founded as we might think. Roosevelt and Leopold evidently did not see the need to treat nature and culture as antinomies. Unless their Darwinism is sufficient explanation for their view, perhaps Emerson can help provide a deeper basis for appreciating that unity than either author could provide. Is T.R.'s famous will a reflection of Emersonian creativity? Can Leopold's liberal education in wildlife be seen as a facet of the moral lessons Emerson says are to be found in nature?

Taking such possibilities seriously at least allows us to examine our own assumptions about the split within conservationism more critically. While preservationists seem to speak for nature and utilitarians for culture, both can in fact imagine cultural constellations that are reconciled to nature's "needs" and constraints. The same is true of reform environmentalists and deep ecologists; the *hope* to reconcile nature and culture that Emerson's work embodies is at least alive and well. But the reconciliations offered in his stead take place in a different realm and in a different manner from the sort that Emerson offers. On the one hand, Emerson does not believe that human purposes have to be subjugated to the rest of nature for the two to be in harmony, and to that extent his position cannot be subsumed to that of the preservationists/deep ecologists. On the other hand, he does not argue that comfortable self-preservation (which includes healthy and pleasant natural surroundings) achieved through the conquest of nature is the end of the best human life, and hence he parts company with the gospel of efficiency/reform environmentalists.

Emerson and Environmentalists

To put it another way, by reconciling nature and culture in the realm of Reason/Spirit, Emerson rejects the "consumer" mentality that is central to the familiar oppositions, i.e., he rejects their guiding assumption that our life is defined primarily by bodily concerns. It may be for this reason that Emerson points us always to endless "prospects," while today's thinkers are more likely to point toward some "steady-state" future in which a "balance," static or dynamic, between man and nature exists. That same point distinguishes his thinking from the "new age" varieties of deep ecology that, with an almost Emersonian creativity, claim to take their cues from ancient traditions, primal peoples, spiritualism. However, the syncretism of these writers is predicated on the search for "wisdom," in the form of determinate guidance along life's path—just the kind of "retrospective" thinking that Emerson disdains.

There are additional reasons to think that Emerson's ideas reach more deeply into the relation between nature and culture than what has followed. The supposed clarity of our terms of debate cannot withstand critical scrutiny. Increasingly it is coming to be understood, for example, that much of what in the past might have been considered "wilderness" in this country is in fact a result at least in part of the activities of indigenous human populations. To "leave nature alone" is not to return to some premodern condition of human life, but to create a standard for human activity that has likely not been met for as long as there have been human beings. On the other side, it seems to stretch the meaning of nature very far to claim that a well designed solar power station is somehow more "natural" than a nuclear plant.

It is also not the case that our readily available categories avoid the kind of mystery that Emerson at least openly acknowledges in bringing forward the relationship of humanity to the universal soul. The antitheses that contend today do not lack in mystery, but we lack the will to face their mysteries head on. Those who believe in "managing planet earth" depend on the mystery of the source of the ever-widening and deepening progress that will be necessary to bring our affairs and nature's under control. There is a faith behind "sustainable development" that problems of the present will yield to finite solutions in the future, completely contrary to our experience of tradeoffs, unintended consequences, decay, and sheer human folly. To those who look to ecoegalitarianism, both past and future will necessarily remain mysterious. For it is difficult to explain how, apart from accident, "primal" human beings could have been able to act so "unnaturally" as to produce the present deeply "unnatural" culture. And it remains mysterious just how we are to be the only consciously ecoegalitarian beings on earth, without a sense that we are thereby profoundly unequal to the rest of creation.

Emerson, in contrast, faces the mystery that is implicit in the account of human beings as ensouled bodies. He attempts to follow through the tensions that are intrinsic to this two-sidedness. To chose nature *or* culture, childlike realism *or* idealism is by his showing to simplify and distort the character of human life. The fact that the readily available environmental ideologies of today are predicated on just such simplifications may help account for how readily they are lead to extremes that bear little resemblance to human life as we know it. Mistaking a part for the whole, they build an unsteady and lopsided structure.

An additional problem is that contemporary attempts to reconcile nature and culture tend to claim to start from what science teaches about natural ecosystems, and draw conclusions from that about optimal population levels, energy production methods, economic systems, social organization, etc. Yet modern science is what it is today because over the centuries since Descartes it has sought to purge itself of just the kind of morally normative understanding of nature that would allow such conclusions to be drawn. These political reform programs must have logical priority over the science, because the human purposes and needs they claim to satisfy must be known first in order to understand the significance of natural constraints. Perhaps the availability of fresh water in some parts of the world is a limit on population. But modern science cannot tell us whether it is better to have more people who must consume less water, or who mine water from icebergs, or fewer people who are free to consume as much as they wish. This choice is said to depend on a "value judgement," which has an entirely different status than the "facts" about water availability.

This point, insufficiently appreciated by most environmentalist writers and their critics, helps account for the utopian character of so much of the discussion in this area. Mistakenly under the belief that their political projects somehow derive from scientific investigation of environmental problems, authors are free to use their imaginations to envision cultural constellations that are more "in tune" with nature, because in fact the science is barely constraining in the normative realm. Commonly, the existence of that scientific fig leaf preempts the examination of the politics or morality of these utopian reconciliations on their own terms. Even in "deep ecology," which prides itself on a more serious examination of assumptions than "reform environmentalism," there is a distrust of philosophical investigation of the value commitments that will lead to action at remaking society.

The problems that stem from a nature shorn of moral content are certainly not Emerson's. Because he has not abandoned a normative conception of nature, he does not have to make leaps from what he says about nature to what he advocates for humanity. His writings about nature are of a piece with his broader political project of protecting the ability of a commercial, democratic society to appreciate and produce creative individuals. That creativity is what nature is all about, its final cause.

It is more difficult than some might hope to dismiss Emerson's position as compared with its readily available alternatives. Its frustrating open-endedness may be preferred to the premature closure that characterizes much of today's environmentalist discourse. The "pragmatism" that we praise in our outlook may be a smug adherence to comfortable and well-worn alternatives. Yet recognizing the comparative strength of Emerson's position reveals what is most problematic in it. Nature's lesson of disciplined creativity can express itself in many ways. Up to a point Emerson can rank order them: creation of material goods is lower than beauty, beauty second to the creation of a moral world. Still, in this highest category at least, Emerson is far less interested in content than in process. He will not stop to judge among the creations of the cobbler, the farmer, the scholar, and Caesar, so long as each builds his own world. Reason is not useful to confront the disagreement among the great thinkers Emerson sets up as models, nor are they models for the particular content of their thought. Instead, reason comes into its own when it brings us to confront the misty prospects just beyond the horizon of what is currently known.

Emerson's normative understanding of nature, then, does not make of nature a teacher of constraints or limits—quite the contrary. In this way he again departs seriously from the lesson that almost all varieties of contemporary environmentalism seek to inculcate. And, however ill grounded such lessons in the contemporary exhortations may be, there would seem to be good grounds for doubting Emerson on this point. The lesson of creativity drawn from nature is a curiously democratic cure to the ills of democracy. Its relativism opens the door to that most democratic of sentiments, "do your own thing." One reads the Gita in the morning, backpacks in the afternoon, agitates for animal rights in the evening, and meditates after dinner.

This outlook on creativity may ultimately have more in common with the utopian aspects of contemporary environmentalism than the more superficial disagreement over the status of natural constraints would suggest. From Paul Ehrlich's discussions of birth control to Barry Commoner's or E.F. Schumacher's recommendations for social, political, and economic revolutions, there is a tendency among environmental thinkers to argue, with Emerson, as if human practices and institutions were easily malleable. The imperative in one case is "build your own world"—in the other, natural constraints. This is hardly a trivial difference, but there is a shared impatience with the employment of reason in a critical capacity that might stand in the way of the projects at reconstruction, whether they aim at achieving some equilibrium state, or at Emerson's apparently infinite task.

Emerson's *skepsis* (for which he was admired by no less an authority than Nietzsche[19]) may allow us to observe flaws in contemporary thinking about nature, without necessarily providing us with a sound, ready-made alternative. Thinking about the weakness in Emerson's argument might suggest what form a more satisfactory alternative would take. Like Emerson, and unlike contemporary environmentalism, we might seek an understanding of nature as intrinsically normative. Like contemporary environmentalism, but unlike Emerson, we wonder whether the normative content of nature can suggest constraints, in the manner of any non-relativistic moral thinking. A serious investigation of these questions could do worse than start from an examination of premodern thinking about nature in the West.

Notes

1. John Stuart Mill, "Nature," in *Essays on Ethics, Religion and Society* (Toronto: University of Toronto Press, 1969), 373-402.

2. Roderick Nash, *Wilderness and the American Mind*, 3rd ed. (New Haven: Yale University Press, 1982), 85-86.

3. Hans Huth, *Nature and the American: Three Centuries of Changing Attitudes* (Berkeley: University of California Press, 1957), 88-89.

4. Michael Lopez, *Emerson and Power: Creative Antagonism in the Nineteenth Century* (DeKalb: Northern Illinois University Press, 1996), 88.

5. John Muir, *Our National Parks* (Madison: University of Wisconsin Press, 1981), 131-36. See also Stephen Fox, *John Muir and His Legacy:*

The American Conservation Movement (Boston: Little, Brown and Co., 1981), 4-6.

6. All citations in the text are to Ralph Waldo Emerson, *Essays and Lectures* (New York: The Library of America, 1983). In that edition, *Nature* runs from pages 5 to 49 and "Nature" from 541 to 555.

7. Passages such as this were satirized even in Emerson's own day; see the wonderful drawings by Cranch in Merton M. Sealts Jr. and Alfred R. Ferguson, *Emerson's Nature—Origin, Growth, Meaning* (New York: Dodd, Mead and Co., 1969), 9, 29, 36.

8. Compare George Kateb, *Emerson and Self-Reliance* (Thousand Oaks, Calif.: Sage Publications, 1995), 95.

9. See B.L. Packer, *Emerson's Fall: A New Interpretation of the Major Essays* (New York: Continuum, 1982), 1-21, 26-27; and Kateb, *Emerson and Self-Reliance*, 2-3.

10. For Emerson's difficulty in coming to grips with Napoleon—a grave problem, given his ultimate emphasis on creative genius—see Perry Miller, "Emersonian Genius and the American Democracy," in Milton R. Konvitz and Stephen E. Wicher, eds., *Emerson: A Collection of Critical Essays* (Englewood Cliffs: Prentice-Hall, Inc., 1962), 72-84.

11. Winston S. Churchill, *A History of the English Speaking Peoples: The New World* (New York: Dodd, Mead and Co., 1956), 378.

12. Compare Joel Porte, "Nature as Symbol: Emerson's Noble Doubt," in Sealts and Ferguson, *Emerson's Nature*, 147; and John Michael, *Emerson and Skepticism: The Cipher of the World* (Baltimore: Johns Hopkins University Press, 1988), 66-67.

13. Compare Sherman Paul, "The Angle of Vision," in Sealts and Ferguson, *Emerson's Nature*, 132-33.

14. For example, Porte, "Nature as Symbol," 146. For an argument closer to mine see Alan D. Hodder, *Emerson's Rhetoric of Revelation: Nature, the Reader, and the Apocalypse Within* (University Park: Pennsylvania State University Press, 1989), 153-54. In William T. Harris, "Emerson's Philosophy of Nature" (Sealts and Ferguson, *Emerson's Nature*, 126ff.), the suggestion is made that the crack is evident in the chapter titled "Prospects."

15. For Emerson's ongoing attempts to reconcile spiritual and material things see David M. Robinson, *Emerson and the Conduct of Life: Pragmatism and Ethical Purpose in the Later Work* (Cambridge: Cambridge University Press, 1993), 184. For the problem of bodies and souls see Joseph Cropsey, "Political Life and a Natural Order," *Journal of Politics* 23, 1961: 46-56.

16. Compare Harold Bloom's treatment of this passage. Bloom rather arbitrarily makes "eloquence" the centerpiece of the examples, but he also notes, "A contemporary Carlyle might react to this list by querying: 'But why has he left out flying saucers?'" Harold Bloom, "Emerson: The American Religion," in Harold Bloom, ed., *Emerson: Modern Critical Views* (New York: Chelsea House Publishers, 1985), 112.

17. Alan D. Hodder, *Emerson's Rhetoric of Revelation: Nature, the Reader, and the Apocalypse Within* (University Park: Pennsylvania State University Press, 1989), 22. The point was anticipated by Oliver Wendell Holmes. See his "A Strange Sort of Philosophy in the Language of Poetry" in Sealts and Ferguson, *Emerson's Nature*, 121.

18. Samuel P. Hays, *Conservation and the Gospel of Efficiency: The Progressive Conservation Movement 1890-1920* (Cambridge: Harvard University Press, 1959).

19. Friedrich Nietzsche, *On the Genealogy of Morals/Ecce Homo*, ed. and trans. Walter Kaufmann (New York: Vintage Books, 1967), 399. Stanley Cavell, *Conditions Handsome and Unhandsome: The Constitution of Emersonian Perfectionism* (Chicago: University of Chicago Press, 1990), 38, is probably correct to note a similarity between the thinking of Emerson and Heidegger.

7

Henry David Thoreau's Use of Nature

Bob Pepperman Taylor

It is obvious that Henry Thoreau (1817-1862) occupies a hero's role in much environmentalist literature. Max Oelschlaeger writes, for example, that "It is no exaggeration to say that today all thought of the wilderness flows in *Walden*'s wake."[1] Roderick Frazier Nash argues that "Thoreau's organicism or holism, reinforced by both science and religion, led him to refer to nature and its creatures as his society, transcending the usual human connotation of that term. . . . There was no hierarchy nor any discrimination in Thoreau's concept of community."[2] He concludes from these claims that Thoreau "would have been sympathetic to both the ends and the means of modern environmental radicals."[3] Likewise, Donald Worster writes that Thoreau represents an early and important expression of biocentrism:

> Like St. Francis of Assisi, he embraced the entire animate world on the most tolerant and democratic terms. Nature was a vast community of equals, and more, a universal, consanguineous family. . . . Thoreau's makeup would not allow him to so elevate man above the rest of the earth, or to claim for him any unique rights. He could not accept the idea that man had been given license to reshape the world to suit his own tastes and to seize for his exclusive use the resources provided for all. In this respect, too, Thoreau was a representative voice for an important aspect of Romanticism: in its campaign to restore man to nature, Romanticism was fundamentally biocentric.[4]

These writers, and many others like them, present Thoreau as a forbear of the kind of environmentalism currently promoted by many radical environmental ethicists. This view, of course, is not surprising. It is perfectly understandable that environmentalists like Oelschlaeger, Nash, and Worster want to claim Thoreau as their own, as one of the founders of the bio-centrism and wilderness preservationism they advocate. There is no greater American nature writer, and it is certainly a rhetorical coup, at the very least, to secure his name in support of their particular theories and perspectives.

This appeal to Thoreau is part of a larger and familiar story in the environmentalist literature, in which the American tradition of thought about the environment is conventionally divided between the conservation tradition, whose founder is often identified as Gifford Pinchot, and the modern environmental movement, which has roots in Thoreau and Muir and Leopold, but which comes to maturity after the 1960s with the systematic development of biocentric environmental ethics. The conservation tradition is generally portrayed as crudely utilitarian, while environmentalism defends deeper and broader ethical grounds for respecting and protecting the natural world. Mark Sagoff, for example, writes, "The environmental, or 'ecology,' movement that arose in the 1960s and 1970s differs from conservationism in defending a nonutilitarian conception of man's relationship to nature."[5] As this story is usually told, a morally deficient anthropocentrism is now in the process of being replaced by a more sophisticated and morally defensible biocentrism.[6]

It is not obvious, however, that Thoreau will do for those who tell this story all that they want him to. Perry Miller once bitingly wrote that nobody exploited nature for his own purposes more than Thoreau:

> This lover of Nature was not a lover of nature itself: as he said, he ever sought the 'raw materials of tropes and figures.' For him these metaphors . . . were the rewards of an exploitation of natural resources, as self-centered, as profit seeking, as that of any railroad builder or lumber-baron, as that of any John Jacob Astor. . . . He strove to transcend not only experience, but all potential experience; had he achieved what he intended, he would have become pure act, and his beloved Nature could then have been consigned to oblivion.[7]

While I believe Miller exaggerates the degree to which nature had no independent status for Thoreau outside of his own literary ambitions, I will argue below that he is certainly correct to suggest that Thoreau approached nature out of a concern for deeply human purposes. Jane Bennett hints at this problem for environmentalists when, in her study of Thoreau's understand-ing of nature, she observes that "Thoreau does not advertise the fact that

Nature is always something of a work of art; he quietly acknowledges it."[8] If she is right, her observation casts at least a little doubt on claims about the biocentric character of Thoreau's thought.

Thoreau and Environmentalism

Lawrence Buell brings these tensions to the surface of biocentric environmentalism in his book, *The Environmental Imagination*.[9] Here we can see the problems that Thoreau creates for modern environmentalists when they use him to defend their own views. Buell begins by criticizing those interpreters who think that Thoreau "was not really *that* interested in nature as such; nature was a screen for something else."[10] Buell wants to claim that nature had biocentric integrity for Thoreau, entirely outside of any human uses and importance it may have. But this understanding only came late and incompletely for Thoreau. In fact, Buell casts doubt upon this initial argument when he complains that Thoreau never really could "get past the Emersonian axiom that 'nature must be viewed humanly to be viewed at all.'"[11] The portrait Buell ends up painting is of a thinker who was significantly confused about his own attraction to nature, at least in part because he was drawn toward it out of "multiple, shifting, and at times conflicting motives."[12] But even though Thoreau was confused about nature, we can see that in his later works he "became less interested in himself as he became more interested in nature."[13] While Thoreau never fully held or understood the "deep ecology" perspective that Buell finds the seeds of in the mature writings, he was moving in the direction that would inspire others in developing a more consistent and powerful environmentalism. "So Thoreau was not John Muir. Yet Thoreau leads to Muir; indeed, Thoreau became one of Muir's heroes."[14]

So for Buell, Thoreau is important not because of what he said, but because of what he might have said had he conformed more to what Buell believes to be an appropriate environmentalism. "You were groping toward an ecological vision you never grasped; your environmentalism was fitful, your biocentrism half-baked. Fine. We mustn't succumb to mindless hero-worship."[15] While Buell hopes that by reading Thoreau, we "can move in all the necessary directions,"[16] this is more because we can now see that certain elements in Thoreau's writings point one way or another, rather than because Thoreau actually pursued these paths himself. In the final analysis, Thoreau is more of a symbol than a thinker, a man associated in our culture with nature and the wild rather than a philosopher in his own right. "Thoreau's importance as an environmental saint lies in being remembered, in the affectionate simplicity of public mythmaking, as helping to make the space of nature ethically resonant."[17]

What is most striking about this reading of Thoreau is how anachronistic and opportunistic it is. Buell begins the analysis with his own conception of an appropriate environmental ethic. He then uses this conception to measure Thoreau and, unsurprisingly, discovers that Thoreau fails to fit the mold. Unwilling to abandon Thoreau as a symbol, however, Buell ends up stripping him of his integrity as an independent and original thinker. Thoreau can only be made to play his appointed role in Buell's story by failing to take him seriously on his own terms. Instead of attempting to find a coherence in Thoreau's work, instead of working to discover what he was self-consciously trying to say and do, Thoreau is made to fit, awkwardly at best, contemporary intellectual and political agendas. In the end, rather than being a figure capable of generating a genuine moral and intellectual inspiration, Thoreau is made to be no more than a childlike version of ourselves. It is our own supposed sophistication that is really being praised, in comparison to Thoreau's presumed ethical immaturity. Contemporary environmentalists like Buell can exploit Thoreau as a particular kind of environmentalist only by failing to read him seriously.

In this chapter I provide a reading of Thoreau that avoids some of these problems. I will explain what I believe Thoreau thought about nature and the role it played in his work as a whole. I will argue that for Thoreau, nature is first and foremost a resource to be employed for the purpose of encouraging the creation and health of a democratic polity. I will also argue that when we read Thoreau in this way, it is clear that he has little to say about contemporary debates between anthropocentric and biocentric environmental ethics. Rather, his commitment is to a form of democratic conversation that greatly distrusts these types of ideological debates altogether. Not only does Thoreau fail to fit neatly into the stories commonly told about the traditions of conservationism and environmentalism; he actually promotes political views that may make us wary about this project in the first place.

Nature and Democratic Citizenship

In a famous passage in *Walden*, Thoreau explains his retreat to Walden Pond:

> I went to the woods because I wished to live deliberately, to front only the essential facts of life, and see if I could not learn what it had to teach, and not, when I came to die, discover that I had

not lived. I did not wish to live that which was not life, living is so dear; nor did I wish to practice resignation, unless it was quite necessary. I wanted to live deep and suck out all the marrow of life, to live so sturdily and Spartan-like as to put to rout all that was not life. . . .[18]

Moving to his cabin provides Thoreau with some distance from the routines of Concord village, and the natural surroundings of Walden inspire him to think of his own prospects in ways different than are likely within the context of mundane village life. By making a break with his own routines, and placing himself at some distance from everyday social affairs and institutions, he hopes to be able to experience the full measure of life.

There are two simple, even obvious, but important initial observations we can make about these comments. First, Thoreau clearly believes that his own life is in need of renewal. He writes, for example, of his own disappointments with himself: "I never knew, and shall never know, a worse man than myself" (384). While living at the pond, however, he "grew in those seasons like corn in the night" (411), and eventually comes to think of himself as more independent than "any farmer in Concord" (366). By radically simplifying his life, he learns that "It is life near the bone where it is sweetest" (584), and thus he achieves his aim of learning to cultivate the full intensity and experience and enjoyment of life, at least to some significant degree. Going to Walden is Thoreau's personal "Declaration of Independence"; he ironically tells us that he began spending nights at his cabin "by accident" on July 4, 1845 (389). Such a declaration, of course, is only necessary because of some perceived limitation or unfreedom that must be overthrown in order for a more dignified, free, and "sturdy" life to be established.

Second, the physical context in which Thoreau learns these important lessons is the natural world, a world at least partially removed from human artifice. We must not forget that the land around Walden Pond was not by any stretch of the imagination what most of us would think of as wilderness; there was a railroad running along one end of the pond, the shores had been heavily logged, and the area was surrounded by a humanly sculpted mosaic of open farmland and woodlots. Nonetheless, it is "the woods" to which Thoreau is drawn as a place to live deliberately. This is partly because the woods offer a solitude that is conducive to the kind of reflection required by an individual seeking to set his or her life on a new course. "I have, as it were, my own sun and moon and stars, and a little world all to myself" (426). But this solitude should not be exaggerated. Thoreau claims that he is "naturally no hermit,"[19] and there is a constant stream of visitors—friends, passersby, curiosity seekers, hunters, fishermen, ice harvesters, and others—passing by the pond and through his cabin. Walden provides Thoreau with a critical distance from the center of society, but it never provides a complete withdrawal from this society, nor does he seem to believe that it should.

In fact, while Thoreau values the privacy living at Walden affords him, the relief from some of the distractions of conventional New England life, his purpose is less to forget New England than to gain a critical vantage point from which to view it. The nature represented by Walden grants him such a perspective, a place in which to experience a liberating independence of thought and lifestyle, even while participating in human society. We should not forget that Thoreau's bean field, one of the key symbols of his independence, generated produce that was exchanged on the market for the rice he preferred (451). Another of these symbols, Thoreau's cabin, was produced from logs cut with a borrowed ax, and constructed with help from his friends (354-58). Wild nature, for Thoreau, is by no means an unpeopled wilderness beyond the frontiers of society. It is a location for a freer individual and social life, a place of experimentation beyond the constraints of traditional roles and options. In this sense, Walden Pond functions for Thoreau much the way the Piraeus functions as a setting for Socrates' conversation in *The Republic*: even while staying within the sphere of the city's influence and activities, it is far enough removed from the center of society to allow for a serious discussion of ways of life that might appear outrageous or obnoxious from more socially respectable and conventional points of view.

In addition to providing a location for experiencing a sense of solitude and moral independence, nature generates, perhaps even more importantly, inspirational symbols for Thoreau. Consider just two powerful examples, the morning sun and the frozen pond transformed by the warmth of spring. There are continual references throughout *Walden* to sleep and death, as contrasted with the vigorous, intense life Thoreau seeks. "Moral reform is the effort to throw off sleep," Thoreau tells us, and "I have never yet met a man who was quite awake. How could I have looked him in the face?" (394).[20] Again he observes, "The commonest sense is the sense of men asleep, which they express by snoring" (581). The final sentences of the book, however, find hope in the symbol of the rising sun. "Only that day dawns to which we are awake. There is more day to dawn. The sun is but a morning star" (587). In a similar manner, the climax of the book is reached when spring arrives at Walden, melting the ice from the pond. "Walden was dead and is alive again" (570). The drama of *Walden* is the drama of awaking, even of resurrection, and this drama is conveyed through Thoreau's loving description of and reflection on his natural surroundings.

Nature thus provides Thoreau with a continual and complex array of symbols, infused with life as a result of his own moral projects. Nature's beauty, for example, provides Thoreau with the contrast to our own suffocating conventions and practices:

> Nature has no human inhabitant who appreciates her. The birds with their plumage and their notes are in harmony with the flowers, but what youth or maiden conspires with the wild luxuriant beauty of Nature? She flourishes most alone, far from the towns where they reside. Talk of heaven! Ye disgrace earth. (482)

The natural world also provides objects that serve as symbolic role models, as when Thoreau tells us to "Grow wild according to thy nature, like these sedges and brakes, which will never become English hay" (488). In a like manner, Thoreau is continually drawing upon the images of nature and natural phenomena to symbolize the potential freedom, beauty, vitality, and joy of life. The independence *Walden* promotes is illustrated and illuminated by the natural world in which the story is set. Nature in this way provides Thoreau with a sort of education, but it is more an education about Thoreau's own longings and intentions than it is about giving up such human preoccupations and "becoming one with nature." (Certainly to the dismay of some modern readers, Thoreau tells us that "He is blessed who is assured that the animal is dying out in him day by day, and the divine being established" [497-98] and that "Nature is hard to be overcome, but she must be overcome" [498]) As Thoreau says in his chapter on "The Pond in Winter," "I am thankful that this pond was made deep and pure for a symbol" (551).

So *Walden* is a story of Thoreau's moral reform, and nature plays a central role in this reform, both in providing an appropriate location for this drama and as a store of inspirational symbols upon which he may draw. But *Walden* is far from being a merely personal quest. In fact, Thoreau believes his private story is important precisely because of its relevance for the lives of his fellow citizens. He says on the first page of the book that he "should not obtrude my affairs so much on the notice of my readers if very particular inquiries had not been made by my townsmen concerning my mode of life, which some would call impertinent, though they do not appear to me at all impertinent, but, considering the circumstances, very natural and pertinent" (325). That is, although he finds himself disagreeing with his neighbors, their disagreements are over matters of mutual interest and concern. He is interested in speaking primarily to those who live in New England, under conditions similar to his own and in an environment he can, without being presumptuous, claim some understanding of.[21] He is writing to the "mass of men" whom he believes live "lives of quiet desperation" (329). This desperation is unnecessary: "But men labor under a mistake . . . . Most men, even in this comparatively free country, through mere ignorance and mistake, are so occupied with the factitious cares and superfluously coarse labors of life that its finer fruits cannot be plucked by them" (327). Thoreau writes *Walden*, not because he believes that the fundamental values of his neighbors are perverse. Rather, he shares these values—ultimately the commitment to independence and liberty—and believes New England society is pursuing them in a manner which is destined to be self-defeating. As he writes in his *Journal*, "There is nothing but confusion in our New England life. The hogs are in the parlor."[22] The assumption throughout *Walden* is that the report of his private "Declaration of Independence" is of the greatest public import: "If I seem to boast more than is becoming, my excuse is that I brag for humanity rather than for myself; and my shortcomings and inconsistencies do not affect the truth of my statement" (361).

Thoreau's own struggle to overcome "sleep" or moral lethargy is thus presented as paradigmatic. The assumption is that his neighbors are just as capable of being awoken as he is, that their lives are sufficiently similar to his own to make his story potentially significant for them. "As I have said, I do not propose to write an ode to dejection, but to brag as lustily as chanticleer in the morning, standing on his roost, if only to wake my neighbors up" (389). When, at the end of the book, he observes that "We think that we can change our clothes only" (586), he is speaking for all of us, assuming that he is not the first person to find it hard to shake off habits and conventions and desires that are preventing him from living as he ought and achieving the goals he values. Thoreau presents himself as a representative man, and the news of his own experiment is therefore a message of hope for anyone who, like him, fears that "The better part of the man is soon ploughed into the soil for compost" (327): "I learned this, at least, by my experiment; that if one advances confidently in the direction of his dreams, and endeavors to live the life he has imagined, he will meet with a success unexpected in common hours" (580). Thoreau's successes are intended to inspire precisely because of his egalitarian presuppositions. The message of *Walden* is a message of hope for all those who lead lives of "quiet desperation." Thoreau is suggesting that if he can break the cycle of private desperation, so can any other citizen of New England. Far from being a book about Thoreau's unique, inspired, or superior qualities,[23] *Walden* is self-consciously a lesson about the possibilities before every man and woman.

It is within this context that we can appreciate why Thoreau cares as deeply as he does about the natural world. As *Walden* illustrates, he believes that nature makes possible a break from convention, a fresh perspective, an opportunity to discover and assert our own direction and independence and sense of autonomy. It presents each of us, as it were, with access to "the Piraeus." Now nature is by no means the only vehicle through which an individual can be encouraged to discover such things. As the chapter on "Reading" makes clear, great literature also offers such opportunities for those who are able to take advantage of them: "By such a pile [of great books] we may hope to scale heaven at last" (406). But this option is available only to those who can read the ancient languages,[24] and although Thoreau would like our towns and villages to promote literary culture more rigorously than they do,[25] he never suggests that such a culture is available to the democratic many or is in any way a prerequisite for wisdom or democratic citizenship. In fact, although he keeps a copy of the *Iliad* on his table, he explains that he hoed beans rather than read during the entire first summer (411). *Walden*, that is, is about options available to those of us without Harvard educations, and what makes the natural world such a significant tool for helping us to escape the narrow confines of convention and common sense is that it is democratically distributed among the citizenry. "The setting sun is reflected from the windows of the alms-house as brightly as from the rich man's abode; the snow melts before its door as early in the spring" (583). Just as Thoreau finds a location and an inspiration for independence in the natural world, so he is confident that any individual can discover the same truths he finds at Walden. While he explicitly tells us that *Walden* is intended to convey a message of hopefulness rather than provide a model for others to literally copy (378), Thoreau does believe that nature, even the tamed pastoral nature around Concord, is potentially a powerful force in all walks of life for encouraging the creation of citizens with independent characters. For this reason, we need to value and protect the nature that surrounds us. "Our village life would stagnate if it were not for the unexplored forests and meadows which surround it. We need the tonic of wildness" (573).[26] Thoreau is not telling us to retreat to our own private Walden Ponds; he only stays at the pond for a little over two years himself, before moving on to other opportunities and experiences.[27] He is writing to an audience that is surrounded by a magnificent natural environment, and he uses this environment as the tool with which he and they may expand their understandings of their own potentials and prospects, regardless of where and under what conditions they live.

Understood in this way, *Walden* can be viewed as a work of what we might think of as political education in the deepest sense. Augustine writes, in *The City of God*, that a political community is defined by the objects loved in common within that community.[28] *Walden* is an elaborate attempt to convince American citizens that they need to understand their own commitments to liberty in a manner that will lead to greater rewards and be more morally compelling than the mere promotion of the market freedoms of a budding capitalist society.

The problem with a capitalist economy is not that it is "individualistic" or encourages us to be preoccupied with our liberty. On the contrary, the problem is that it encourages us to aim way too low in our understanding of the promise and possibilities of individual freedom. Capitalism encourages a crudely materialist and consumerist understanding of freedom, and gives up almost entirely on the cultivation of an understanding and practice of moral autonomy. As Thoreau writes in "Life Without Principle," "I think that there is nothing, not even crime, more opposed to poetry, to philosophy, ay, to life itself, than this incessant business."[29] The United States, regardless of whatever virtues it embodies, is as guilty as any other political community in failing to nurture seriously the moral character of its citizens. "The chief want, in every State that I have been into, was a high and earnest purpose in its inhabitants."[30] *Walden* is one of Thoreau's attempts to promote such a "high and earnest purpose," to define the American Dream in a morally inspiring manner. Such a project goes to the heart of America's understanding of itself, its citizens' shared visions and values. Thoreau is obviously not a conventional political activist (he abstained from voting, and he is notorious for his lack of sustained involvement with organized protest politics), but he is a profound and engaged social and political critic, deeply concerned about the character of the American political community. *Walden* is just one, albeit the greatest, expression of his commitment to trying to influence the moral character of this community's citizens.

From Thoreau's perspective, such a project is of the greatest importance, since America's failures grow, he believes, more from a corruption of the democratic citizenry than from any other cause. In "Civil Disobedience" he is concerned that the "Mass of men serve the State thus, not as men mainly, but as machines, with their bodies,"[31] and he fears that our growing affluence is resulting in our moral deterioration: "Absolutely speaking, the more money, the less virtue; for money comes between a man and his objects, and obtains them for him."[32] In this famous polemic, Thoreau does not present a detailed theory of "civil disobedience," or the rudiments of an understanding of the nature of justice. What he provides, instead, is a claim that our problem is cowardice and corruption more than a lack of knowledge and theory. "I do not wish to quarrel with any man or nation. I do not wish to split hairs, to make fine distinctions, or set myself up as better than my neighbors. I seek, rather, I may say, even an excuse for conforming to the laws of the land. I am but too ready to conform to them."[33] This tendency to conform is the source of our sickness, the reason that slavery continues to curse the land. "Those who, while they disapprove of the character and measures of a government, yield to it their allegiance and support, are undoubtedly its most conscientious supporters, and so frequently the most serious obstacles to reform."[34] What is needed is not fine political theory but strong, independent, and courageous citizens. "O for a man who is a *man*, and, as my neighbor says, has a bone in his back which you cannot pass your hand through."[35] The sad situation is that we, today, have "nine hundred and ninety-nine patrons of virtue to one virtuous man."[36] In "Civil Disobedience," as in all of his overtly political writings, Thoreau is not concerned to teach us new principles, but rather, to force us to face the violence with which we violate the principles upon which we claim to agree.[37]

Thoreau's primary concerns as a critic are, negatively, to shame us when we fail (as in "Civil Disobedience" and his greatest political essay, "Slavery in Massachusetts") and, positively, to suggest ways in which we can gain the independence of thought and character necessary to rebel against tyranny and political evil. As he says in "Civil Disobedience," "You must live within yourself, and depend upon yourself, always tucked up and ready for a start, and not have many affairs."[38] This exhortation brings us back to *Walden* and the central role nature plays in Thoreau's understanding of his own project: nature is his one hope for providing a method, a tool, for the American citizenry to establish the degree of independence required by free individuals if they are to be responsible and clearheaded and courageous in their response to injustice. An image Thoreau uses throughout his writings is of civilized or cultivated objects that return to a partially wild condition: his bean field in *Walden*,[39] the bateau of the boatmen in "Ktaadn," the wild apples described in a late essay named for them. All these objects originate as products of American and European civilization, but all then become shaped by the wildness of the American landscape. As Thoreau writes in "Wild Apples," "*our* wild apple is wild only like myself, perchance, who belong not to the aboriginal race here, but have strayed into the woods from the cultivated stock."[40] The point is not to return to some primitive or primeval life. Rather, it is to cultivate the advantages of both the wild and the civilized. Speaking of the materials with which he constructs his home at Walden, Thoreau writes, "With a little more wit we might use these materials so as to become richer than the richest now are, and make our civilization a blessing. The civilized man is a more experienced and wiser savage" (354). Nature is potentially the "pill" that can make our democratic society well (432).

So nature is central to Thoreau's project because it provides the medium through which he hopes to achieve his primary task of promoting strong, independent minded citizens. Without such citizens, democratic society is in danger of being seduced by the prospect of unlimited and unearned wealth ("The gold-digger is the enemy of the honest laborer, whatever checks and compensations there may be"[41]), of suffering the alienation and sense of powerlessness produced by market society ("There is no more fatal blunderer than he who consumes the greater part of his life getting his living"[42]), and of being distracted from the primary possibilities and purposes of a full and rewarding life ("Why should we live with such hurry and waste of life? We are determined to be starved before we are hungry" [396]). But most importantly, only strong and autonomous citizens are capable of honestly identifying political evils like slavery and imperial war for what they are, and refusing to grant these crimes legitimacy. Democratic citizens must try, like Thoreau, to emulate the wild apple; although they are clearly the products of their society, they must learn to be wild enough to maintain a strong sense of independent integrity and judgment.

Thoreau clearly believes that nature suits him well in the task of promoting this kind of independence. In his *Journal* he writes, "Surely faith is not dead. Wood, water, earth, air are essentially what they were; only society has degenerated. The lament for a golden age is only a lament for golden men."[43] Nature, that is, provides us with a constant, a sense of stability, the recognition that to the degree that we despair, this despair has to do with our own human failures, and not with the basic potentials presented to us over and over again by creation. Elsewhere, he writes, "I must live above all in the present,"[44] and he frequently suggests that when we experience nature we are potentially released from our preoccupation with conventional affairs, released for a moment into the pure experience and enjoyment of living.[45] Nature also reminds us that we are not gods, that the world is not ours to shape into any form we wish, that wisdom and health require a certain humility: "With so little effort does nature reassert her rule and blot out the traces of man."[46] And, as we find in *Walden*, Thoreau also writes in "Autumnal Tints" that nature is profoundly egalitarian, available to rich and poor alike as a resource of inspiration and renewal: "Wealth indoors may be the inheritance of few, but it is equally distributed on the Common. All children alike can revel in this golden harvest."[47] In "Walking" he makes the point this way: "As a true patriot, I should be ashamed to think that Adam in paradise was more favorably situated on the whole than the backwoodsman in this country."[48]

Of all the services nature performs, however, by far the greatest is that it gives our lives what Thoreau calls, in *A Week on the Concord and Merrimack Rivers*, "a suitable background."[49] Here he argues that the "world is but canvas to our imaginations,"[50] a background that challenges the customary life Thoreau fears we are all "partially buried" within.[51] In *Walden*, the move to the pond provides Thoreau with a physical location on the periphery of society, not entirely removed but far enough away to gain a fresh and semi-detached perspective on the conventions and tendencies of American society. In addition, he gains the psychological and intellectual room to develop a strong sense of his own beliefs and convictions, independent of common wisdom and the prejudices of the village. Nature functions throughout Thoreau's works in a similar manner, providing a physical and imaginative space for Americans to cultivate the independence we must expect from responsible democratic citizens. Thoreau spent the better part of his career encouraging Americans to experience nature in particular ways, since he saw this as the most hopeful technique for encouraging his fellow citizens to resist the type of economic developments and political crimes we were disastrously, in his view, embracing. This is why he claims, famously, that "in Wildness is the preservation of the World."[52]

Regardless of how sympathetic we may be with Thoreau's overall political project—certainly it is not crazy to worry about the moral independence and integrity of the American citizenry, in Thoreau's time as well as our own—there are nonetheless reasons to be critical of his use of nature in pursuing this project. Thoreau himself recognized, from time to time, the degree to which nature was not safe from permanent human alteration, and this situation, of course, is dramatically more obvious in our own time than it was in his.[53] More significantly, it is not at all clear that the experience of nature provides the kind of limits and humility Thoreau desires, or that these limits are even compatible with other claims he makes for nature's influence. On the one hand, he suggests that nature takes us outside ourselves, forces our eye outward to an independent and wonderful world that is not of our own making, but of which we are a part. Observing the frozen pond in winter, Thoreau writes, "Heaven is under our feet as well as over our heads" (547). This natural world "under our feet" can inspire and console, but above all it provides an antidote to human arrogance by properly framing human life within a greater natural context. On the other hand, if the world is but "canvas to our imaginations," it is difficult to see how it can provide us with any limits whatsoever. On the contrary, in this incarnation nature can potentially become a medium within which human pride may run riot, as when Thoreau himself writes, "Let us wander where we will, the universe is built round us, and we are central still."[54] Thoreau's own understandings of nature may at times be running at cross-purposes.

When we view Thoreau's discussion of nature from the perspective of his broader political project, however, it becomes clear that these tensions are not the result of a simple incoherence in Thoreau's theory of nature. On the contrary, they reflect and grow out of the tensions endemic to the democratic society he's addressing in the first place. Democratic society, after all, is committed to the proposition that the wills of individuals are of the highest authority. Yet such a society also finds itself needing to restrain and educate these wills if democracy is not to deteriorate into the kind of moral and political chaos predicted by democracy's enemies.[55] This well-known paradox of democracy is the source of the paradoxes in Thoreau's use of nature, and this greater paradox is yet to be resolved, to my knowledge, by democratic theory. Rousseau is no more able to square this circle than Thoreau, but each writer's greatness grows from his powerful recognition of this problem and his mighty, if ultimately unfinished, battle to resolve it.[56]

Environmentalism, Conservationism, and Democracy

For my present purposes, however, there are some significant conclusions we can draw from this discussion. First, Thoreau's use of nature is a technique within his overriding political project, rather than an end in-and-of itself. This is not to say that Thoreau did not have a genuine and intrinsic love of nature, or that he was in some sense crudely exploitative of the natural world (as Perry Miller suggests in the quotation referred to at the outset). But it does mean that at the end of the day, Thoreau was a deeply humanist thinker. In his *Journal* he writes, "Nature must be viewed humanly to be viewed at all; that is, her scenes must be associated with human affections, such as are associated with one's native place, for instance. She is most significant to a lover. A lover of Nature is preeminently a lover of man. If I have no friend, what is Nature to me? She ceases to be morally significant."[57] There is no reason to believe that Thoreau's perspective on these issues ever changed much over the course of his life (Worster and Buell to the contrary notwithstanding). Although there are "biocentric moments" scattered throughout Thoreau's works, it requires a radically selective reading of this corpus to make Thoreau into a biocentric theorist, or even a thinker moving in that direction.[58]

Some of the most beautiful, and rarely noted, comments from the *Journal* are reflections on music. Listening to his neighbor's clarinet, Thoreau writes that our music "is perhaps the most admirable accomplishment of man."[59] Consider his comparison of this music to the various sounds of nature. "Certainly the voice of no bird or beast can be compared with that of man for true melody. . . . The bird's song is a mere interjectional shout of joy; man's a glorious expression of the foundations of his joy."[60] Or his sheer pleasure at hearing a group of men and women swimmers singing: "Man's voice, thus uttered, fits well the spaces. It fills nature. And, after all, the singing of men is something far grander than any natural sound."[61] Thoreau certainly loves the birds' songs and other sounds in nature, but he holds throughout the *Journal* that the final purpose of nature is to serve as a location for people, for "Man, the crowning fact, the god we know."[62] This is as true in the earlier *Journal* as it is in the later years.[63] Thoreau's love of music is emblematic of his deep and consistent humanism. In contrast to modern biocentric theory, Thoreau's concerns with nature neither grow out of an ecological crisis nor convey a preference for unpeopled wilderness over pastoral rural countryside. In this sense, his interests and worries are too dissimilar from biocentrism to make him a genuine forbear of these modern views.

And this leads to a second important conclusion: Thoreau's uses of nature illustrate not only his differences with contemporary biocentrism, but the degree to which his views stand in opposition to important tendencies within contemporary radical environmentalism. The point of Thoreau's work is to encourage the establishment of strong and independent citizens. In his *Journal*, Thoreau praises the lives of a number of his neighbors. His friend Minott has learned how to love his life, how to play in nature, how to be an "old-fashioned man" who has "not scrubbed up and improved his land as many, or most, have."[64] Rice and his sons have learned to live their lives as a sport,[65] but this does not mean Thoreau fails to appreciate hard work, since he respects Flannery as the "hardest working man I know."[66] He pays his neighbor Hosmer the highest compliment, suggesting that he is a man of heroic and timeless sensibilities: "Human life may be transitory and full of trouble, but the perennial mind, whose survey extends from that spring to this, from Columella [a Roman agricultural writer] to Hosmer, is superior to change. I will identify myself with that which did not die with Columella and will not die with Hosmer."[67] Thoreau's admiration for these individuals is based upon their autonomy, their refusal to be swept along with the emerging market economy, their independence of character and lifestyle. When Thoreau writes, "I wish my neighbors were wilder,"[68] these are his role models for what a "wilder" life looks like. These are the individuals who display the type of character Thoreau believes is being lost in a society dependent upon slavery, engaged in imperialist warfare, losing subsistence agriculture to markets for labor and commodities, and generating a consumer culture that threatens to unleash unlimited and untamed material desire. This is why, in "Slavery in Massachusetts," he trusts the political judgment of rural folk more than that of sophisticated urbanites: "When, in some obscure country town, the farmers come together to a special town meeting, to express their opinion on some subject which is vexing the land, that, I think, is the true Congress, and the most respectable one that is ever assembled in the United States."[69] Thoreau had, and knew he had, "wild" neighbors; his fear was that they were a dying breed in the new America.

This populist, perhaps even Jeffersonian, perspective is in the strongest contrast with the temper of modern radical environmentalism. Instead of being concerned about cultivating a democratic citizenry of character and courage, much radical environmentalism—what Carolyn Merchant calls "radical ecology"—is committed instead to promoting a particular "world view." Biocentric environmental ethics, for example, has taken as its fundamental task to challenge the "anthropocentrism" of conventional ethics and replace it with some form of biocentrism or ecocentrism.[70] Criticizing what she calls the "mechanistic worldview" of modern science, Carolyn Merchant writes, "The mechanistic worldview continues today as the legitimating ideology of industrial capitalism and its inherent ethic of the domination of nature. . . . The egocentric ethic associated with this worldview, however, has been challenged by the ecocentric ethic of the ecology movement . . . and the worldview itself by deep ecology."[71] The project such environmentalism sets for itself is fundamentally ideological insofar as its primary goal is to replace one (older, anthropocentric, anti-environmentalist, bad) ideology with another (new—or perhaps archaic—biocentric, ecologically sound, good) one. Whatever commitment such an environmentalism has to democracy, this is necessarily subordinate to the overall goal of promoting environmentally sound world views.[72] Philosophy is preferred to democracy, in the event the two should lead in different directions. In fact, the presupposition of this form of environmental ethics is that the way most people think, their conventional wisdom, the current democratic worldview, is hopelessly unsound. In contrast, environmental ethicists claim to have found a privileged philosophical foundation upon which to develop a new way of looking at the world. "The many" will not understand these environmental truths unless and until they abandon the values and principles at the core of their current belief systems. Robyn Eckersley puts the point bluntly: "The problem with the general ecoanarchist approach of 'leave it to the locals who are affected'" is that it only "makes sense when the locals possess an appropriate social and ecological conscious-ness."[73]

Thoreau is not terribly concerned about discovering and promoting a particular set of truths that may stand in opposition to the truths held by others. Instead, as he says in *Walden*, his task is to try to "wake his neighbors up," to shake them out of what he believes is their moral lethargy and cowardice. His fights with these neighbors are fights over the content and meaning of shared values, rather than about the values they should hold in the first place. His fear is a democrat's fear, that his fellow citizens won't have the courage of their convictions, that they will be tempted by wealth or corrupted by power to neglect their duties and obligations. "There is nothing," he bitterly records in his *Journal*, "to redeem the bigotry and moral cowardice of New-Englanders in my eyes."[74] Thoreau's concerns about cowardice and bigotry, however, stand in the sharpest contrast to the "philosopher's" (more accurately, the ideologue's) fear, that one's fellows simply don't have the resources or abilities to know what is right in the first place. Thoreau is the democratic critic par excellence, in that he plays the prophetic role, using all his rhetorical skills in an attempt to cajole his audience back to what he believes is the community's historic promise. Many of the environmentalists who claim Thoreau as a forbear, in contrast, have abandoned this promise altogether in favor of an entirely new faith. This puts them in the position of either converting or compelling, rather than arguing with, their audience.[75] In this important sense, Thoreau's work actually stands as a powerful democratic rebuke to many of those who claim him as a hero.

It should also be noted that those who take the animating spirit of Thoreau's work seriously will be reluctant to take the bait of those for whom the crucial environmental battles are fundamentally ideological, between, say, "environmentalism" and "conservationism," or between biocentrism and anthropocentrism. The important environmental questions facing us today have very little to do with these abstract issues, and a great deal to do with particular problems requiring serious democratic discussion, analysis, and debate. Various connections can easily be drawn from Thoreau's work to both the conservationist and the environmentalist traditions, as these are defined in the scholarly literature. But Thoreau's most important message as one of America's foremost democratic critics is that we should beware of those who insist on thinking of our political problems in this way, as matters to be decided by the clash of competing ideologies which are themselves the constructions of elites and intellectuals and potential philosopher kings.

A final conclusion is that Thoreau's concern about, interest in, and uses of nature are simply not the strongest elements of his thought. Although Thoreau is often thought of as a profound "nature writer" with eccentric (at best) political views, it seems to me that something approaching the opposite is closer to the truth. We know that for all Thoreau teaches us to love and listen to the natural world, he was powerless to prevent himself, let alone the rest of us, from treating that world as just one more medium within which to express our will and desires. There is no reason to believe that this particular medium will necessarily tame the human arrogance and tutor the moral character Thoreau worried about so much. On the other hand, it is still very much the case that democratic society must contend with the problem of character among its citizens. Just consider, for example, the remarkable popularity of William Bennett's *Book of Virtues*, and it is obvious that American society is terribly nervous about its moral health. And when the field of principled "resistance to civil government" is ceded almost entirely to the likes of Montana "Freemen," those who blow up federal office buildings to avenge the deaths at Waco, and alienated former professors who wage one man wars against modern technology by blowing up targeted individuals, it is perhaps not too soon for us to sympathize with Thoreau's concern about the moral integrity of American citizens. This problem certainly has implications for the ways in which we treat the natural world, but it goes much deeper, straight to the heart of the prospects for and potential contained within our democratic aspirations.

Notes

1. Max Oelschlaeger, *The Idea of Wilderness* (New Haven, CT: Yale University Press, 1991), 171.

2. Roderick Frazier Nash, *The Rights of Nature* (Madison: University of Wisconsin Press, 1989), 37.

3. Nash, *Rights of Nature*, 167.

4. Donald Worster, *Nature's Economy* (New York: Cambridge University Press, 1994), 84-85.

5. Mark Sagoff, *The Economy of the Earth* (New York: Cambridge University Press, 1988), 154.

6. See Nash, *Rights of Nature*, passim and 8-9: "One of the most useful insights into recent American history concerns the qualitative difference between 'environmentalism', as it emerged in the 1960s, and what used to be called 'conservation.' When Gifford Pinchot named it in 1907, conservation stood squarely in the American mainstream. The Progressive conservationists made every effort to plant their seedling notion in the fertile soil of national growth and strength. Utilitarianism and anthropocentrism marked the early movement. Time and again, Pinchot, the first Chief of the U.S. Forest Service, pointed out that conservation did not mean protecting or preserving nature. On the contrary, it stood for wise and efficient *use* of natural resources. The idea was to control nature and serve the material interests of humankind but with an eye to long-term needs. Under this philosophy the dam-building Bureau of Reclamation and the timber-producing Forest Service became the showcases of early twentieth-century conservation. But a half century later these same agencies found themselves under heavy fire from a new breed of environmentalists. Impoundments and clearcuts, they alleged, infringed not only on the rights of people to experience and enjoy nature but on the rights of nature itself."

For another version of the same story, see Carolyn Merchant, *Radical Ecology* (New York: Routledge, 1992), chapter 3.

7. Perry Miller, *Consciousness in Concord* (Boston: Houghton Mifflin Co., 1958), 33.

8. Jane Bennett, *Thoreau's Nature* (Thousand Oaks, CA: Sage Publications, 1994), 64.

9. Lawrence Buell, *The Environmental Imagination* (Cambridge, MA: Harvard University Press, 1995).

10. Buell, *Environmental Imagination*, 11.

11. Buell, *Environmental Imagination*, 125.

12. Buell, *Environmental Imagination*, 134.

13. Buell, *Environmental Imagination*, 384.

14. Buell, *Environmental Imagination*, 137.

15. Buell, *Environmental Imagination*, 139.

16. Buell, *Environmental Imagination*, 395.

17. Buell, *Environmental Imagination*, 394.

18. Henry David Thoreau, *Walden; or Life in the Woods,* in *A Week on the Concord and Merrimack Rivers; Walden; or Life in the Woods; The Maine Woods; Cape Cod* (New York: Library of America, 1985), 394. All citations in the text are to this work.

19. "I think that I love society as much as most, and am ready enough to fasten myself like a bloodsucker for the time to any full-blooded man that

comes my way." Thoreau, *Walden*, 434.

20. It is perhaps not unimportant that Thoreau suffered from narcolepsy. See Robert D. Richardson, *Henry Thoreau* (Berkeley: University of California Press, 1986), 126.

21. "I have travelled a good deal in Concord." Thoreau, *Walden*, 326.

22. Henry D. Thoreau, *The Journal of Henry D. Thoreau, XII*, Bradford Torrey and Francis H. Allen, eds. (Boston: Houghton Mifflin Co., 1949), 331.

23. It is common in the secondary literature for interpreters to accuse Thoreau of holding a heroic view of himself and, conversely, a disdainful view of his neighbors. For one of the most sophisticated examples of this argument, see Nancy Rosenblum, "Thoreau's Militant Conscience," *Political Theory* 9 (February 1981): passim and 100, where she argues that Thoreau believes "the noble soul is exclusive" and "enjoys no society and recognizes few peers."

24. Thoreau comments that we need to be able to read the ancient languages in order to understand the history of the world. Thoreau, *Walden*, 405.

25. "In this country, the village should in some respects take the place of the nobleman of Europe. It should be the patron of the fine arts. It is rich enough." Thoreau, *Walden*, 409-10.

26. Thoreau, of course, strongly supported the creation of parks and wilderness preserves. In *The Maine Woods*, for example, he writes: "The kings of England formerly had their forests 'to hold the king's game,' for sport or food, sometimes destroying villages to create or extend them; and I think that they were impelled by a true instinct. Why should not we, who have renounced the king's authority, have our national preserves . . . our forests, not to hold the king's game merely, but to hold and preserve the king himself also, the lord of creation,—not for idle sport or food, but for inspiration and our own true re-creation? or shall we, like villains, grub them all up, poaching on our own national domains?" Henry David Thoreau, *The Maine Woods*, in *A Week*, 712.

27. "I left the woods for as good a reason as I went there. Perhaps it seemed to me that I had several more lives to live, and could not spare any more time for that one." Thoreau, *Walden*, 579.

28. "'A people is the association of a multitude of rational beings united by a common agreement on the objects of their love.' . . . And, obviously, the better the objects of this agreement, the better the people, the worse the objects of this love, the worse the people." Augustine, *City of God* (New York: Penguin Books, 1981), 890.

29. Henry D. Thoreau, "Life Without Principle," in *Reform Papers* (Princeton, NJ: Princeton University Press, 1973), 156.

30. Thoreau, "Life Without Principle," 177.

31. Thoreau, "Civil Disobedience," in *Reform Papers*, 66.

32. Thoreau, "Civil Disobedience," 77.

33. Thoreau, "Civil Disobedience," 86.

34. Thoreau, "Civil Disobedience," 72.

35. Thoreau, "Civil Disobedience," 70.

36. Thoreau, "Civil Disobedience," 69.

37. "The majority of men of the North, and of the South, and East, and West, are not men of principle." "Slavery in Massachusetts," in *Reform Papers*, 102; concerning John Brown, Thoreau writes, "I should say that he was an old-fashioned man in his respect for the Constitution, and his faith in the permanence of this Union. Slavery he deemed to be wholly opposed to these, and he was its determined foe." "A Plea for Captain John Brown," in *Reform Papers*, 112.

38. Thoreau, "Civil Disobedience," 78.

39. "Mine was, as it were, the connecting link between wild and cultivated fields; as some states are civilized, and others savage or barbarous, so my field was, though not in a bad sense, a half-cultivated field." Thoreau, *Walden*, 448.

40. Henry David Thoreau, "Wild Apples," in *Excursions* (Boston and New York: Houghton Mifflin Co., 1893), 369-70.

41. Thoreau, "Life Without Principle," 163.

42. Thoreau, "Life Without Principle," 160.

43. Thoreau, *Journal, I*, 244.

44. Thoreau, *Journal, II*, 138.

45. "Must be out-of-doors enough to get experience of wholesome reality, as a ballast to thought and sentiment. Health requires this relaxation, this aimless life. This life in the present." Thoreau, *Journal, IV*, 409-10.

46. Thoreau, "A Winter Walk," in *Excursions*, 221. See *Cape Cod* as Thoreau's most powerful work concerning the limits imposed upon humanity by nature: "But I wished to see the seashore where all man's works are wrecks." Henry David Thoreau, *Cape Cod* in *A Week*, passim and 893.

47. Thoreau, "Autumnal Tints," in *Excursions*, 334.

48. Thoreau, "Walking," in *Excursions*, 273.

49. Henry David Thoreau, *A Week on the Concord and Merrimack Rivers*, in *A Week*, 38.

50. Thoreau, *Concord and Merrimack*, 238.

51. "All men are partially buried in the grave of custom." Thoreau, *Concord and Merrimack*, 107.

52. Thoreau, "Walking," 275.

53. "Nowadays almost all man's improvements, so called, as the building of houses, and the cutting down of the forest and of all large trees, simply deform the landscape, and make it more and more tame and cheap." Thoreau, "Walking," 259. For a poignant recent reflection on this problem, see Bill McKibbin, *The End of Nature* (New York: Random House, 1989).

54. Thoreau, *Concord and Merrimack*, 270.

55. Most famously, see Plato's *Republic*, Book VIII.

56. I have in mind Rousseau's promise in the introduction to *The Social Contract* to "take men as they are and laws as they might be." By the end of the book, however, Rousseau has failed to live up to this promise, using Legislators and Civil Religion, as well as demographic and sociological preconditions, in the attempt to shape, if only in his imagination, a citizenry capable of responsible democratic participation and decision making.

57. Thoreau, *Journal, IV*, 163.

58. *The Maine Woods* is the most biocentric of Thoreau's texts in that it contains such famous comments as this: "Is it the lumberman . . . who is the friend and lover of the pine, stands nearest to it, and understands its nature best? . . . No, it is the poet, who loves them as his own shadow in the air, and lets them stand. . . . It is not their bones or hide or tallow that I love most. It is the living spirit of the tree, not its spirit of turpentine, with which I sympathize, and which heals my cuts. It is as immortal as I am, and perchance will go to as high a heaven, there to tower above me still." Aside from the fact that here he is explicitly speaking poetically, rather than literally, it is important to note that by the end of this book, Thoreau is happy to retreat from the wilderness of Maine to pastoral Massachusetts. "Nevertheless, it was a relief to get back to our smooth, but still varied landscape. For a permanent residence, it seemed to me that there could be no comparison between this and the wilderness, necessary as the latter is for a resource and a background, the raw material of all our civilization. The wilderness is simple, almost to barrenness. The partially cultivated country it is which chiefly has inspired, and will continue to inspire, the strains of poets, such as compose the mass of any literature." In short, at the end of his reflections on the wilderness in Maine, Thoreau appears to have retreated from any significant commitment to biocentrism. Thoreau, *The Maine Woods*, 685, 711.

59. Thoreau, *Journal, IV*, 114.

60. Thoreau, *Journal, II*, 480-81.

61. Thoreau, *Journal, II*, 474.

62. Thoreau, *Journal, II*, 207.

63. Compare the previous comment from volume II (1851) with the following: In volume V (1853) he writes: "What is Nature unless there is an eventful human life passing within her?" (Thoreau, *Journal, V*, 472). In volume IX (1856) he writes: "It is in vain to dream of wildness distant from ourselves. There is none such" (Thoreau, *Journal, IX*, 43). In volume XIII (1860) he writes about animals, "You must tell what it is to man. Surely the most important part of an animal is its *anima*, its vital spirit, on which is based its character and all the peculiarities by which it most concerns us" (Thoreau, *Journal, XIII*, 154). Throughout the fourteen volumes, that is, Thoreau's humanism is fairly clear and steady.

64. Thoreau, *Journal, III*, 41-43; *X*, 168; *XIV*, 67.

65. Thoreau, *Journal, IIX*, 26-27.

66. Thoreau, *Journal, X*, 187.

67. Thoreau, *Journal, VIII*, 245.

68. Thoreau, *Journal, II*, 171.

69. Thoreau, "Slavery in Massachusetts," 99.

70. Again, see Nash, *The Rights of Nature* for an intellectual history of environmental ethics.

71. Merchant, *Radical Ecology*, 59.

72. See my "Democracy and Environmental Ethics," in William Lafferty and James Meadowcroft, eds., *Democracy and the Environment* (Cheltenham, UK and Brookfield, VT: Edward Elger,1996), 86-107.

73. Robyn Eckersley, *Environmentalism and Political Theory* (Albany: State University of New York Press, 1992), 173.

74. Thoreau, *Journal, XI*, 326.

75. See Michael Walzer's distinction between "prophets" and "priests" in his magnificent *Exodus and Revolution* (New York: Basic Books, 1985).

8

Frederick Law Olmsted:
Civic Environmentalist

Marc Landy

In its modern incarnation, environmentalism displays a curious lack of concern for people and how they live. Although the role of humans in altering ecosystems is widely discussed, that role is almost entirely considered in terms of the depredations it causes to the rest of nature. The concern is with man's impact on nature. The impact of the physical surround on man has been shunted off to the urbanologists. Jane Jacobs, William Whyte and Andres Duany have brilliantly depicted how the pattern of streets, sidewalks, and other public spaces affect the quality of life in cities and towns, but their focus is entirely on the built not the natural environment.[1] It is only in very recent years that the environmental movement has even begun to overcome this artificial dichotomy between ecology and urbanology. The environmental justice movement is perhaps the most politically visible of the new efforts to link a concern for physical systems with a concern for how people live.[2]

This dichotomy has not always characterized thinking about man and nature. As Bob Pepperman Taylor convincingly shows, Thoreau in particular was vitally concerned with the relationship between nature and moral character.[3] But Taylor also reveals that Thoreau's nature was a curiously abstract thing—a source of symbols and a philosophical vantage point from which to criticize modern commercial life. Frederick Law Olmsted (1822-1903) shared Thoreau's concern about the impact of materialism and urbanism on human character, but his concern for nature was more palpable. His great legacy consists not only of the parks he designed and the natural wonders he helped to preserve, but also the subtle and complex thinking and writing he produced regarding the relationship of people and nature.

Olmsted's writing lacks Thoreau's rhetorical bite, for like Pinchot he was a founder, not a prophet. In place of Thoreau's jeremiads, Olmsted offered the founding principles for a new profession, landscape architecture. The landscape architect would design the parks, universities, street patterns, and new towns that an expanding democracy required. Practicing in the midst of a commercial society, landscape architects would inevitably be called upon to serve the rich. Indeed Olmsted himself designed many great estates including one of the grandest, Biltmore. But creating private playgrounds was not landscape architecture's highest calling. Its central purpose was to design not just commodious space but democratic space. It was responsible for shaping and preserving the physical forms that would best foster democratic-republican purposes. It combined the principles of political science with those of horticulture, aesthetics, and engineering.

Democratic Environmentalism

Olmsted read Tocqueville, and his concerns are uncannily similar. He called Tocqueville the "clearest and most painstaking writer" about the American national character.[4] Like the Frenchman, but unlike Thoreau, his critique of modern commercial society was measured. Olmsted was keenly aware of the advantages that modern technology and modern egalitarianism brought to the lives of ordinary people, and that those advantages were most available in cities. But he shared Tocqueville's recognition that these benefices also pose grave dangers for American democracy in the form of materialism and self-regardingness.

> The love of money is the root of considerable evil. How it does narrow and degrade and blind most everybody here (in America). They actually let nothing come in competition with *business*. They will not pay their respect to God until they have free leave from Mammon. The common people are ill natured, desperately selfish and incapable of friendship of more than words. Not so beastly and stupid as the English but more crafty and hypocritical, yet better according to their light than the rich.[5]

Like Tocqueville, Olmsted aimed to understand what obstacles could be placed in the way of such excessive atomism and what possibilities there were for nurturing the public spirited and culturally uplifting aspects of people's souls. He designed parks, college campuses, and suburban communities specifically for those purposes. His project to elevate mass tastes and habits might be mistaken for elitism. But it is precisely the opposite of elitism, since it sought to enable ordinary people to enjoy amenities previously restricted to an elite—ample outdoor recreation and tranquil commodious habitation.[6] It was *democratic* environmentalism.

Although deeply appreciative of the rights conferred by the Declaration of Independence, Olmsted conceived of the American democracy less in terms of abstract entitlements and more in terms of concrete democratic practice. Like Tocqueville he wanted to know how American citizens actually lived and what could be done to encourage them to act responsibly. Tocqueville located much of what was good about American democratic practice in the customs and institutions of its towns. Writing several decades later when the emigration to cities was already well under way, Olmsted recognized that the bulk of the population would not be living in such towns. He sought to preserve the republican essence of town life by altering the physical shape of the city, crafting the physical space of educational communities, and recreating townships in the form of suburbs.

In the previous quote Olmsted claimed that the ordinary city dweller was incapable of friendship. Making allowance for overblown rhetoric, what he really meant was that a particular kind of friendship was lost in the transformation from small town to city living—civic friendship. Judging from his other encomiums to urban life, he well knew that some forms of friendship are indeed enhanced by cities. Because of their great cultural and vocational diversity one is far more likely to meet people there who share one's own intellectual and vocational and avocational interests. In contemporary life, professional and cultural pursuits have become perhaps the most fertile of all sources of friendship.[7]

But civic friendship promotes citizenship in a way that other forms do not. Because it is rooted in place, it encourages the types of fellow feeling that helps build neighborly harmony. If my neighbor is my friend I am discouraged from making selfish decisions about the space we share and the local institutions upon which we both depend. I have a strong incentive to find mutually beneficial solutions to common problems and to view those problems as opportunities for cooperation rather than for resort to lawyers and courts. The promotion of such local ties can extend out into the broader community providing the substrate of goodwill and trust that makes deliberation and compromise possible.[8]

Because friendships require great mutual concern and devotion, the number of friends one can support is small. Deep friendships are experienced by others as exclusionary and therefore have a problematic impact on citizenship. Civic friendship is more inclusive precisely because it is more casual and undemanding. It is formed and enjoyed largely on the basis of unpremeditated encounters, the sort that take place in public or quasi public spaces—sidewalks, stoops, playgrounds, post offices, and supermarkets.

Perhaps Olmsted's deepest contribution both to democratic theory and to conservationism was to recognize that civic friendship could be successfully cultivated even in the barren soil of the city. Thus when he faced the difficult choice between devoting his career to improving the lot of the freed slaves or to superintending the New York city streets he chose the latter. Even the critical task of helping blacks to learn to live as free persons was secondary to creating the physical substrate that would enable all Americans of whatever color to exercise the rights and obligations of citizenship (IV, 24).

Parks and Civic Friendship

Olmsted's clearest statement regarding the influence on democratic life of its physical surroundings is contained in a speech he gave entitled "Public Parks and the Enlargement of Towns."[9] It begins by acknowledging the inevitability, indeed the desirability, of urbanization. The "enlargement of towns" is an integral part of the progress that has occurred since medieval times, whose fruits include: mass education, political liberty, and faster transportation.[10] The access the city offers to schools, museums and music, and other specialized services vastly improves the quality of life of rural migrants. The rate of migration will undoubtedly accelerate as the city's superior qualities become more widely recognized.[11]

Despite its great advantages, life in the city also gives rise to terrible evils. Disease, misery, vice, and crime are more prevalent there. Most terribly, the very nature of urban social intercourse is destructive of civic friendship.

> Whenever we walk through the denser part of town, to merely avoid collision with those we meet and pass upon the sidewalks, we have constantly to watch, to foresee, and to guard against their movements. *This involves a consideration of their intentions, a calculation of their strengths and weaknesses. . . . Our minds are thus brought into close dealings with other minds without any flowing toward them, but rather a drawing from them. Much of the intercourse between men when engaged in the pursuits of commerce has the same tendency . . . to regard others in a hard if not always hardening way* [italics mine].[12]

Such problems, stemming from the impersonality, the commercialism, and the sheer density of cities, can only get worse as population increases and economic life intensifies. To some extent these can be mitigated by encouraging the segregation of commercial and residential neighborhoods and endowing the latter with greater public amenities, such as wider tree-lined sidewalks. But, most importantly, cities can counteract the enervating impact of urban life through the provision of adequate opportunities for recreation.

Olmsted approached the issue of recreation with great precision. First he divided the topic into two distinct subcategories, each of which made a positive contribution to human well-being. *Exertive* recreation, which was necessary to stimulate the body and the mind, required facilities for mental games like chess and physical games like baseball. Such facilities should be provided in every neighborhood so that residents did not have to travel far to make use of them. *Receptive* recreation, whose contribution was distinctively civic in nature, had different requirements. Olmsted divided it into two additional subcategories—gregarious and neighborly. Gregarious receptive recreation referred to the love people have of being in crowds. Crowds are not mobs. Olmsted recognized that national solidarity and pride could be encouraged through the provision of great promenades like the Champs Elysee or those adjacent to Central Park and Prospect Park where:

> . . . all classes (are) largely represented, with a common purpose, not at all intellectual, competitive with none, disposing to jealousy and spiritual or intellectual pride toward none, each individual adding by his mere presence to the pleasure of all others . . . poor and rich, young and old, Jew and Gentile.[13]

By contrast, he described neighborly receptive recreation as that in which

> the prattle of the children mingles with the easy conversation of the more sedate, the bodily requirements satisfied with good cheer, fresh air, agreeable light, moderate temperature, snug shelter. . . . The circumstances all favorable to a pleasurable wakefulness of the mind without stimulating exertion, the close relation of family life, the association of children, of mothers, of lovers . . . stimulate and keep alive the more tender sympathies and give play to faculties such as may be dormant in business or on the promenade.[14]

This form of recreation is most conducive to civic friendship and it should be the central purpose of the public park.

> We want a ground to which people may easily go after day's
> work is done and where they may stroll for an hour, seeing, hear-
> ing and feeling nothing of the bustle and jar of the streets. . . .
> We want the greatest possible contrast with the streets and the
> shops and the rooms of the town . . . especially . . . with the
> restraining and confining conditions of the town . . . which
> compel us to walk circumspectly, watchfully, jealously . . . to
> look closely on others without sympathy.[15]

Olmsted recognized that although each of these forms of recreation was intrinsically valuable, their requirements were to an important extent mutually exclusive. Promenades could be placed adjacent to parks, but if put in their midst, they would destroy the peace and quiet so essential to neighborly receptive recreation. He recognized that his role as landscape architect was as much involved with keeping competing activities out of the park as it was with determining what the park should include. Many of the most acrimonious battles he engaged were about preventing otherwise useful edifices like statues, restaurants, and museums from cluttering up the parkland.

Democracy's Highest Purpose

Olmsted was enraptured by the English countryside and by the great architects and landscape designers who had done so much to shape it. His parks were self-consciously modeled on those of the great English estates. The picturesque and pastoral elements that comprise them were his palette. At first glance it might seem odd that the democratic environmentalist should so favor the haunts of the English nobility. But his aesthetic and political concerns were of a piece. Like Tocqueville, Olmsted's greatest ambition was to elevate democratic life and that meant elevating taste. He was not satisfied merely to encourage good citizenship. He believed that ordinary people could nourish their spirits in a manner previously considered the exclusive preserve of the aristocracy.

> Men who are rich enough . . . provide places of this needed
> recreation for themselves. There are in . . . Great Britain more
> than one thousand private parks and notable grounds devoted to
> luxury and recreation . . . The enjoyment of the choicest natural
> scenes in the country . . . is thus a monopoly . . . of a very few
> very rich people. The great mass of society, including those to
> whom it would be of the greatest benefit, is excluded . . . The

establishment by government of great public grounds for the free enjoyment of the people under certain circumstances is thus justified and enforced as a public duty.[16]

It is a scientific fact that the occasional contemplation of natural scenes of an impressive character . . . is favorable to the health and vigor of men and especially to the health and vigor of their intellect beyond any other conditions that can be offered them, that it not only gives pleasure for the time being but increases their subsequent capacity for happiness and the means of securing happiness.[17]

The tranquility and beauty that he required of parks served an even greater end than civic friendship; they fostered contemplation.

Pastures would dominate his greatest parks because of all kinds of scenery they best stimulated contemplation.

> As Art deals with the manners and morals of men through the imagination; this is one of many reasons why the expression of amplitude and free sweep in the scenery of a Park, *which can only be produced by broad meadow like surfaces with shadowy and uncertain limits,* is an artistic requirement of the first importance. (VI, 233)

Although nominally a free thinker, it is to the Bible that Olmsted turned for his most eloquent pastoral encomium.

> It consists of combinations of trees, standing singly or in groups, and casting their shadows over broad stretches of turf, or repeating their beauty by reflection upon the calm surface of pools, and the predominant associations are in the highest degree tranquilizing and grateful. *As expressed by the Hebrew poet: 'He maketh me to lie down in green pastures, he leadeth me beside the still waters. '*[18]

This is God's chosen landscape. It restores souls.

An American Romantic

Olmsted's life prior to his becoming a landscape architect, though curiously aimless, did provide formative political and aesthetic experiences which shaped his approach to landscape architecture.[19] Born in 1822, his mother died when he was a small boy and he was sent off to live with various clergymen. Yet he remained attached to his father, a successful merchant and nature lover who took the boy on trips to such scenic locales as the White Mountains, the Coast of Maine, and upstate New York (I, 5).

His young manhood was dilettantish to a distinctly un-American degree. He dropped out of Yale ostensibly because of an eye ailment. But after he recovered, he did not return, despite the fact that his brother John and his best friend, Charles Loring Brace, both matriculated there and he was often in New Haven to keep their company. After sailing to China as a merchant seamen he determined to become a farmer. He apprenticed for a year on a farm in upstate New York and then, in 1847, his father bought him his own farm on Staten Island, New York.

Although he sought to impress his friends and family with his dedication to agriculture, and devoted himself to learning and applying the most progressive agrarian techniques of the day, Olmsted never exhibited the single-mindedness characteristic of the successful farmer. After only a couple of years of farming he chose to leave the farm in the care of others and accompany his brother John and their friend Brace on a walking tour of England. This trip would later result in his first book, *Walks and Talks of an American Farmer in England*, which appeared in 1852 (I, 48).

Olmsted's trip to England brought his love of English romantic landscape to full flower. He had become a passionate adherent of the style of landscape design pioneer by Capability Brown and championed by Henry Repton. He read and praised the discussion of the picturesque written by Uvedale Price. He decried the excessive ornamentation and botanical exoticism that was threatening the simple pastoral unpretentiousness of the great English gardens. He applauded the departure from classicism's rigorous commitment to straight lines embodied in the Gothic revival's love of curvilinearity. He praised its effort to discover "the genius of the place" as opposed to classicism's imposition of artificial lines and contours.[20]

Olmsted's book on England is imbued with his appreciation of the great parks he visited there.

> Probably there is no object of art that Americans of cultivated taste generally more long to see in Europe than an English Park. What artist so noble, has often been my thought, as he who, with far-reaching conception of beauty and designing power, sketches the outline, writes the colours, and directs the shadows of a picture so great that Nature shall be employed upon it for generations, before the work he has arranged for her shall realize his intentions. (I, 10)

When he returned from England, Olmsted was nearly thirty. Although he had no vocation, he had decided to devote himself to social reform in some guise. His dear friend Brace was soon to dedicate his life to the cause of child welfare, serving as the founder and longtime director of the Children's Aid Society. Although Olmsted evinced interest in the whole panoply of reform causes that were gathering force among enlightened urbanites, the two that were to preoccupy him for the next several years were anti-slavery and parks. It did not become clear until well into the next decade that, of the two, parks would prevail to form his lifetime obsession.

In 1852, once again leaving his farm in the care of others, Olmsted went south as a roving reporter for the *New York Times*. He would ultimately make three separate trips to various parts of the South and write a book based on each of them.[21] This *oeuvre* constitutes perhaps the most comprehensive description of ante-bellum southern life. Particularly because of its lack of polemic, it served as a very convincing and influential indictment of slavery.

Olmsted's southern reportage is worthy of study on its own merits, but its chief contribution to his democratic environmentalism is epitomized by a conversation he had in Nashville with a southern gentleman whom he had known at Yale, Samuel Perkins Allison. Allison's critique of northern society and culture forced Olmsted to admit that the superiority of the North over the South was less clear-cut than he would wish to admit.

> The conversation making me acknowledge the rowdyism, ruffianism, want of high honorable sentiment and chivalry of the common farming and laboring people of the North, as I was obliged to, made me very melancholy. (II, 234)

The flaws of both North and South were very different but equally debilitating.

> With such low, material, and selfish aims in statesmanship (as the best men of the South have), and with such a low, prejudiced, party enslaved, and material people (at the North), what does the success of our Democratic nationality amount to—and what is to become of us? (II, 234)

Olmsted saw no hope of improving southern society as it was then constituted. Although he liked and admired men like Allison, he found their aristocratic pretensions to be false. Allison's idea of honor was "mere deference to time honored rules and conventionalisms" (II, 234). The result of slavery had been to make men like him "prodigal, improvident and ostentatiously generous . . . habitually impulsive, impetuous and enthusiastic" (II, 239-40).

> I need to be more of an Aristocrat or more of a Democrat than I have been—a Socialist Democrat.[22] We need institutions that shall more directly assist the poor and degraded to elevate themselves. Our educational principle must be enlarged and made to include more than these miserable common schools. The poor and wicked need more than to be let alone. (II, 234)

In fact, Olmsted's contact with the slave South and the incumbent need to defend the North made him decide to become more of an aristocrat *and* more of a democrat. The size and scale of the changes required to elevate the democracy were indeed greater and more urgent than he had previously recognized and therefore the birth of a major new democratic political movement was necessary. It required leadership, and to perform that role a true aristocracy, not the Southern sham variety, would need to come to the fore.

Olmsted would later interrupt his involvement with Central Park to spend the first two years of the Civil War as the executive director of the Sanitary Commission, a privately sponsored but publicly sanctioned organization devoted to improving the public health conditions of the soldiers. His efforts included directing the provision of hospital ships for McClellan's army during the Peninsular Campaign.

His involvement with the war effort immersed him again in the issue of slavery. When the Union captured the slave-laden Georgia Sea Islands early in the war, Olmsted saw it as a perfect opportunity to experiment with how best to assist slaves in adjusting to the rigors of freedom. He wrote legislation creating the so-called Port Royal experiment and lobbied hard to be made the director of the model community the legislation would create. At the same time, he was approached by New York city officials to consider becoming superintendent of streets. Although the grid pattern adopted by the city in the early 1800s had pretty much determined the layout of city streets in a mechanistic manner that was anathema to Olmsted, the final disposition of many avenues had not yet taken place. He hoped to redesign several of them in a curvilinear fashion and to use this and other means to reduce symmetry and avoid high density in the as yet undeveloped parts of the city.

In the event, Olmsted was offered neither the leadership of the Port Royal experiment nor the New York superintendency of streets. But it is worth noting that he appears to have been prepared to turn down the Port Royal opportunity to accept the New York position. He seems to have determined that his own greatest contribution to public welfare would come from helping to physically shape urban America.

Founding Landscape Architecture

Olmsted's founding of the landscape architecture profession was achieved through his involvement with the first great American public park, Central Park in New York City. Although he did not participate in the initial decision to create the park, he and Calvert Vaux designed it and he presided over its establishment, serving as its first superintendent. The first official use of the title "Landscape Architect" dates to the letter of resignation that Olmsted and Vaux submitted to the Central Park Board of Commissioners on May 12, 1863, which they signed "Messrs. Olmsted and Vaux, Landscape Architects."[23]

In 1855 Olmsted abandoned the farm to his brother's care and became a partner in the publishing firm of Dix and Edwards which published *Putnam's Magazine* as well as books by many of the leading authors of the day. He obtained the partnership by investing $5,000 of his father's money in the firm. Within two years the firm went bankrupt (I, 17).

This dismal failure was to be the proximate cause of his becoming a landscape architect. Out of work, and with no immediate prospects, Olmsted lodged at an inn on the Connecticut coast to proofread his third book of southern travels. By sheer coincidence, Charles Wyllys Elliott met him there. Elliott was a member of the Central Park Commission and an admirer of Olmsted's reformist writings. He urged Olmsted to apply for the post of park superintendent. Construction of the park had just begun and no overall plan for it had yet been approved. The superintendent's job consisted mainly of overseeing the construction crews. He reported to the park engineer, who was responsible for the overall project.

Despite his lack of administrative experience, Olmsted determined to apply. He quickly returned to New York to mobilize support. The park commission, appointed by the state legislature, was dominated by Republicans. The New York City administration, which provided the labor for the project, was Democratic. Although Olmsted had virtually no qualifications for the position he had acquired a reputation as a high-minded reformer by dint of his writing and editorial work. Most importantly he enjoyed the enthusiastic support of such luminaries as William Cullen Bryant and Washington Irving. In the end he seems to have gotten the job because he represented a suitable compromise between the commissioners who wanted a staunch Republican, which he was, and the New York City Democrats who would agree to a Republican only if he was ineffectual, which he was reputed to be.

Downing and Democratic Virtues

Although the specific circumstances surrounding his appointment were accidental, Olmsted had, prior to his appointment, formed strong opinions about parks and their place in a democratic society. He was a devotee of the works of Andrew Jackson Downing, the first great proponent of parks for American cities. He subscribed to Downing's magazine, *The Horticulturalist and Journal of Rural Taste and Rural Art*, and also contributed articles to it.[24] Olmsted's partner in designing Central Park and Prospect Park, Calvert Vaux, had previously been Downing's partner. It is a tragic irony that were it not for Downing's untimely death in a steamboat accident on the Hudson, he rather than Olmsted would, in all likelihood, have won the commission to build Central Park.

When the park was nearly finished, Olmsted wrote a circular which he sent to several prominent friends of Downing proposing that a bust of Downing be placed in the park, "in one of the shaded recesses of the Ramble," and that it be inscribed with a long quote from one of Downing's essays. The proposed inscription contains many of the most important ideas and themes that would come to dominate Olmsted's own thought and work.

Downing urged his readers to:

> plant spacious parks in your cities and unloose their gates as wide as the gates of morning to the whole people . . . so education and culture will banish the plague spots of democracy, and the dread of the ignorant exclusive, who has no faith in the refinement of a republic will stand abashed in the next century before a whole people whose system of voluntary education embraces . . . not only common schools of rudimentary knowledge, but common enjoyments of all classes in the higher realism of art, letters, science, social recreation and enjoyments. (III, 251-52)

Downing had won fame not as a social reformer or park advocate but as an architect of private homes. He had sought to develop a school of rural architecture capable of dignifying the American rural landscape. But even in this milieu his aims were not solely aesthetic. He wanted to build dwellings capable of encouraging a sense of domesticity and stability that would countervail what he took to be the excessively frenetic and aimless character of American life. Downing had also read Tocqueville.[25] He feared that "the spirit of unrest, followed into the bosom of society makes of man a feverish being, in whose Tantalus' cup repose is the unattainable drop." His aim prefigured one of Leopold's: to create homes and gardens that would root men in "one spot of earth . . . [an] Eden of interest and delights."[26]

Downing sought a similar result at the level of village as well. He designed a village with a park of twenty to fifty acres that would be "the nucleus or heart of the village." Park frontage would be divided into lots of at least a quarter acre, while those lots on wide streets emanating from the park on each side would have sufficient frontage to ensure that the village retained a "rural character." Downing hoped that, over time, the villagers would come to see the park as their common pleasure garden and would endow it with trees, flowers, shrubs, and "rustic seats and arbors."[27]

Olmsted himself did not design dwellings. But his plans for suburban developments, most notably Riverside, Illinois, as well as his park designs, share the aims articulated by Downing. He saw parks as akin to schoolrooms in their ability to edify and improve those who patronized them. And he viewed the suburb as a village whose closeness to nature and intimate character provided a welcome and necessary antidote to the work life spent in the city.

Encountering Nature: Park Planning and Stewardship

Olmsted teamed up with Downing's former partner, Calvert Vaux, and they submitted a plan for the park, entitled Greensward, which triumphed in the open competition that was held. Its sweeping meadows embodied Olmsted's commitment to the pastoral ideal. In keeping with Olmsted's understanding of landscape architecture, the plan blended aesthetic brilliance and sociological subtlety. Each aspect of the design was aimed to create a sense of separation between the park and the surrounding buildings (this despite the fact that the city had not yet reached anywhere near the border of the park). Stone walls separated it from the street so that, once one was in the park, life outside it was screened from view. The traffic crossings that the city demanded be included at regular intervals to accommodate crosstown traffic were sunk so as to be virtually invisible. In keeping with his objective of segregating different forms of recreation, the plan contained no sports facilities (III, 117-88).

The park was no wilderness. In fact almost every acre of it was subject to aggressive recontouring in accordance with Olmsted's plan. Its most noteworthy individual elements—the Ramble, the Sheep Meadow, the Lake—were artfully conceived to encourage tranquility and to spark the imagination.

Olmsted did not limit the park plan only to issues of physical design. He was very sensitive to the criticism levied by its opponents that the park would simply become a haven for the nineteenth-century equivalent of gang members, dope addicts, and muggers. To meet this objection he conceived of a special park police force whose responsibility it would be to enforce a high level of civility among park users. In addition to patrolling the park, they would man all the entrances and exits.

He acknowledged that preventing the abuse and degradation of the park by its visitors was "the most vulnerable point of the undertaking."[28] Therefore adequate supervision and maintenance were as crucial to the park's ability to accomplish its civilizing mission as was its initial design. Properly understood, the landscape architect's responsibility encompassed management as well as design.

The landscape architect needed to be the steward of his park in other ways as well. Indeed the most aggravating controversies that Olmsted engaged in with city government involved proposed encroachments on park land.

> Having become the resort of large assemblages of people, the Park is considered too advantageous a field for advertising to be neglected by those who would force their wants and wares upon the public at every turn. . . . If all the applications for the erection and maintenances of towers, houses, drinking fountains, Aeolian harps, gymnasiums, observatories, (and) weighing scales for the sale of eatables, velocipedes, perambulators, Indian work, tobacco and segars, for the privilege of using steam-engines, snowshoes (and) ice boats, and for the use of the ice for fancy dress carnivals, were granted, they would occupy a large portion of the surface of the Park, establish a very extensive and very various business, and give it the appearance of the grounds of a country fair, or of a Militia training field.[29]

Olmsted had no objection to country fairs and militia training. Indeed, as the Civil War was winding down, he sent E.L. Godkin, the editor of the *Nation*, a detailed proposal for the creation of a peacetime militia (V, 369). But parkland was sacred. To use it for purposes incompatible with receptive recreation and contemplation was to diminish its capacity to perform its central objectives.

Olmsted's objections were equally vociferous regarding the placement of fine buildings, monuments, statues, or even a zoo. In none of these instances did he dispute the intrinsic merit of the proposed encroachment. He opposed them solely because they would distract park visitors away from the pastoral tranquility and beauty that were its *raison d'etre*.

Olmsted's objection to encroachments extended even to horticultural matters. He opposed specimen planting and flower bedding because they detracted from the "spirit of place." Olmsted compared the impression made by a common wildflower in a mossy bank and an exotic hybrid of the same flower placed in a vase under glass. The brilliance and rarity of the latter dazzled the eye, but the former, so inconspicuous as to not even interrupt conversation or require a special stop, was far more soothing and refreshing. The task of a landscape architect was akin to that of a musical composer, blending tonalities and melodies to achieve the most balanced and harmonious overall composition rather than producing this or that brilliant passage.[30]

Olmsted worked to create national parks as well as urban ones. The design issues that the two types of parks presented were very different. In the urban setting the parks literally had to be created and engineered whereas the national parks involved the preservation of pre-existing scenic splendor. But the highest purposes to be fulfilled by each were essentially the same—the latter simply operated on a grander scale.

Joseph Sax describes how Olmsted's concern for the way in which natural wonders would be encountered is evidenced in his proposal for managing the park at Niagara Falls. Niagara was already among the most popular tourist attractions in America, and Olmsted had no desire to keep people away. Nonetheless, he opposed allowing visitors to watch the falls without leaving their carriages. Viewpoints suitable for carriages would inevitably become crowded and busy and distract viewers from the grandeur of the occasion. Watching from a carriage, viewers might merely glimpse the falls. Making them dismount and walk to an observation area would encourage them to slow down and become absorbed in the view. He wanted to restore the experience to what it had been when:

> a visit to the Falls was a series of expeditions, and in each
> expedition hours were occupied in wandering slowly among the
> trees, going from place to place, with many intervals of rest. . . .
> here was not only a much greater degree of enjoyment, there was
> different kind of enjoyment. . . . People were then loath to leave
> the place; many lingered on from day to day . . . revisiting ground
> they had gone over before, turning and returning.[31]

Unless one recognizes the specific human ends which the national parks were to serve, Olmsted's discussion of them seems incoherent. In his report on "The Yosemite Valley and the Mariposa Big Trees," Olmsted sounded, at times, like John Muir. He advocated "the preservation and maintenance as exactly as is possible of the natural scenery," basing that claim on "the rights of posterity."[32] But two pages later he advocated building a road to the valley in order to better accommodate visitors.[33] In his mind, of course, there was no contradiction between preserving the scenery and inviting people to see it, provided that visitors were encouraged and, if need be, gently coerced into appreciating the natural wonders of the park in an appropriately unobtrusive, contemplative fashion.

Civic Reform: Colleges and Suburbs

Olmsted's landscape architecture extended beyond parks. His most ambitious planning schemes involved stemming the tide of rural to urban migration that created excessive urban congestion in the first place. Instead of bringing rural people to the city to enjoy urban amenities, he sought physically to disperse those amenities to revive existing rural communities and to create a whole new residential genre, the suburb.

The Morrill Act passed during the Civil War gave Federal land to the states, the proceeds of which they could use to build colleges that combined liberal and practical education. In what was still a predominantly farming nation, practical education meant, above all, agricultural education. Olmsted viewed these new "land grant" colleges as great opportunities for redeploying urban technical and cultural assets to the countryside.

In his view, the land grant college would not only provide farmers with access to modern agricultural innovations. It would also demonstrate to its rural neighbors what a modern "urbanized" rural community could and should be like. Students would live neither in off-campus boarding houses nor large impersonal dormitories but in houses that resembled attractive private domiciles replete with private bedrooms, common rooms, and dining rooms. The purpose of these houses was not just to make the students comfortable, but to educate them in the art of genteel domestic living so that when they later settled in the countryside they would bring with them a level of taste and refinement that rural living currently lacked.

Olmsted's own model for this endeavor was the New England town as Tocqueville had described it and as he himself had witnessed it in his youth. Unlike rural communities in the rest of the country, those in New England were specifically designed to promote civic friendship. They were compact, encouraging interaction among residents. Farmsteads were not isolated but built on the road near to town, close to neighbors, church, school, and meeting house. The rural communities he had seen in the South and Midwest had "few public edifices or public works of any kind" (VI, 13). By contrast, the New England towns brought civilization to the countryside in the form of libraries, lyceums, and monuments.

If the land grant colleges were built as secluded self-contained campuses far from existing communities, they would resemble southern plantations. Olmsted had visited plantations on his trips south and he had noticed how little those islands of wealth and gentility added to the life of the surrounding areas. Instead the campuses should be New England towns writ large, placed in the midst of existing communities, closely linking the populace to great educational opportunities and providing common ground for the exchange of ideas and opinions. Properly designed and situated, they would help stem the tide of rural migration to the city by endowing the countryside with the best aspects of urban life. Olmsted was able to translate this vision into the designs for several different college campuses including what was then called the College of California at Berkeley and two new land grant schools, the Massachusetts Agricultural College at Amherst and the Maine College of Agricultural and Mechanic Arts at Orono (VI, 10-16).

Olmsted's attraction to the suburb came from his recognition that it was an essentially urban creation. The advent of the commuter railroad and the streetcar meant that there were no longer any physical reasons for cities to be so dense and compact. Suburbs were really urban neighborhoods characterized by lower density and turbulence. Properly conceived, a suburb would offer the civic advantages of the small town with easy access to urban amenities and the bucolic charm of rural living. Thus it represented "not a regression but an advance upon those qualities which are characteristic of town life."[34] A suburb could and should provide "elbow room about a house without going to the country, without sacrifice of butchers, bakers and theaters" (VI, 36-37).

These aspirations were contained in his design for Riverside, a suburban development near Chicago. In addition to the railroad, Olmsted proposed a grand promenade to connect Riverside to downtown. Such a promenade would be composed of pedestrian, equestrian, and commercial lanes. Thus it would afford opportunities for gregarious and exertive recreation as well as permitting commuters to enjoy the pleasures of scenic beauty on their way to and from work. A commercial block would be established near the train station both to enable residents to buy necessities without traveling to Chicago and to serve as a focal point for sociability. Small parks, playgrounds, and commons were strewn throughout the park; but the major recreational area was a 160-acre park along the Des Plaines river. As a further effort to create a restful and bucolic image, the streets were laid out in gentle curvilinear patterns as opposed to the urban grid (VI, 273-90).

Little of what Olmsted envisioned in his designs for residential colleges or suburbs was ever actually realized. But his elaborate plans, and the theorizing that lay behind them, demonstrate the breadth of his ambition for reconfiguring the physical as well as the cultural and political life of the nation.

Human Nature and Conservationist Reform

Olmsted's human-centered consideration of nature places him squarely in American conservationist tradition. He cherished the pastoral and the picturesque landscape for its power to affect the mind and soul of man. He had no objection to using human engineering to alter the landscape. Built before the advent of the bulldozer and backhoe, Central Park is a monument to the ability of human sweat and toil to rearrange nature. Olmsted quarreled with Charles S. Sargent, Director of the Arnold Arboretum, because Sargent insisted that only native plants be used along the Riverway park that they both were working on. Olmsted wanted to use whatever plants, foreign or domestic, most suited his design.[35]

But Olmsted's conservationism was no mere "gospel of efficiency." Olmsted was not a utilitarian, as that devoutly secular gospel would imply. Nature was a tool placed at the service of human nature. Olmsted targeted those specific natural elements that had the greatest affinity with man's best nature and that could liberate him, at least temporarily, from the soul-deadening urban bustle.

Olmsted was a thoroughgoing humanist who appreciated the many avenues by which the human spirit was elevated and refined including: art, music, and literature. But he did grant nature a special place in that endeavor because it could be appreciated disinterestedly. Urban life wore people out by forcing them to be so calculating and so concerned with the opinion of others.

> In all social pleasures and all pleasures which are usually enjoyed
> in association with the social pleasures, the care for the opinion
> of others, or the good of others largely mingles. In the pleasures
> of literature, the laying up of ideas and self-important purposes
> which cannot be kept out of view.

By contrast:

> In the interest which natural scenery inspires . . . the attention is
> aroused and the mind occupied without purpose, without a
> continuation of the common process of relating the present
> action, thought or perception to some future end. No other
> pursuits offered such purity of experience.[36]

The enjoyment of scenery employs the mind without fatigue, and yet exercises it; tranquilizes it and yet enlivens it.[37]

Olmsted was a conservationist in another sense as well. Like Pinchot and T.R., his views about nature were integrated into a broader critique of American political, economic, and social life, and into a wider reform agenda shaped by that critique. Such concerns are hardly absent in contemporary environmentalism, where views about nature are often linked to very pointed political and economic criticism. The difference is that modern environmentalism rarely shows conservationism's respect for, and appreciation of, civilization. That was Olmsted's starting point. Modern civilization had done great things. The advance of equality and democracy would not have been possible in the absence of modern technological innovations and the movement of large populations to cities. He had no nostalgia for primitive life and the hardships and barbarities it entails. Nor does he object to capitalism. Instead he criticized excessive materialism and self-regardingness, diseases endemic in supposedly anticapitalist regimes as well as in free market ones. He sought to preserve the virtues of the city while providing refuge from its crowding and impersonalism.

Olmsted's greatest lesson for contemporary environmentalists involves his blending of nature and civilization. Rather than treat them as antithetical, Olmsted viewed nature as civil-izing. Tinkering with nature was fine as long as the proper objectives were kept in mind. Indeed, all of man's efforts to control nature, or to preserve it for that matter, had to be understood in the context of the great democratic republican project that those efforts were to simultaneously sustain and enhance.

Notes

1. Andres Duany and Elizabeth Plater-Zyberk, "The Second Coming of the Small Town," *Wilson Quarterly* XVI, no. 2 (Winter 1992): 19-48; Jane Jacobs, *The Death and Life of Great American Cities* (New York: Vintage Books, 1962); William H. Whyte, *City: Rediscovering the Center* (New

York: Doubleday, 1988).

2. Marc Landy, Marc J. Roberts, and Stephen R. Thomas, *The Environmental Protection Agency: From Nixon to Clinton*, expanded edition (New York: Oxford University Press, 1994), 308.

3. See Taylor's essay in this volume.

4. Charles Capen McLaughlin, ed., Charles E. Beveridge, associate ed., *The Papers of Frederick Law Olmsted: Vol. V, The California Frontier,* (Baltimore: Johns Hopkins University Press, 1977): 596. (All citations in the text are to this edition of the Olmsted papers, referred to by volume number.)

5. Letter to Charles Loring Brace, November 12, 1850 (I, 358-59).

6. Olmsted's political outlook is carefully explored by Geoffrey Blodgett in "Frederick Law Olmsted: Landscape Architecture as Conservative Reform," *Journal of American History* 62, no. 4 (March 1976): 869-89. I also profited greatly from two other excellent treatments of Olmsted's thought and his influence on urban design: David Schuyler, *The New Urban Landscape: The Redefinition of City Form in Nineteenth Century America* (Baltimore: Johns Hopkins University Press, 1986), and Thomas Bender, *Toward and Urban Vision: Ideas and Institutions in Nineteenth Century America* (Baltimore: Johns Hopkins University Press 1975).

7. For a recent discussion of the workplace as a source of community and friendship see Arlie Russell Hochschild, *The Time Bind: When Work Becomes Home and Home Becomes Work* (New York: Metropolitan Books, 1997).

8. I am heavily indebted to Bertrand De Jouvenel for my understanding of civic friendship. See especially his discussion in *Sovereignty* (Chicago: University of Chicago Press, 1957), Chapters 7 and 8.

9. The speech was later turned into an article of the same name published in *Journal of Social Science*, 1871. "Public Parks and Enlargement of Towns" is reprinted in Donald Worster, ed., *American Environmentalism: The Formative Period 1860-1915* (New York: John Wiley, 1973), 111-32.

10. Olmsted, "Public Parks," 115.

11. Olmsted, "Public Parks," 120.

12. Olmsted, "Public Parks," 121.

13. Olmsted, "Public Parks," 127.

14. Olmsted, "Public Parks," 128-29.

15. Olmsted, "Public Parks," 131.

16. Frederick Law Olmsted, "The Yosemite Valley and the Mariposa Big Trees: A Preliminary Report (1865)," reprinted in *Landscape Architecture* 44, no. 1 (1953): 21. Afterwards referred to as "Yosemite Report."

17. Olmsted, "Yosemite Report," 17.

18. Quoted in Charles E. Beveridge and Paul Rocheleau, *Frederick Law Olmsted: Designing the American Landscape* (New York: Rizzoli, 1995), 37.

19. For an informative account of Olmsted's life see Laura Wood Roper, *FLO: A Biography of Frederick Law Olmsted* (Baltimore: Johns Hopkins University Press, 1973).

20. See the excellent discussion of Olmsted's aesthetic views in Beveridge and Rocheleau, *Designing American Landscape*, 32-54. The book is also magnificently illustrated.

21. *A Journey in the Seaboard Slaves States, with Remarks on Their Economy* (New York: Dix and Edwards, 1856); *A Journey Through Texas; or, a Saddle-Trip on the Southwestern Frontier* (New York: Dix Edwards, 1857); *A Journey in the Back Country* (New York: Mason Brothers, 1860).

22. His use of the term "socialist" does not carry the modern connotation of the word but is meant simply to imply a greater concern for the social well-being of the citizenry.

23. Norman T. Newton, *Design on the Land: The Development of Landscape Architecture* (Cambridge MA: The Belknap Press of Harvard University Press, 1971), 273.

24. Beveridge and Rocheleau, *Designing American Landscape*, 20. See also the major new biography of Downing by David Schuyler, *Apostle of Taste: Andrew Jackson Downing, 1815-1852* (Baltimore: Johns Hopkins University Press, 1995).

25. John William Ward, "The Politics of Design," in Laurence B. Holland, *Who Designs America?* (Garden City, NY: Anchor Books, 1966), 62.

26. Ward, "Politics of Design," 63.

27. Andrew Jackson Downing, "Our Country Villages," *The Horticulturist* 4, no. 12 (June 1850): 537-41. (Cited in I, 364.)

28. Frederick Law Olmsted, "Report on Police Force," in Frederick Law Olmsted Jr. and Theodora Kimball, eds., *Forty Years of Landscape: Central Park* (Cambridge, MA: MIT Press, 1973), 442.

29. Olmsted, "Report on Police," 519.

30. Beveridge and Rocheleau, *Designing American Landscape*, 35.

31. Joseph L. Sax, *Mountains Without Handrails* (Ann Arbor, MI: University of Michigan Press, 1980), 23-24.

32. Olmsted, "Yosemite Report," 22.

33. Olmsted, "Yosemite Report," 24.

34. Schuyler, *New Urban Landscape,* 163.

35. Beveridge and Rochelau, *Designing American Landscape*, 101.
36. Olmsted, "Yosemite Report," 20.
37. Olmsted, "Yosemite Report," 20-21.

Afterword

Bob Pepperman Taylor

> To be a part of the democratic tradition is to be a prisoner of
> hope. And you cannot be a prisoner of hope without engaging in
> a form of struggle in the present that keeps the best of the past
> alive.[1]

In his recent history of Western attitudes toward nature, Peter Coates
observes the "Whiggish" character of much of the literature on this topic.
"The often inquisitional search for the roots of disharmony in our relationship with nature has been complemented by an earnest quest for the sources
of enlightenment."[2] The intellectual history of environmental values and
conceptions of nature is commonly presented as a morality play in which
vicious ideas from the past account for our environmental problems, but also
inspire the development of alternative world views. These alternative views,
in turn, are proposed as the foundations for a new and ecologically sound
society. This story is progressive, a tale of sin and (possible) redemption.
History points the way to a new understanding of the human relationship to
nature which will allow us to turn our backs on the ways of our forebears
and forge a new path.

Simon Schama directly challenges this stock element of much environmentalist literature, the claim that the heart of Western culture is hostile at
worst, insensitive at best, to nature.

> . . . the cultural habits of humanity have always made room for
> the sacredness of nature. All our landscapes, from the city park
> to the mountain hike, are imprinted with our tenacious, inescap-
> able obsessions. . . . [T]o take the many and several ills of the

229

> environment seriously does not, I think, require that we trade in
> our cultural legacy or its posterity. It asks instead that we simply
> see it for what it has truly been: not the repudiation, but the
> veneration, of nature.[3]

Contrary to those who would emphasize the "mutually exclusive character
of Western culture and nature," Schama suggests "the strength of the links
that have bound them together."[4] The resources for thinking about our
relation to nature are found within our cultural traditions, rather than in the
rebellion from and rejection of them.

More narrowly focused on New England, Richard Judd has recently
discovered populist roots to the conservation movement. Ever since the
publication of Hays's *Conservation and the Gospel of Efficiency*, it has been
assumed that conservation was an elite movement. But Judd traces much of
the energy of the movement to the very people who farmed, cleared, and
originally abused the New England landscape.

> Pioneering New Englanders, as historians have pointed out,
> devastated the 'virgin' landscape they encountered as they
> pushed out from the heartlands of central New England. Yet
> those who remained on the land after this wave of pioneering
> plunder passed on to the West began reconstituting an equilib-
> rium between nature and culture. Their work is ongoing, but this
> beginning should be recognized for what it was: an important
> commitment among common people to protect and preserve a
> familiar landscape in the face of unsettling social and ecological
> change.[5]

Rather than being only an elite imposition on society, a movement from
above, Judd provides compelling evidence to suggest that conservation (at
least in New England) was in significant part a grassroots movement that
grew from the needs and values and experiences of rural and agricultural
communities.

The common thread in the recent work of these three historians is the
challenge it raises to the view that environmental values and commitments
are best promoted by rejecting our cultural, moral, aesthetic, or political
inheritances. On the contrary, all three argue that it is only by understanding
the complexities and dangers and potentials of these inheritances that we can
begin to properly assess the resources available to us in thinking about,
appreciating, and relating to the natural world.

The project presented by these historians is directly related to the project of this volume. Just as Coates, Schama, and Judd all show, in different ways, how central environmental interest and concern is to our heritage, so most of the authors of the essays in this book present the conservation tradition as a living, vibrant, and rich resource upon which we may profitably draw when addressing our environmental concerns and politics. While the historians challenge us to reject the notion that our political and intellectual traditions are hopelessly corrupt from any acceptable environmentalist perspective, and therefore useless as sources of normative wisdom upon which to draw as we address the environmental problems of our own time, the aim of this volume has been to explore the conceptual wealth within our conservation tradition. By reconsidering conservation, we are offering a focused contribution to the more general reconsideration of the Western tradition of normative discourse on nature proposed by recent historical literature.

The first and most obvious conclusion of this volume, therefore, is a simple extension and elaboration of the message of a broader historical literature: much conventional understanding of the conservation tradition has been misleading and counterproductive. A good deal of the work of these papers has aimed to explain the way particular figures in this tradition have been misunderstood, read too simply, not appreciated for the subtlety or nuance of their ideas. The important point goes one step further: much of our understanding of figures like Henry Thoreau and John Muir has been distorted by contemporary ideological battles. The story so often told of conservationism is that it is in radical opposition to "environmentalism," with the former representing a crude anthropocentrism and the later an enlightened biocentrism. Such a story is, of course, a distortion of the historical record, as the authors of these essays have demonstrated. But this distortion tells a tale of the ideological battles within the environmental movement. The presumption of much environmental ethics in the past generation has been that the conservation tradition has been hopelessly implicated in the environmental deterioration we find around us. Many of the prominent conservationists, after all, were powerful people in positions of political authority, such as Theodore Roosevelt or Gifford Pinchot. If our environmental problems developed during the watch of the "powers that be," then the ideology or world view of these powerful individuals must be implicated in these problems. The solution to these problems must be found, so the logic goes, in an opposition politics and an opposition "world view" or ideology.[6] An oversimplified analysis of the cause of environmental problems has led to a contorted history of the conservation tradition. This, in turn, has hindered our ability to think seriously about our environmental problems and their potential solutions.

There is a second and related theme that is a conceptual consequence of this historical reconsideration: all of the authors of the essays in this volume are committed to thinking about environmental problems within what they take to be our society's democratic traditions. In fact, the appeal of the conservation tradition to most of these authors is precisely its historical connection to democratic commitments and institutions. While some environmentalists and environmental ethicists remain alienated and cynical about these traditions, opting to try to develop alternative politics and radically new ideas,[7] a claim of these papers is that drawing on our deepest moral and political traditions is the most promising way to produce environmental policy that is compelling, widely understandable to broad publics, and politically legitimate. While there is no general agreement among the contributors about the exact political meaning and message of our conservation tradition, there is a commitment to confronting our environmental problems within the context of defensible interpretations of these traditions. The meaning and application of these traditions to public policy analysis is contested, but the need to proceed in this manner is agreed upon. The project as a whole illustrates the richness of these traditions and bolsters a faith that they will yield the resources necessary to thinking reasonably and meaningfully and usefully about nature, our democratic traditions, and the relationship between the two.

Democratic Commitments and Environmental Concern

In his discussion of John Muir, Bruce Pencek presents what he takes to be the foundation of Muir's criticism of urban-dwelling Americans:

> Urban life exacerbates a prior malady: the brute fact that people are social animals who inadequately reflect on their place in the world they willy-nilly transform through their practices and theories. Social life writes large the moral and intellectual vice of pride, whether it take the form of optimism about human mastery and progress or the opposite form of cynicism. Such certitude obstructs individual glimpsing the divine Mind. (17)

In good Christian fashion, Pencek argues, Muir traces our vices to the pride that blinds us to all that is greater than ourselves. So blinded, we plunge headlong into the project of mastering and dominating our environment. Or, what is the flip side of the same coin, we cynically reject human purposes in an equally vain act of believing that our cynicism is itself omnipotent.

This theme of human pride and arrogance emerges at a number of points throughout this volume. Marlo Lewis is clearly impressed by, but deeply critical of Gifford Pinchot's "princely ambitions" (68). Larry Arnhart strikes a serious critical blow when he points out the deeply self-centered character of J. Baird Callicott's "biocentric" interpretation of Leopold's "land ethic" (105-6). Charles Rubin concludes his discussion of Emerson by asking if "nature can suggest constraints, in the manner of any non-relativistic moral thinking " (179). Despite the significant and obvious differences among the authors of these essays and the thinkers they are discussing, a common concern about human arrogance emerges quite clearly in a number of the essays.

If humility is the cure for pride, a false or exaggerated humility is the corresponding vice of the humble. When humility turns to self-loathing, a fear of human evils threatens to destroy a sense of human potentials and goods. A sensitivity to this vice, too, is found throughout this volume. Marc Landy dryly begins his essay by observing that "In its modern incarnation, environmentalism displays a curious lack of concern for people and how they live" (207). The virtue of Olmsted's "democratic environmentalism" (208), Landy argues, is that it aims to promote civic friendship (209) and an appropriate respect for and appreciation of civilization (225). Jeffrey Salmon claims that although Theodore Roosevelt "did not provide a simple guide for how one should reconcile the clash between a dedication to human progress and a desire to preserve wild nature as a source of strength and wisdom in the human character," he did, however, "live this tension, giving each element its due in his writing and in his politics" (35-36). Arnhart maintains that "Leopold shows that conservationism rightly understood transcends the false dilemma of choosing between the preservation of wild nature and the cultivation of civilized life" (111). In a different reading of Muir than that provided by Pencek, James Lennox criticizes Muir for replacing the deification of man with the deification of nature and praises Darwin for refusing to deify either (146). Only this Darwinist perspective, he holds, can promote a realistic and morally satisfying integration of human activity with the natural world (151). Rubin learns from Emerson that "Human beings can create culture, and its dominion over nature, because nature prepares us for that task" (168). Here and elsewhere, the authors in this book express a concern for finding an appropriate understanding of human purposes and culture which draw upon our proper uses and cultivation of nature.

The task these related themes suggest is the need to balance, to negotiate, the difficult tension that is raised by recognizing, first, that human beings are not the be all and end all of creation, and second, that despite the fact that we are not the center of the universe, we have a proper, justifiable, distinctive, and perhaps even good role to play within this creation. If true, this teaching may not be terribly welcome to all. It dissatisfies to the degree that it refuses to replace the business of politics with the certainty of a philosophical system. Our relationship to nature is always morally ambiguous, always subject to revision and adjustment as new problems arise. If the message of this book is correct, democratic virtues that help us reach balanced judgements are much more important to the project of protecting and conserving the environment then is the development of a specialized and esoteric language of environmental ethics or an opposition environmentalism.

This commitment to arguing about environmental policy within the context and practices of American democracy, and thus to arguing about the nature and practices of this American democracy itself, nicely reflects the more general distrust both of human arrogance and false modesty mentioned above. In fact, this distrust is an expression of a kind of democratic sensibility. At first blush, democracy looks to be as arrogant a form of humanism as one could wish to imagine: after all, human will itself is enshrined as the ultimate determinant of public policy. What could be more arrogant than the idea that humans may govern their world with no more discipline or guidance than thinking that what they want to do is fine simply because they want to do it? One need not introduce any principle external to the concerns for democracy itself, however, to see that there are moderating democratic virtues, reasons to think of one's own desires and wants as being disciplined in part by the democratic process. Although it is true that democratic principles encourage me to think for myself, promote my own interests, defend my own opinions and will, they also remind me that all other citizens are encouraged in exactly the same way. My own wants, opinions, and desires will not infrequently conflict with those held by and felt by others. It is in part my recognition of our equality, our common humanity, with all its virtues and foibles and weaknesses, that counsels me to accept the outcome of political deliberation even when I fail to have my way. Democracy promotes a kind of epistemic modesty, teaching me to take my own views very seriously, but also refusing to privilege any human view, my own included, in any absolute sense. Only in the context of such epistemic modesty is it imaginable to accept defeat, if not graciously, at least without questioning the fundamental legitimacy of decisions we disagree with. We are taught to tolerate not only those we dislike and with whom we disagree; just as importantly, we are taught a kind of toleration for political outcomes we disagree with. In a democratic regime political resolution, the acceptance of the outcome of a legitimate political process by both those who have won the day and those who have lost, replaces brute imposition. This can only happen to the degree that citizens recognize the possibility that their own opinions are mistaken or incomplete.

It is precisely this kind of modesty that is all too commonly missing in so much contemporary environmental literature. Consider just these two recent examples from widely read environmental ethicists. In *Nature's Keeper*, Peter Wenz argues that "our culture" is hopelessly anthropocentric, and this anthropocentrism is responsible for virtually every evil ever visited upon our society: "those who consider grass to be at our disposal may be led by degrees to similarly view insects, mice, cattle, and deformed human beings, connecting our culture's anthropocentrism to the Holocaust."[8] The breathtaking sweep of this claim leaves Wenz with a problem, however: if our culture is so uniform and so corrupt that our deepest beliefs lead from agriculture to the Nazis, how can we even begin to reform ourselves? The answer, he suggests, is to turn toward indigenous cultures, since they promote a more harmonious understanding of the proper relationship between humans and the rest of creation. Even though he admits that it is in no way obvious what kind of lessons our society could actually take from small, homogenous traditional communities, he believes they offer the only alternative to our own perverse culture.[9] Regardless of how shockingly and crassly simplistic Wenz's historical, political, and anthropological analysis is in this book, perhaps the most important message is that he simply does not believe that the beliefs and sensibilities of his fellow Americans have any resources internal to themselves with which to address our environmental problems in a satisfactory manner. His neighbors, after all, hold views that are implicated in the Holocaust.[10]

J. Baird Callicott faces a similar problem. Like Wenz, he believes that only after our conventional "world views" are replaced by a "new nonanthropocentric, holistic environmental ethic" will we be able to articulate a morally defensible understanding of the natural world.[11] In fact, he believes that the problem he faces as a biocentrist is less philosophical than it is political: he holds that a holistic and nonanthropocentric environ- mental ethic has already been "persuasively articulated by Aldo Leopold, Holmes Rolston, and Val Plumwood, among others."[12] Thus, the philosoph- ical work is already done, and what remains is the "eventual institutionaliza- tion" of this ethic in practice. Callicott suggests that as a matter of practical politics, it may be necessary to speak in more conventional moral languages when explaining the reasons for environmental protection to nonphilosophers:

> Granted, we may not have the leisure to wait for a majority to come over to a new world view and a new nonanthropocentric, holistic ethic. We environmentalists have to reach people where they are, intellectually speaking, right now. So we might persuade Jews, Christians, and Muslims to support the environmental policy agenda by appeal to such concepts as God, creation, and stewardship; and so on. But this is no argument for insisting . . . that environmental philosophers should stop exploring the real reasons why we ought to value other forms of life, ecosystems, and the biosphere as a whole.[13]

In contrast to Wenz, Callicott's strategy is to appeal to traditional values and try to interpret them in an environmental light. The assumption, however, is that this is nothing more than a rhetorical task, since there is no philosophical merit to these claims. Philosophers have already, as he says, "persuasively articulated" the truth on these matters, but the many simply cannot or will not understand these "real reasons" for valuing nature. While philosophers may be able to fool the many into believing that their religions support environmentalism, the philosopher understands that these moral traditions are actually a grave threat to the environment. The strategy Callicott proposes appears at most to provide some breathing room for the philosophers while they try to figure out how to pull off the "eventual institutionalization" of "a new holistic, nonanthropocentric environmental ethic." Callicott's strategy is not to engage democratic citizens in public debate about environmental values and policy. On the contrary, it is to patronize them while he considers how to gain political power. There is no respect for the variety of moral traditions and discourses generated in democratic society.

Callicott and Wenz never attempt to hide their contempt for the moral languages spoken by those around them. This contempt reflects both an oversimplified intellectual history (most easily seen in Wenz's work) and a noticeably arrogant understanding of the nature of philosophy and the philosopher (most obvious in Callicott). Together these qualities combine to suggest at best an impatience, at worst a hostility, toward democratic society, institutions, processes, traditions, and citizens. It is precisely this impatience (to give it its best possible reading) that is challenged by arguments like those presented in this volume. The project of reconsidering conservation is therefore not only of historical or academic interest. It is actually a project in democratic theory and practice. Within it we confront the degree to which we can maintain a commitment to democratic life while talking seriously about our environmental problems. Thinking within our traditions, even if (perhaps especially if) critically, demonstrates a kind of respect not only for those who came before, but also for our current neighbors and fellow citizens, and those who are yet to become members of our society. For democratic citizens, these traditions (of which conservation is an example and illustration) are the only real currency of serious moral deliberation. Democratic respect and modesty suggest the importance of reconsidering conservation.

Human Limits and Human Purposes

Bill McKibben has recently written that "Living as if you were the most important thing on earth is, literally, blasphemy."[14] Modern environmentalists have often drawn our attention to this problem of human arrogance, in one form or another, since well before David Ehrenfeld wrote *The Arrogance of Humanism*.[15] And it is certainly a message American (and obviously not only American) society has needed, and continues to need, to hear and learn from. There is no doubt that we have too often treated our natural environment cavalierly and thoughtlessly, if not with actual contempt and insolence. The environmental problems we face are real and difficult, and they have at least in part grown out of a kind of self worship or idolatry. We owe a great debt to the recent environmental literature for keeping this problem before us, reminding us that proper respect for the natural world requires a taming of our own wants, a sense of proportion in our understanding of our own importance.

Too often, however, the anger or the fear driving the contemporary environmental critique has led to its own excesses, such as those noted above in Callicott's and Wenz's work. In cases like these, the arrogance of our society has led to an equally arrogant intellectual response, a haughty damnation from the pure of heart and philosophically sophisticated. The crude and dangerous exploitation of our environment produces, in turn, an equally crass and arrogant response from those who are filled with disgust at the damage and alarm at the danger.

Rabbi Menahem Mendel of Kotsk is reported to have said: "The Jew must have two pockets, for use when necessary: in one pocket 'The world was created for me' (Babylonian Talmud, Sanhedrin 37a); and in the other pocket: 'I am but dust and ashes' (Genesis 18:27)."[16] Part of the difficulty of being human, as Rabbi Mendel's saying suggests, is finding a proper balance between humility and pride. Such a balance, the story implies, is never finished, but requires constant adjustment and attending to. There are times when it is necessary to remind ourselves of our rightful place in the world; there are times when it is equally necessary to bring ourselves down a peg or two (or, indeed, even more!) and remember that we are only a part of the greater creation. The work of mediating this tension is never complete, nor is the need for wisdom in understanding what it is that needs to be done at any given moment. Just when we think we have it right, it is probably time to reach into the other pocket for the alternative reminder.

A key lesson to be learned from reconsidering conservation, it seems to me, is something of a political version of Rabbi Mendel's saying. As pointed out above, the theme of pride and humility emerges throughout the volume, reflecting a democratic sensibility about the proper approach to thinking about environmental problems. And this sensibility requires no less of a balancing act than that described by Rabbi Mendel. The optimism in this volume is found in the conviction that the conservation tradition contains more useful tools for thinking about our environmental problems than is often recognized. But it provides these tools within a context of democratic commitments that continually tug against any absolute or final evaluation of nature. Recall Jeffrey Salmon's observation that Theodore Roosevelt was committed to living with the tension between his beliefs in human progress and the preservation of nature, or Landy's discussion of Olmsted's democratic environmentalism. There is no reason for us to think that either Roosevelt or Olmsted got the relationship between democracy and nature right. But there is reason for us to think that they were correct in their formulation of the problem. Just as democratic society must learn limits and higher values from nature, so must our love and concern and respect for nature be infused with and moderated by a commitment to the best of our democratic traditions and respect for our fellow citizens.

Notes

1. Cornel West, "The Moral Obligations of Living in a Democratic Society," in David Batstone and Eduardo Mendieta, eds., *The Good Citizen* (New York: Routledge, 1999), 12.

2. Peter Coates, *Nature* (Berkeley and Los Angeles: University of California Press, 1998), 15.

3. Simon Schama, *Landscape and Memory* (New York: Alfred A. Knopf, 1995), 18.

4. Schama, *Landscape and Memory*, 14.

5. Richard W. Judd, *Common Lands, Common People* (Cambridge, MA: Harvard University Press, 1997), 265-66.

6. Carolyn Merchant writes that "new values that sustain rather than degrade nature and other people are now needed." "The ideas of deep ecology, alternative philosophies, the emerging postclassical sciences, feminism, and reconstructive knowledge point to the possibility of a new worldview that could guide twenty-first century citizens in an ecologically sustainable way of life." Merchant, *Radical Ecology* (New York: Routledge, 1992), 4, 107.

7. "Environmental ethics is both radical and revolutionary." Holmes Rolston, III, *Environmental Ethics* (Philadelphia: Temple University Press, 1988), xii.

8. Peter Wenz, *Nature's Keeper* (Philadelphia: Temple University Press, 1996), 6.

9. Wenz, *Nature's Keeper*, 13.

10. Toward the end of the book, Wenz seems to waffle on this issue by suggesting that certain passages in the Bible support environmental ethics. This observation is undeveloped, most likely because it is contrary to the argument he has defended throughout the book. Wenz, *Nature's Keeper*, 161.

11. J. Baird Callicott, "Environmental Philosophy Is Environmental Activism: The Most Radical and Effective Kind," in Don E. Marietta Jr. and Lester Embree, eds., *Environmental Philosophy and Environmental Activism* (Lanham, Maryland: Rowman & Littlefield, 1995), 24.

12. Callicott, "Environmental Philosophy Is Environmental Activism," 24.

13. Callicott, "Environmental Philosophy Is Environmental Activism," 24.

14. Bill McKibben, *Maybe One* (New York: Simon and Schuster, 1998).

15. David Erenfeld, *The Arrogance of Humanism* (New York: Oxford University Press, 1978).

16. Simcha Raz, ed., *The Sayings of Manahem Mendel of Kotsk* (Northvale, NJ: Jason Aronson, Inc., 1995), 53.

Index

African Game Trails (Roosevelt), 35, 38-39
Agassiz, Louis, 138-39, 150
Agriculture Department, Forestry Division, 81
agriculture, vs. forestry, 73
Amazon River, T. Roosevelt and, 40
American Forest Congress, 87-88
animals, human characteristics attributed to, 121; T. Roosevelt's knowledge of, 35, 38
anthropocentrism, 103, 106, 255; anthropocentric view of nature, 103; vs. ecocentric environmentalism, 116
anti-anthropocentrism, xi, 198, 235
anti-Darwinism, xi; Muir and 150-51
ants, Muir and, 15, 17
Aristotle, 128
Arizona, national forest in, 109
Arnhart, Larry, xi, xii, xiii, 103-32, 233
Arrogance of Humanism, The (Ehrenfeld), 237
art, T. Roosevelt's view of nature's value and, 51-52
Augustine, St., 192
"Autumnal Tints" (Thoreau), 194-95

Baltimore and Ohio Railroad, 86-87
Beagle, H.M.S. (Darwin's ship), 136-37, 139
Bible, Muir and allusions to, 23-25
Biltmore Forest, 74
Biltmore House, 73-74
biocentrism: Thoreau and, 183, 197; biocentric environmental ethics, 198; biocentric view, of nature, 103, 235
Biological Survey, T. Roosevelt and, 35
biology, T. Roosevelt and, 54
biotic community, moral worth of, 103
Blanchard, Governor, 92
Book-Lover's Holiday in the Open (Roosevelt), 35
books, T. Roosevelt and, 47
Boone and Crockett Club, 34, 45, 46, 77; as lobbying organization, 46
Bowers, Edward, 78
Breaking New Ground (Pinchot), 68-69, 89
Browne, W.A., 146
buffalo, extermination of, T. Roosevelt and, 44-45
buffalo herds, xiii
Bull Moose Party, 95

241

About the Contributors

Larry Arnhart is Professor of Political Science at Northern Illinois University. His most recent book is *Darwinian Natural Right: The Biological Ethics of Human Nature* (State University of New York Press).

Marc Landy is Professor of Political Science at Boston College and an author of *Presidential Greatness* (University Press of Kansas) and *EPA From Nixon to Clinton: Asking the Wrong Questions* (Oxford).

James G. Lennox is Professor of History and Philosophy of Science, specializing in the history and philosophy of biology, and Director of the Center for Philosophy of Science at the University of Pittsburgh. His most recent book is a translation and commentary of Aristotle's *De Partibus Animalium* for Oxford University Press's Clarendon Series.

Marlo Lewis Jr. is Staff Director of the U.S. House of Representatives Government Reform Subcommittee on National Economic Growth, Natural Resources, and Regulatory Affairs. He has a Ph.D. in Government from Harvard University.

Bruce Pencek is the information associate at the Center for Business and Economic Research of the University of Nevada, Las Vegas. Before entering librarianship and consulting, he taught political theory and American politics in institutions as diverse as Middlebury College and UNLV.

Charles T. Rubin is Associate Professor of Political Science at Duquesne University, and graduate faculty in the Center for Social and Public Policy, and the Center for Environmental Research and Education. He is author of

The Green Crusade: Rethinking the Roots of Environmentalism (Rowman & Littlefield).

Jeffrey Salmon is Executive Director of the George C. Marshall Institute and Senior Fellow at the Environmental Literacy Council. He is founder of the Civic Environmentalism Working Group.

Bob Pepperman Taylor is Associate Professor of Political Science at the University of Vermont. He is author of *America's Bachelor Uncle: Thoreau and the American Polity* (University Press of Kansas), and *Our Limits Transgressed: Environmental Political Thought in America* (University Press of Kansas).

About The Political Economy Research Center

The Political Economy Research Center (PERC) is the nation's oldest and largest institute dedicated to original research that brings market principles to resolving environmental problems. PERC, located in Bozeman, Montana, pioneered the approach known as free market environmentalism. This approach is based on four main tenets: 1) private property rights encourage stewardship of resources; 2) government subsidies often degrade the environment; 3) market incentives spur individuals to conserve resources and protect environmental quality; and 4) polluters should be liable for the harm they cause others. PERC associates have applied the free market environmentalism approach to a variety of issues, including national parks, water marketing, chemical risk, private provision of wildlife habitat, public land management, and endangered species protection.

PERC's activities encompass three main areas: research and policy analysis, outreach, and environmental education. PERC associates conduct research, write books and articles, and lecture on the role of markets and property rights in environmental protection. PERC holds conferences and seminars for journalists, congressional staff members, state policy makers, business executives, and scholars. PERC also holds an annual free market environmentalism seminar for college students and sponsors a fellowship program that brings graduate students to PERC for three months of research and study on various environmental topics. PERC develops and disseminates environmental education materials for classroom use and provides training for kindergarten through twelfth-grade teachers.

In 1989, PERC organized the first of an annual conference series called the Political Economy Forum aimed at applying the principles of political economy to important policy issues. Each forum brings together scholars in economics, political science, law, history, and other disciplines to discuss and refine academic papers that explore new applications of political economy to policy analysis. The forum papers are then edited and published as a book in PERC's Political Economy Forum series. PERC believes that forums of this type can integrate cutting edge research with crucial policy issues.

From time to time, the series includes books not generated from PERC forums. These books are chosen based on their use of the free market environmentalism approach and their superior scholarship. This volume edited by Charles T. Rubin clearly fits both criteria. The prominent contributors in this collection establish a fundamentally original view of the conservation movement and the impact of public policy on nature. *Conservation Reconsidered* takes a new look at what is problematic about the legacy of American conservationism and explores worthy alternatives to the dominant environmentalist thinking of today.

PERC hopes that scholarship such as this will help advance the environmental policy debate and looks forward to further volumes in this series.